· Bartholomew ·

GLASGOW

Streetfinder

COLOUR STREET ATLAS

GW00419162

Bartholomew

A Division of HarperCollins*Publishers*

Fifth edition 1990
Reprinted with amendments 1992

Printed by Bartholomew, HarperCollins Manufacturing,
in Edinburgh, Scotland

ANC

Glasgow Colour Atlas Contents

Legend

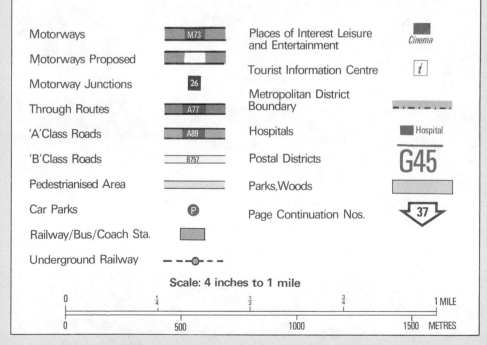

Motorways	M73	
Motorways Proposed		
Motorway Junctions	26	
Through Routes	A77	
'A'Class Roads	A89	
'B'Class Roads	B757	
Pedestrianised Area		
Car Parks	P	
Railway/Bus/Coach Sta.		
Underground Railway	– – –●– – –	

Places of Interest Leisure and Entertainment	Cinema
Tourist Information Centre	i
Metropolitan District Boundary	
Hospitals	Hospital
Postal Districts	G45
Parks, Woods	
Page Continuation Nos.	37

Scale: 4 inches to 1 mile

0   ¼   ½   ¾   1 MILE

0   500   1000   1500   METRES

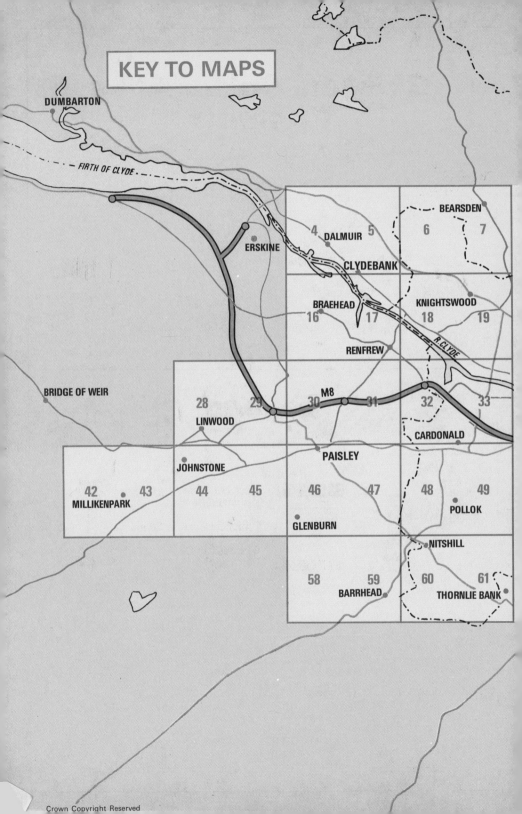

KEY TO MAPS

DUMBARTON

FIRTH OF CLYDE

ERSKINE

BEARSDEN

4 DALMUIR 5 6 7

CLYDEBANK

BRAEHEAD KNIGHTSWOOD
16 17 18 19

RENFREW R.CLYDE

BRIDGE OF WEIR

28 29 30 M8 31 32 33

LINWOOD CARDONALD

PAISLEY

JOHNSTONE

42 43 44 45 46 47 48 49
MILLIKENPARK POLLOK

GLENBURN

NITSHILL

58 59 60 61
BARRHEAD THORNLIEBANK

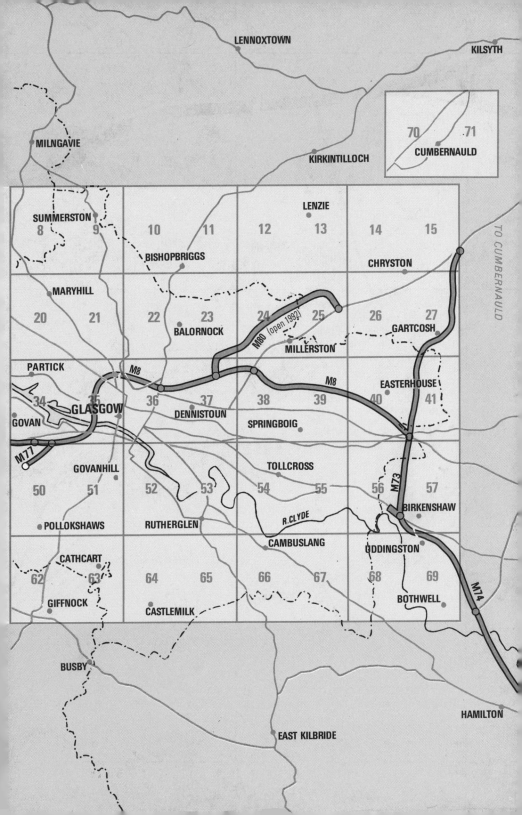

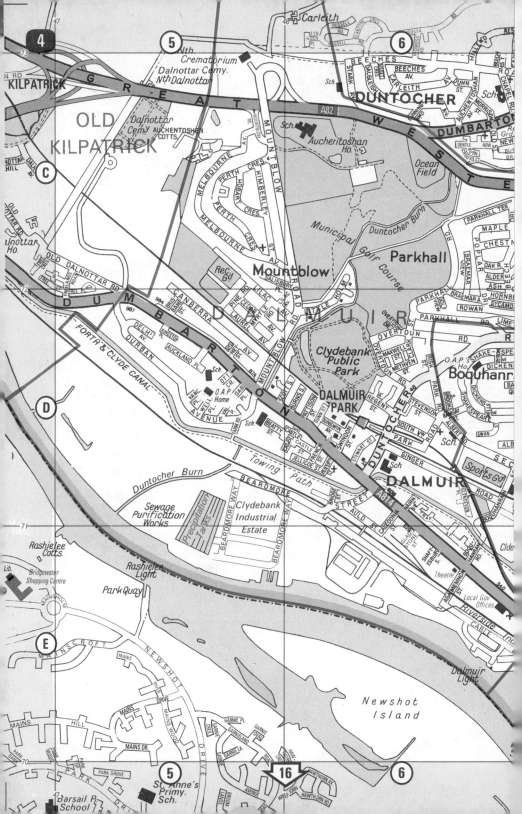

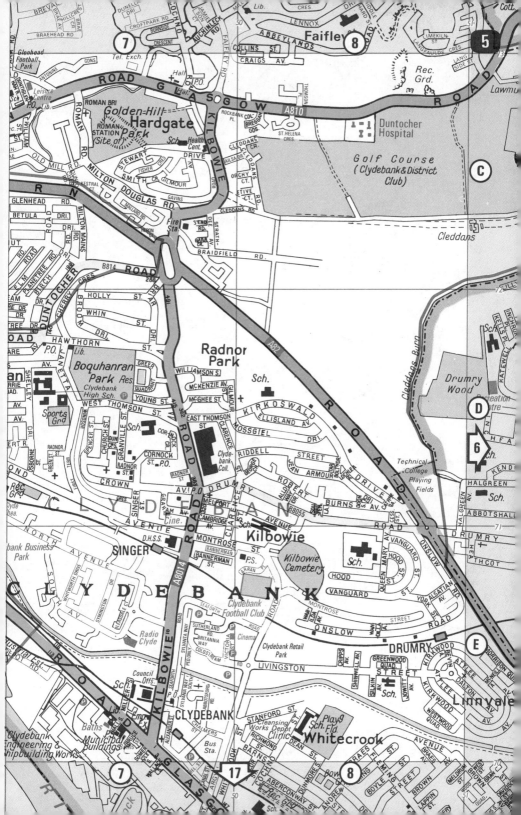

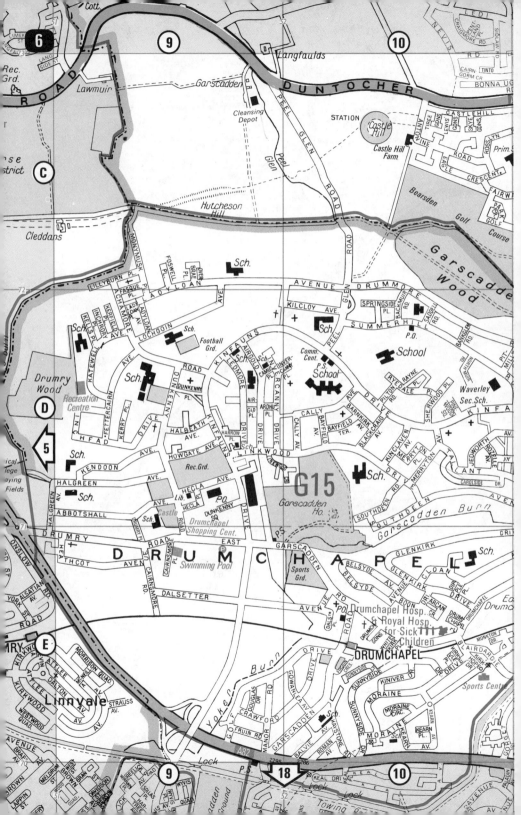

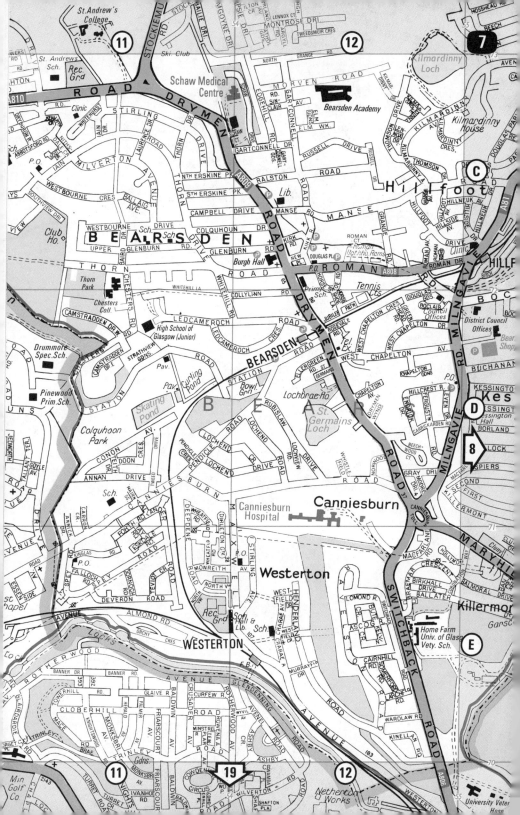

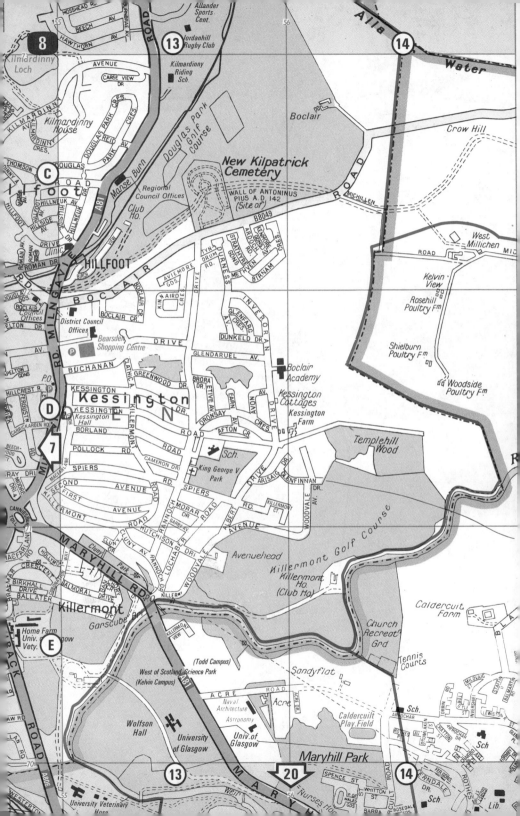

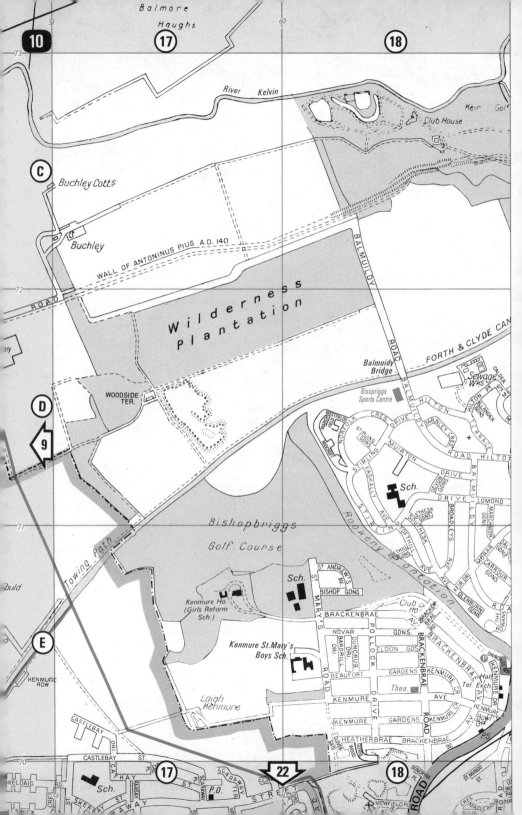

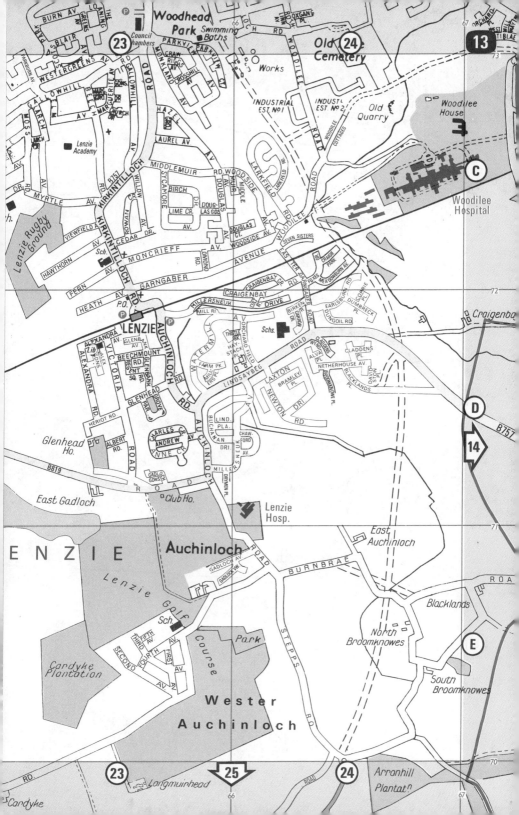

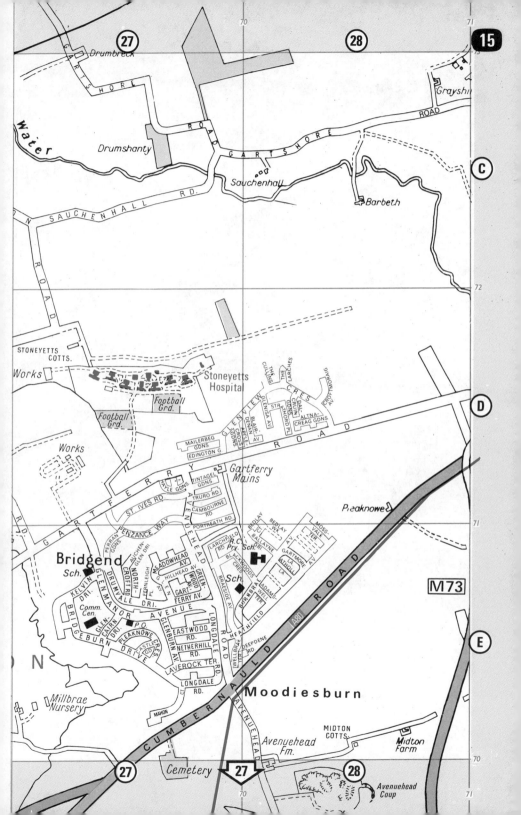

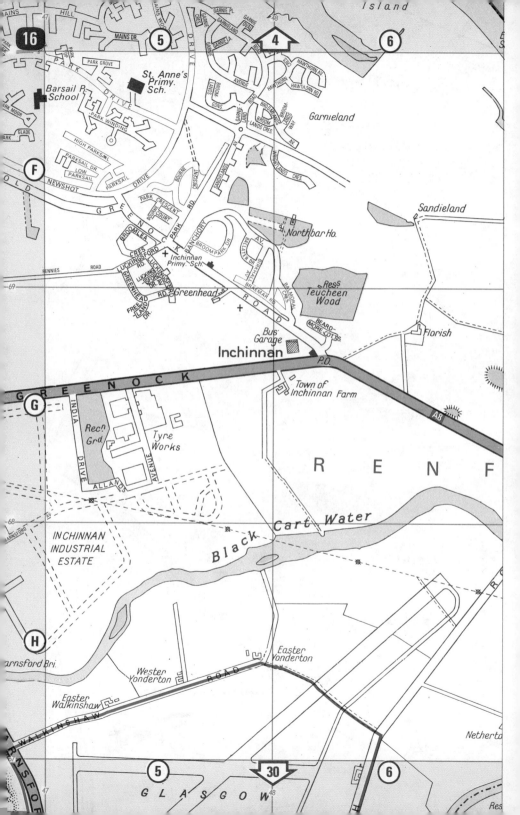

16

5

4

6

HILL

MAINS DR.

PARK GROVE

St. Anne's
Primy. Sch.

Barsail P.
School

PARK DRIVE

PARK WINDING

HIGH PARKSAIL

PARKSAIL DR.
LOW PARKSAIL

PARKSAIL

PARKSAIL DRIVE

F

NEWSHOT

GREENOCK

PARK CRESCENT

PARK COURT

BOURNE

CRESCENT

PARK RD.

BANCHORY

SANDIELANDS

GARNIE LANDS

AVENUE

BROOM
GDNS

BROADLANDS RD

GARNIE PL.
GARNIE OVAL
GARNIE LA.
GARNIE CRES

HAWTHORN AV.

HAWTHORN
HAWTHORN RD.

BROOM-
LANDS
WAY

BROOMLANDS
CRES.

WRIGHTLANDS CRES.

Garnieland

Island

Sandieland

BROMLEA
CRES

LUCKINGSFORD

LUCKINGSFORD
RD.

GREENHEAD

FREE-
LANDS
DR.

LUCKINGSFORD
DR.

GEORGE ST.

GREENHEAD
RD.

Inchinnan
Primy. Sch.

Greenhead

BROOM PARK DR.

AV.

BALFATE LANE

BRAEMAR RD.

BALMORAL

Northbar Ho.

Ress
Teucheen
Wood

BEARD-
MORE COTS.

Florish

ROAD

Bus
Garage

P.O.

Inchinnan

Town of
Inchinnan Farm

A8

GREENOCK

G

INDIA
DRIVE

Rec.n
Grd.

Tyre
Works

AVENUE

ALLANDS

RENF

RENNIES

ROAD

INCHINNAN
INDUSTRIAL
ESTATE

Black Cart Water

BARNSFORD AV

H

arnsford Bri.

Wester
Yonderton

Easter
Yonderton

ROAD

Easter
Walkinshaw

WALKINSHAW

NSFOR

Netherto

5

30

6

G L A S G O W

RESS

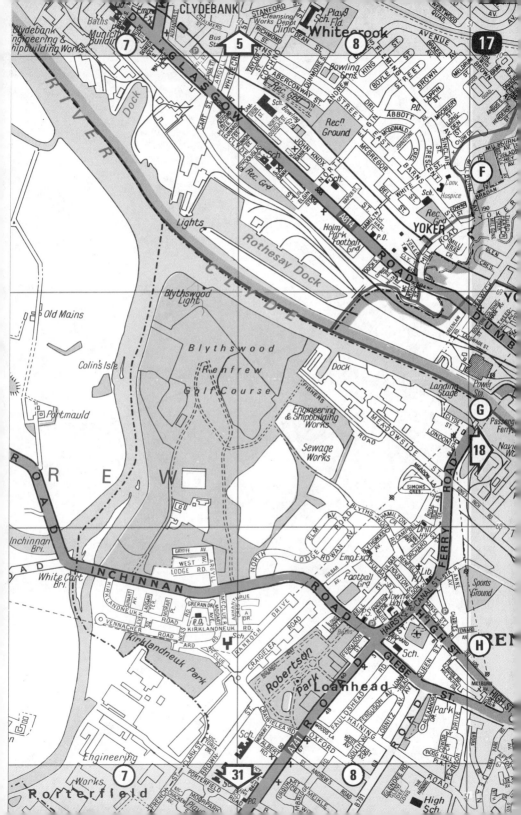

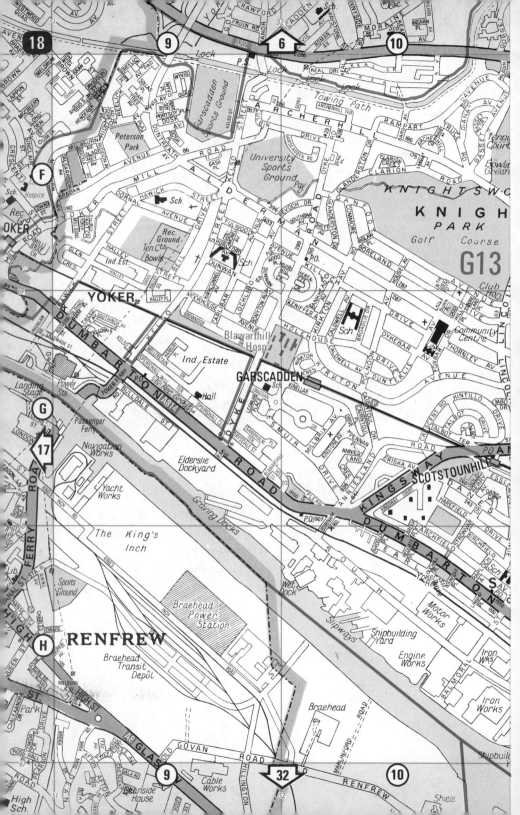

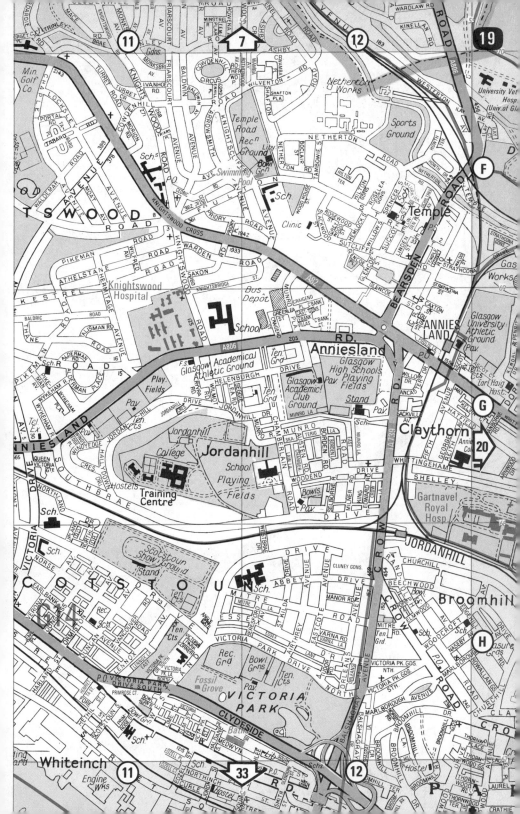

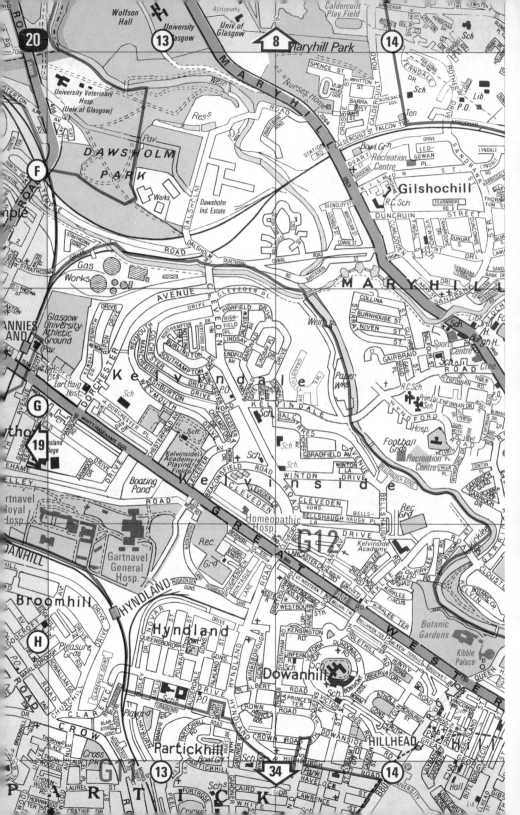

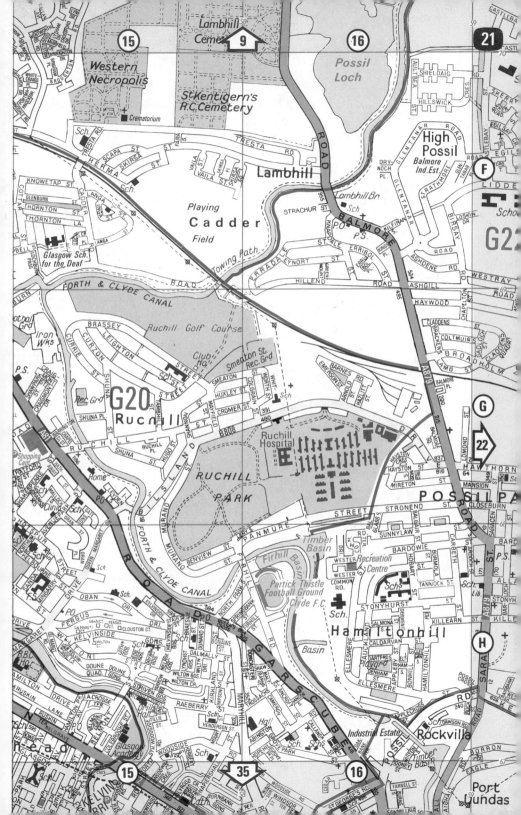

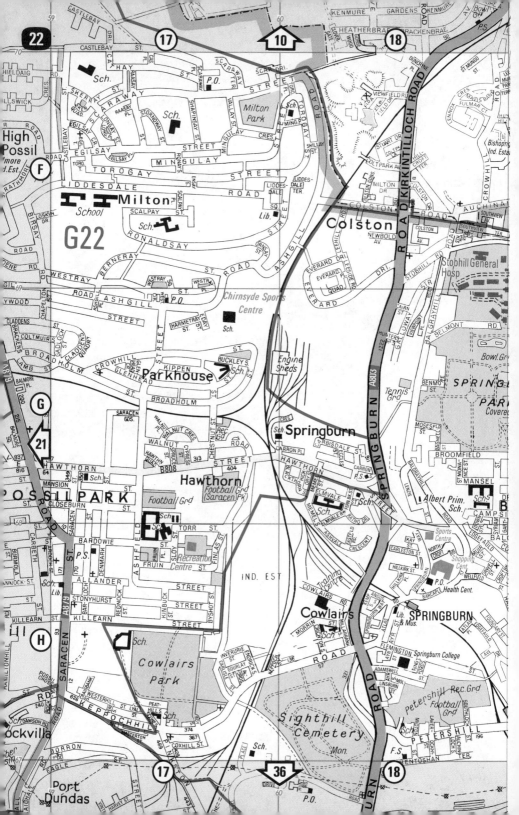

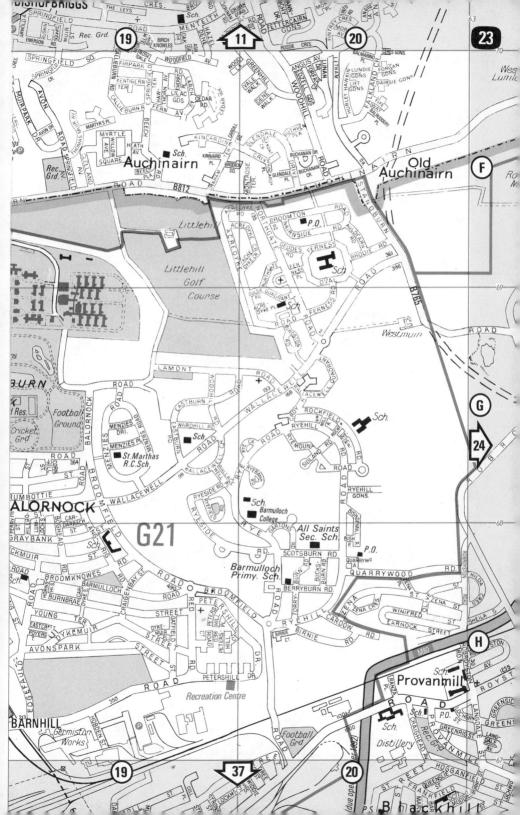

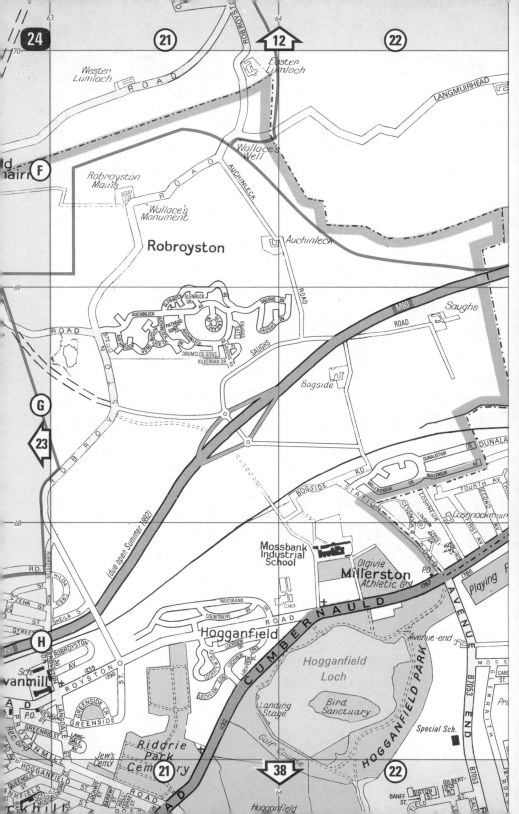

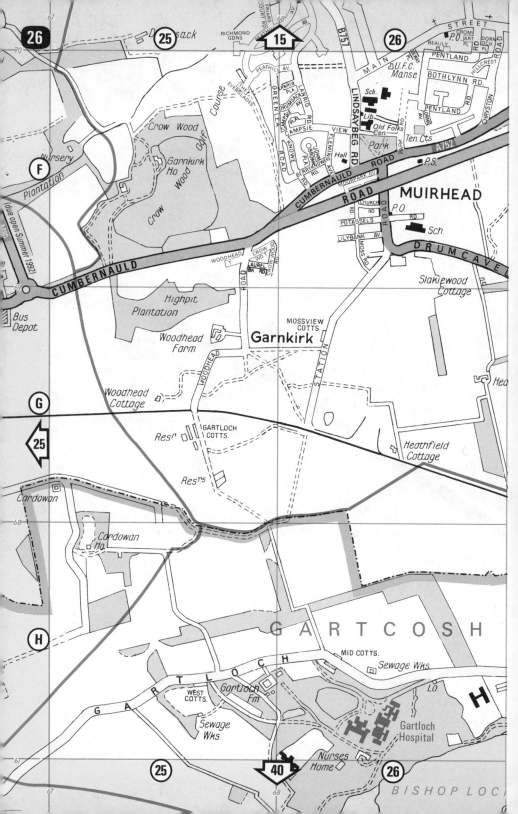

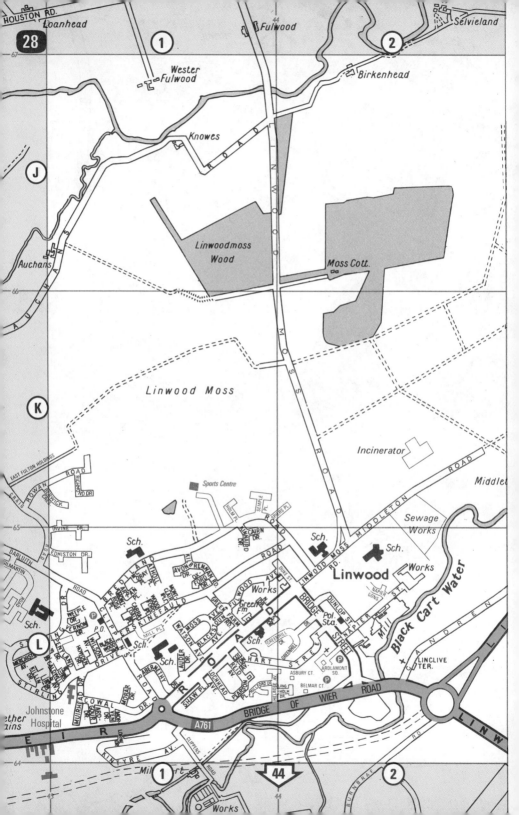

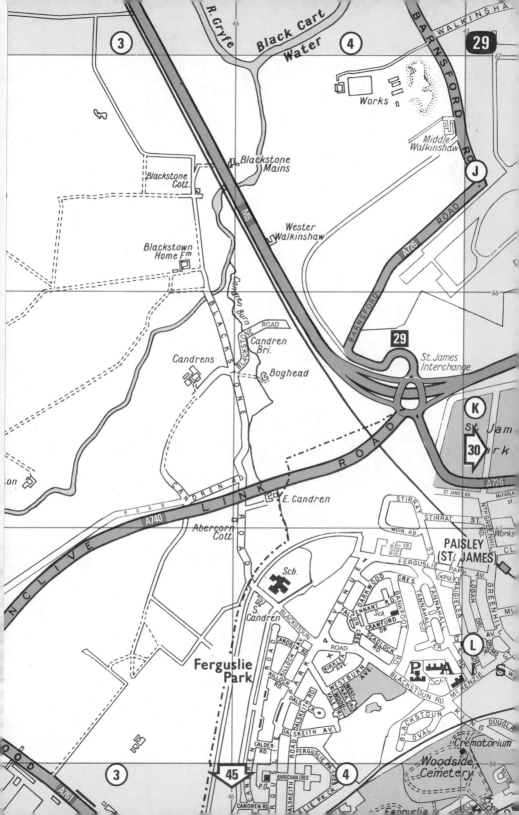

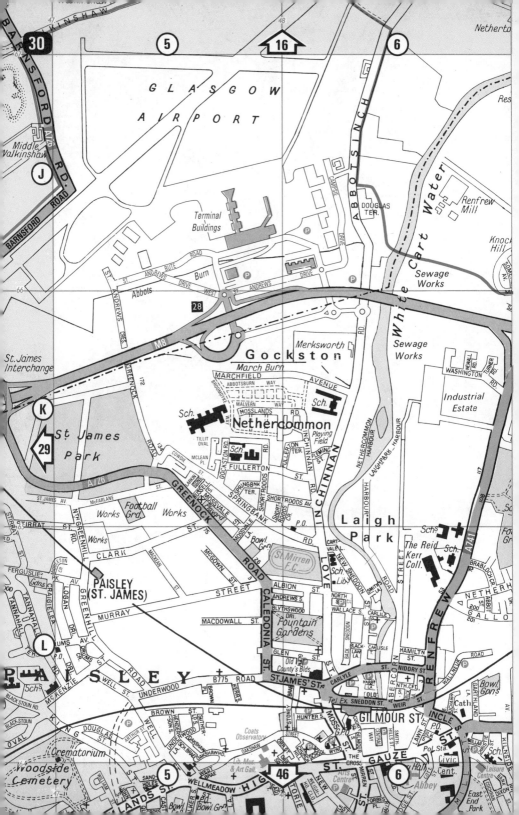

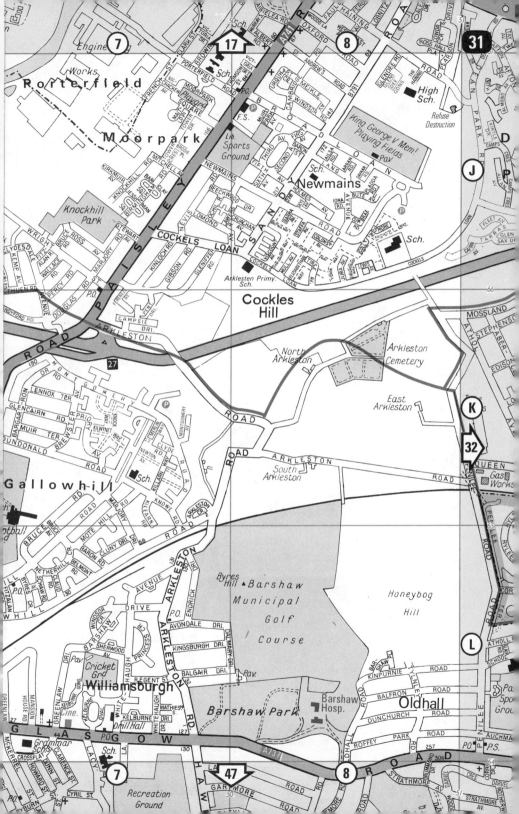

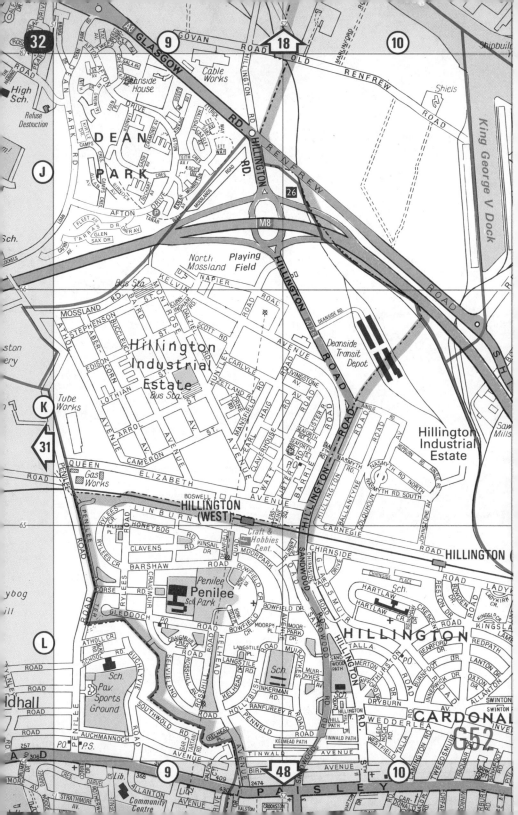

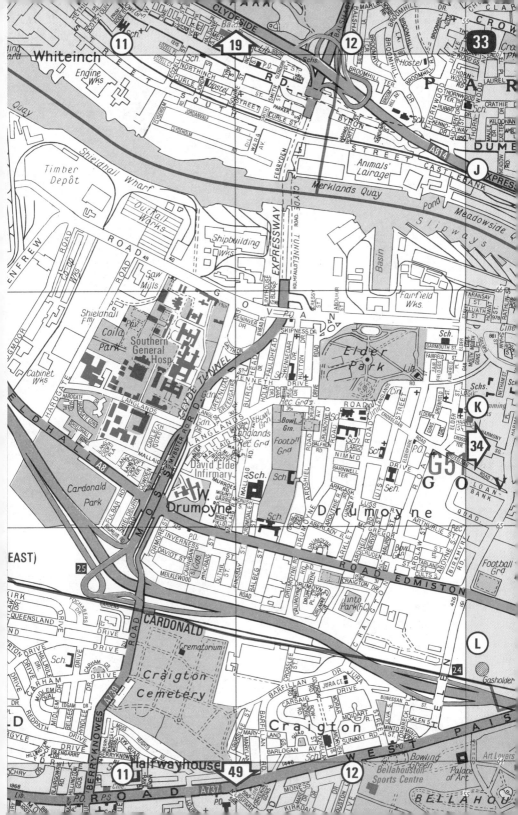

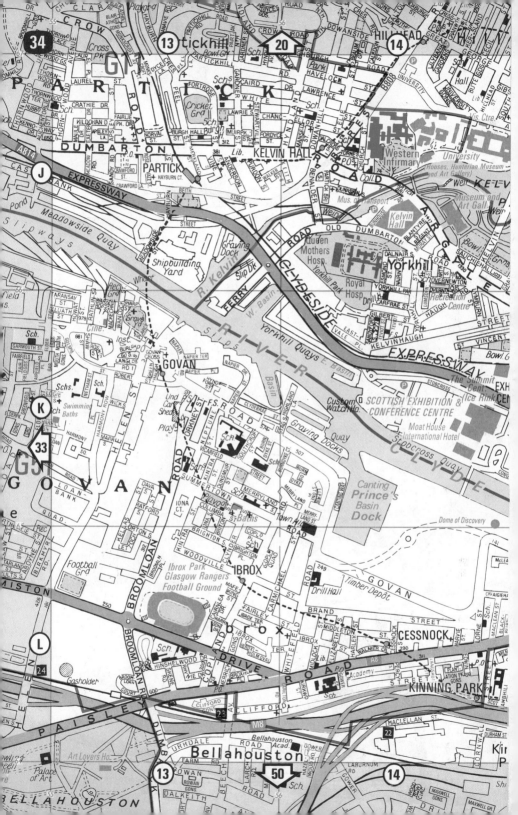

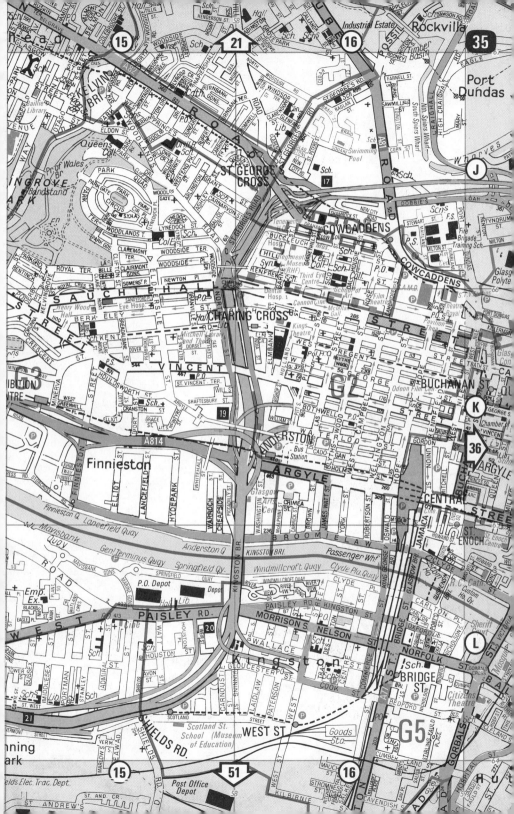

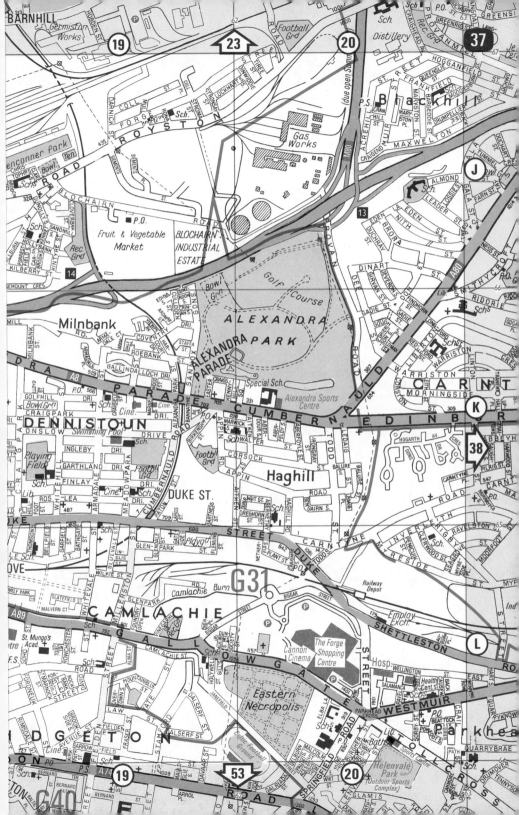

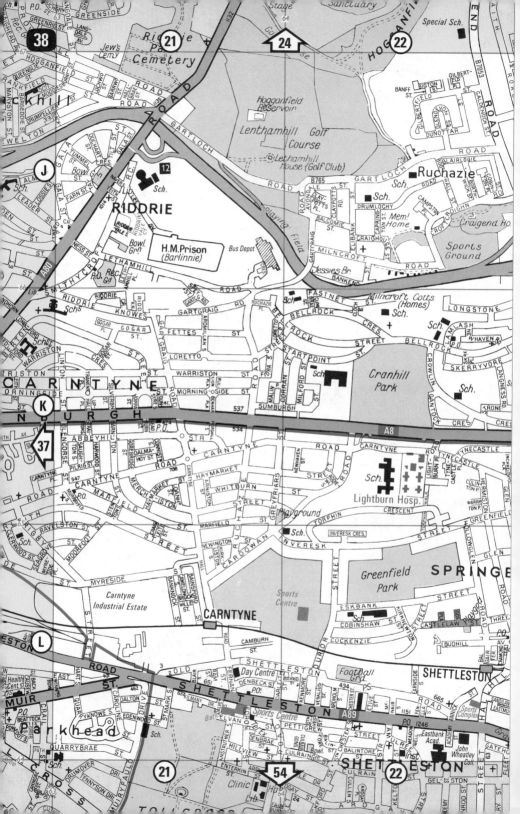

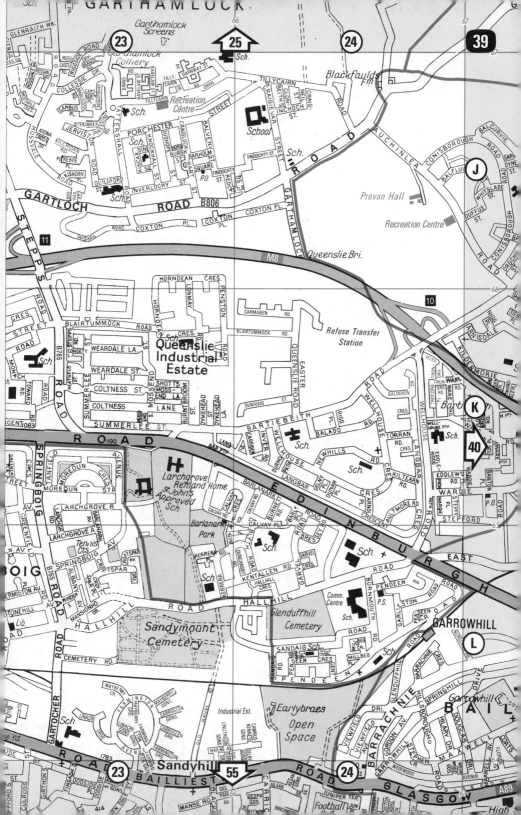

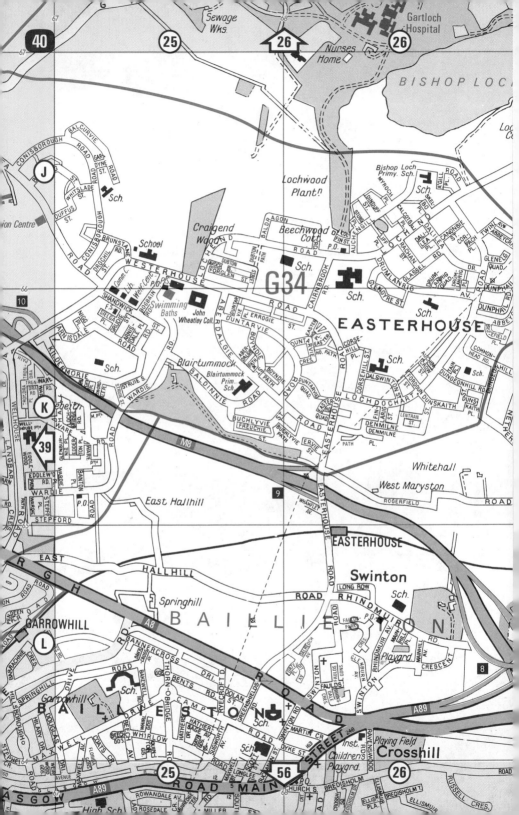

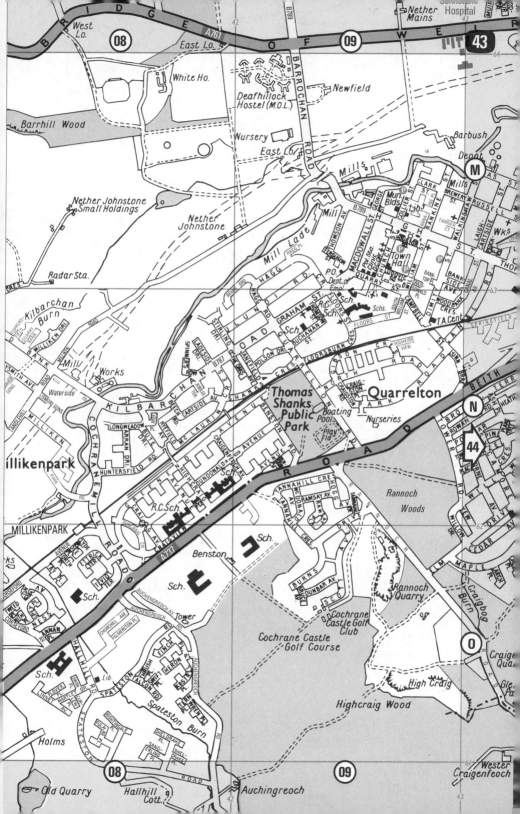

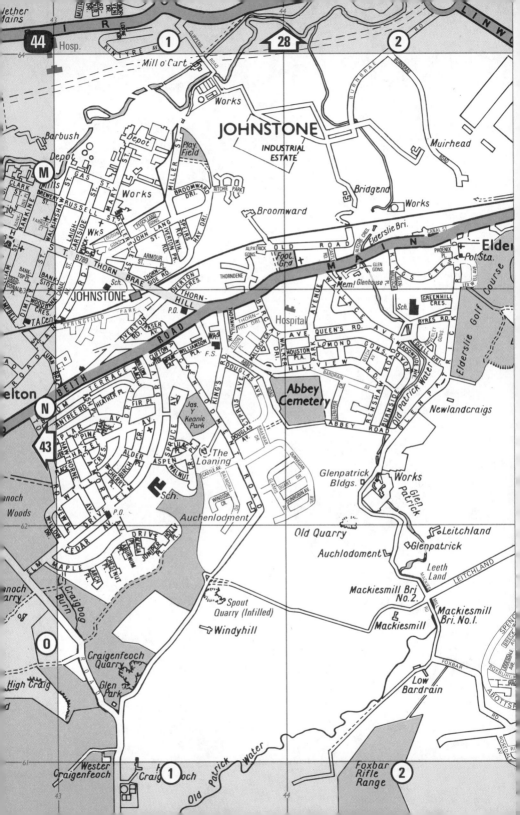

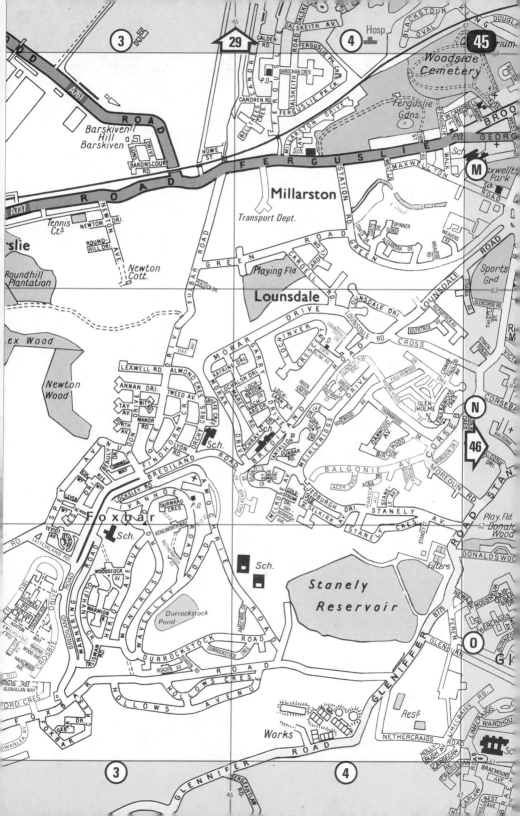

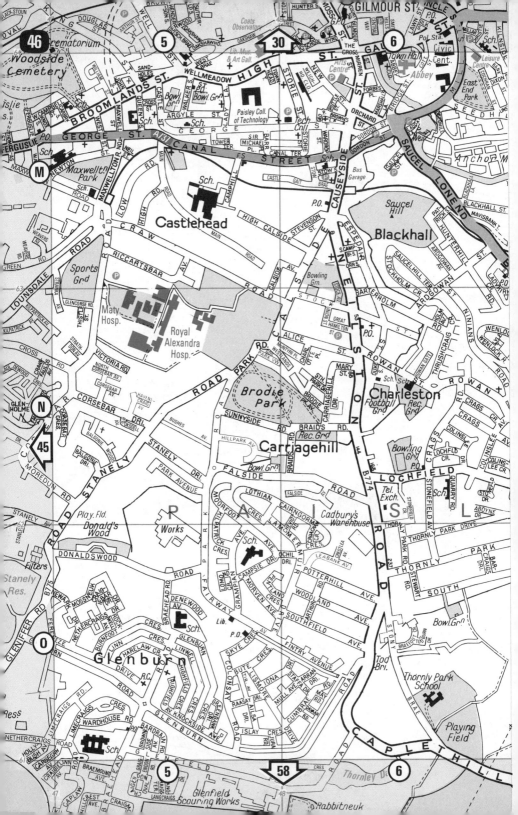

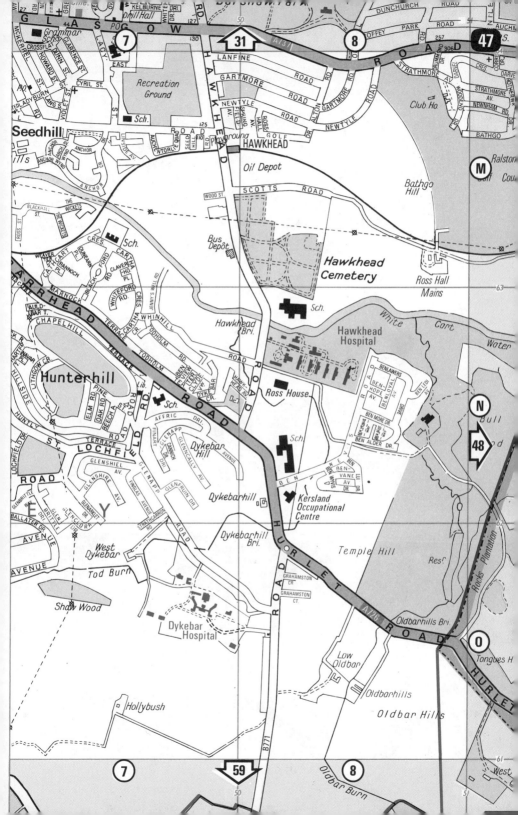

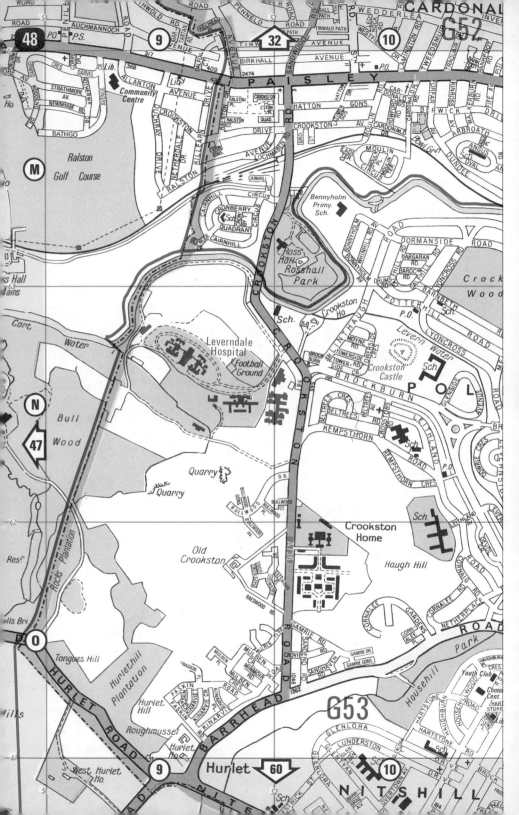

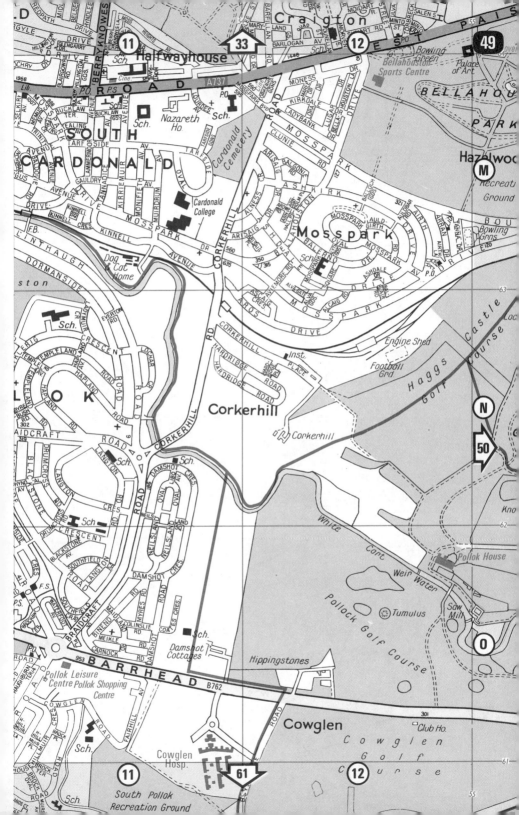

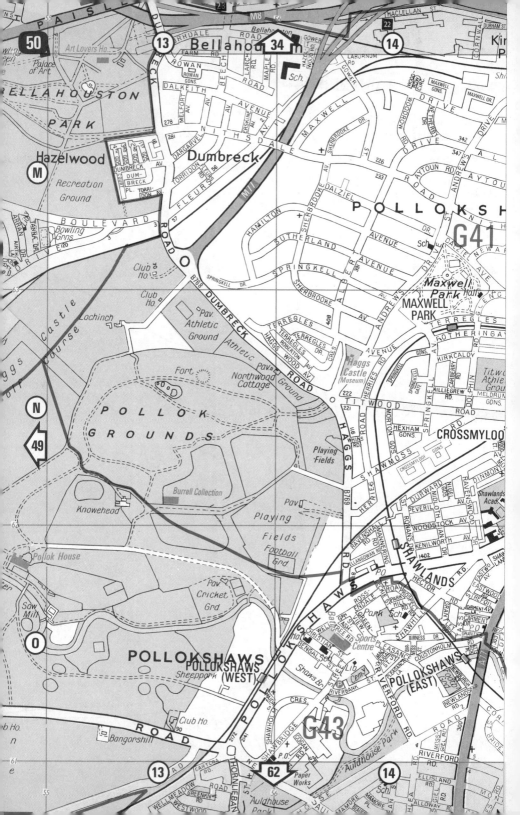

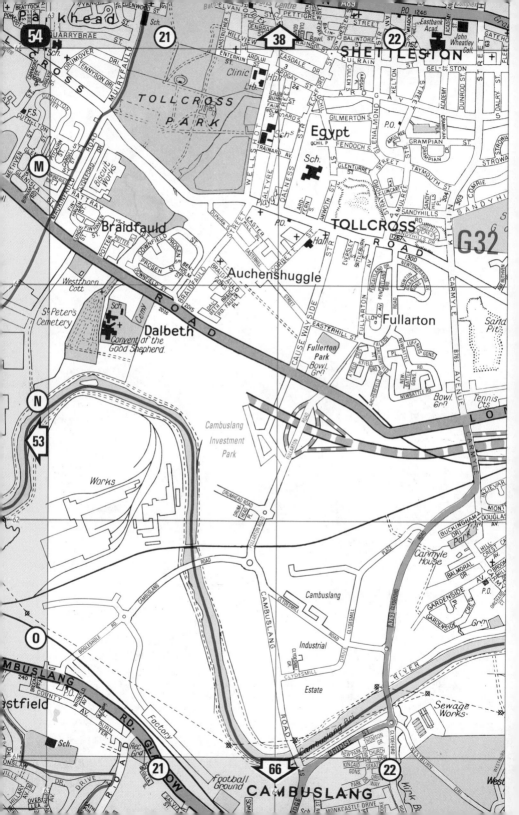

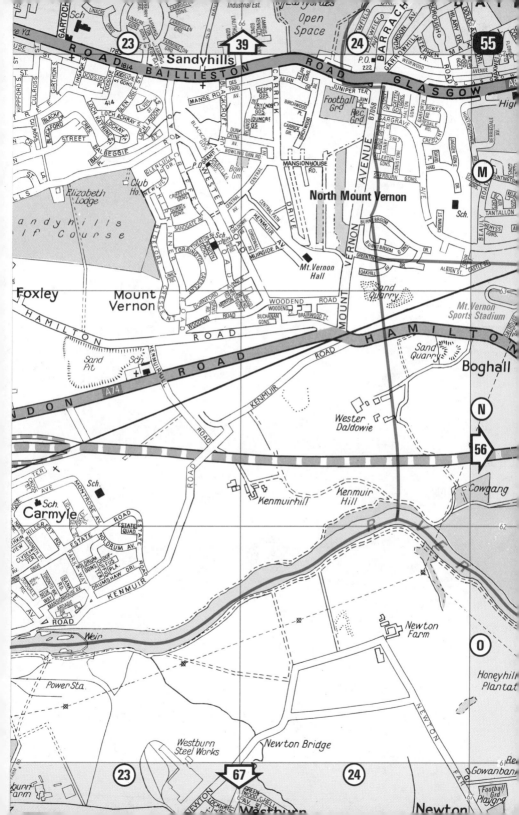

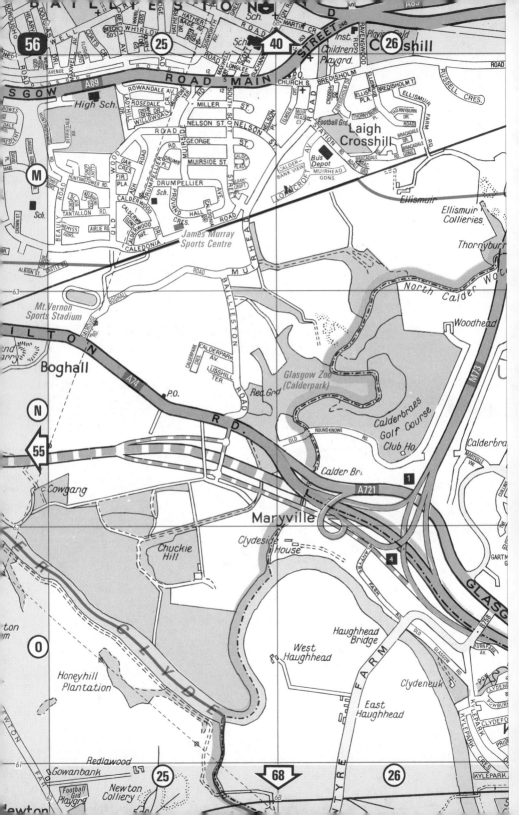

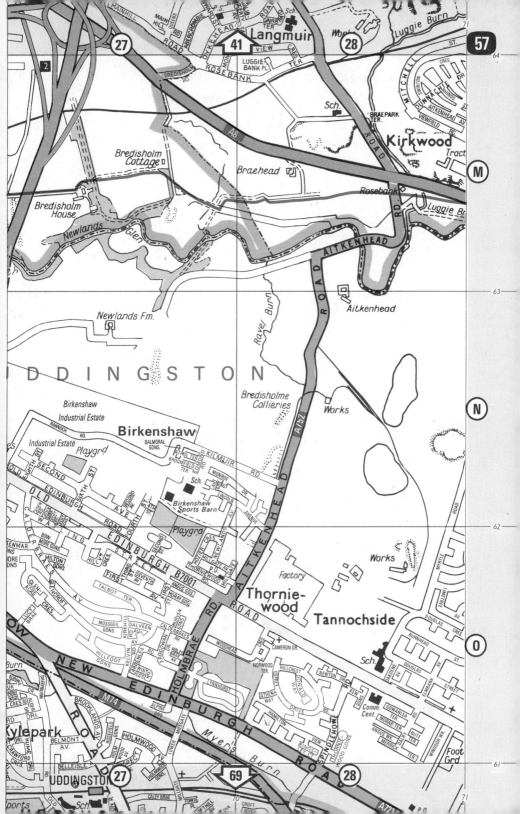

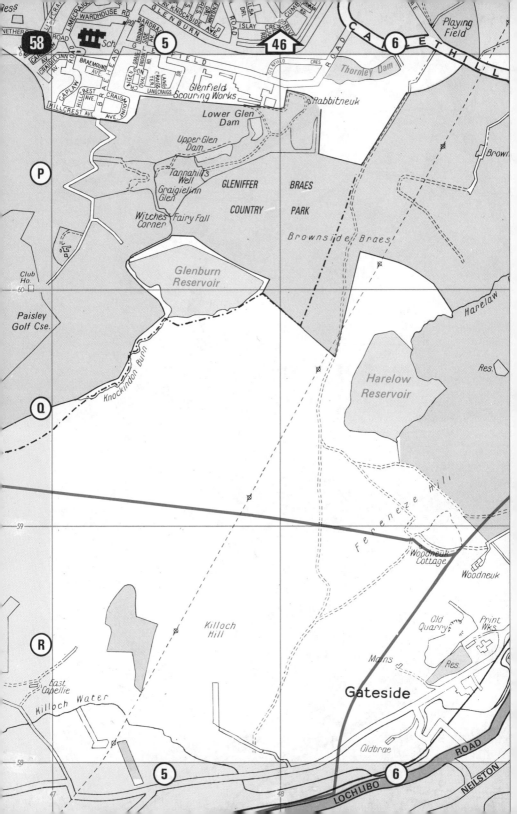

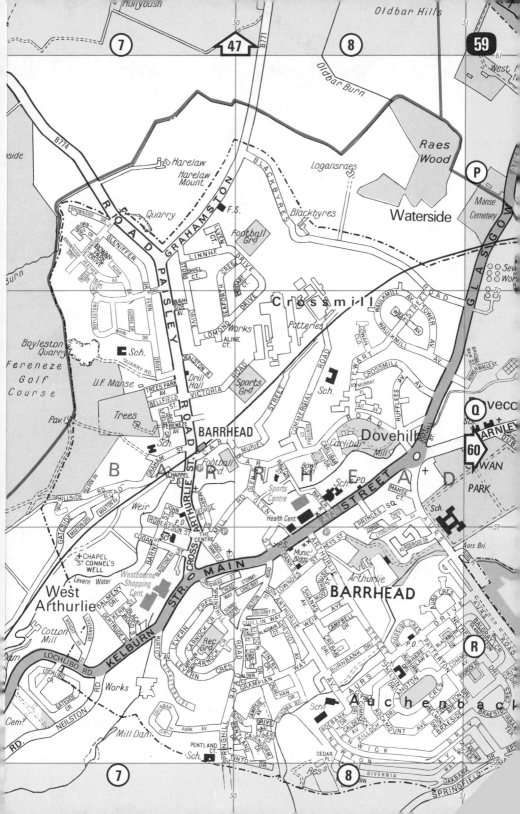

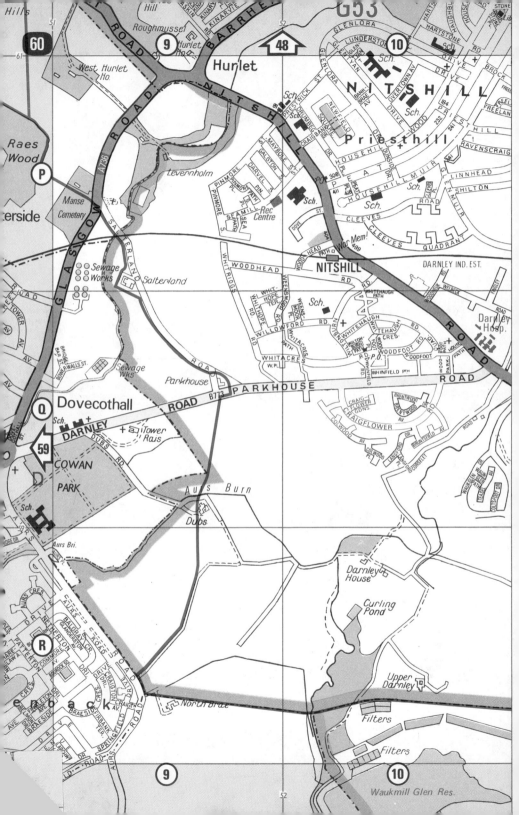

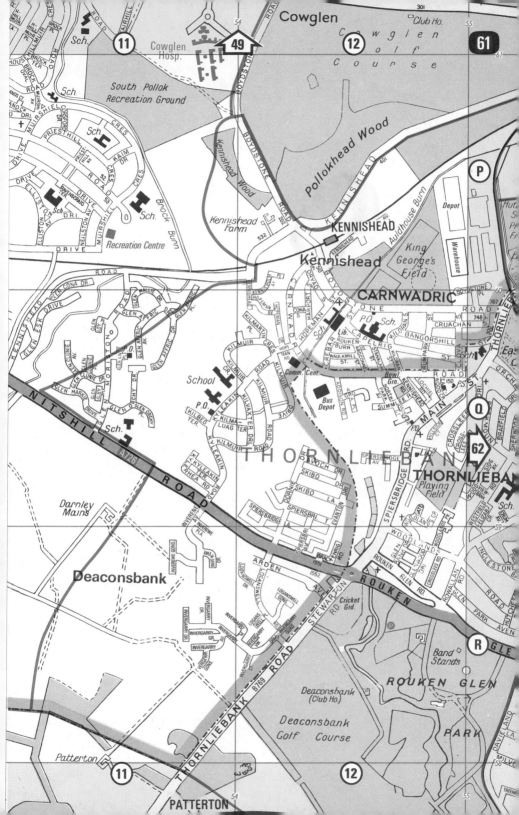

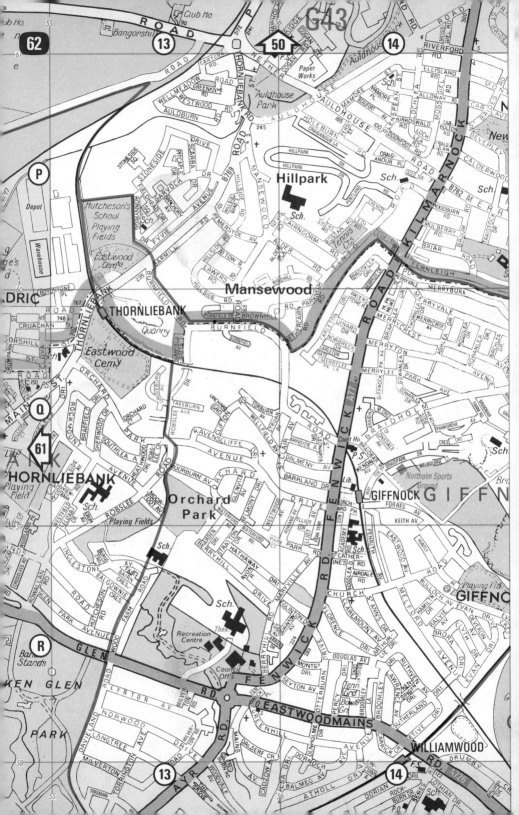

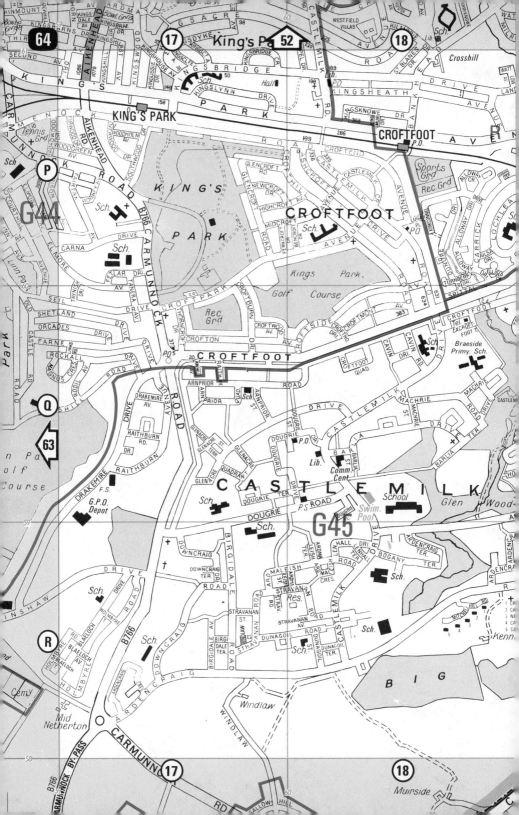

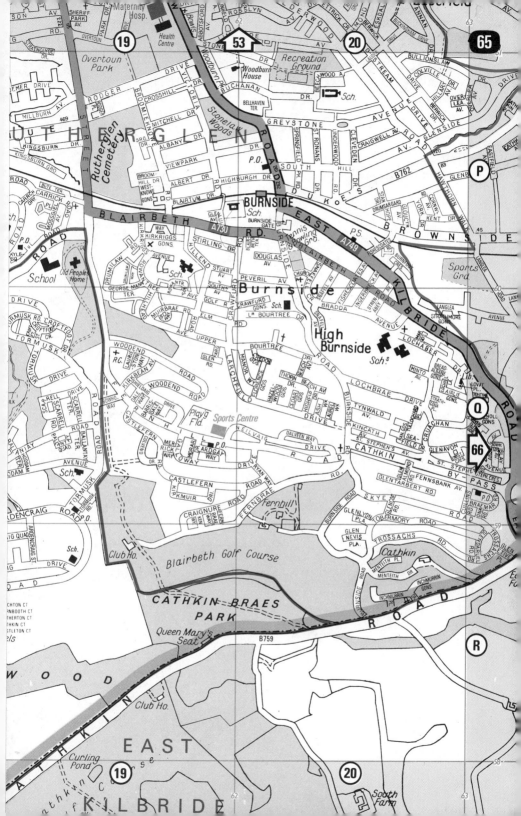

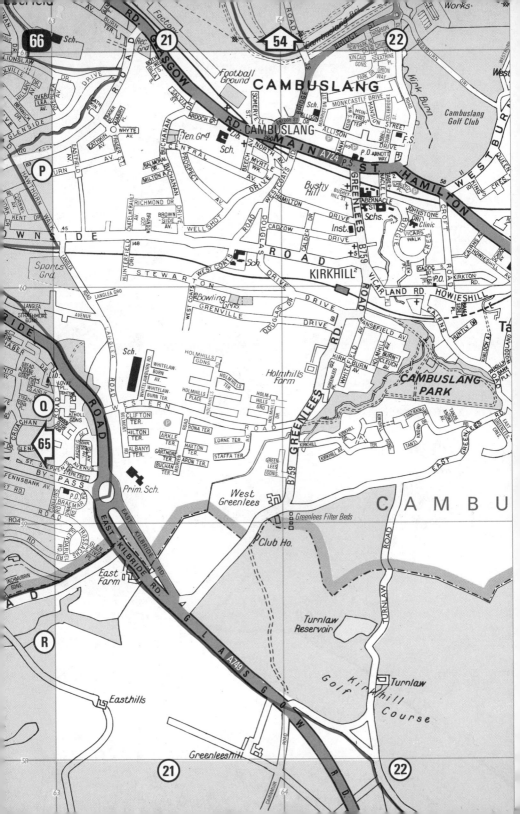

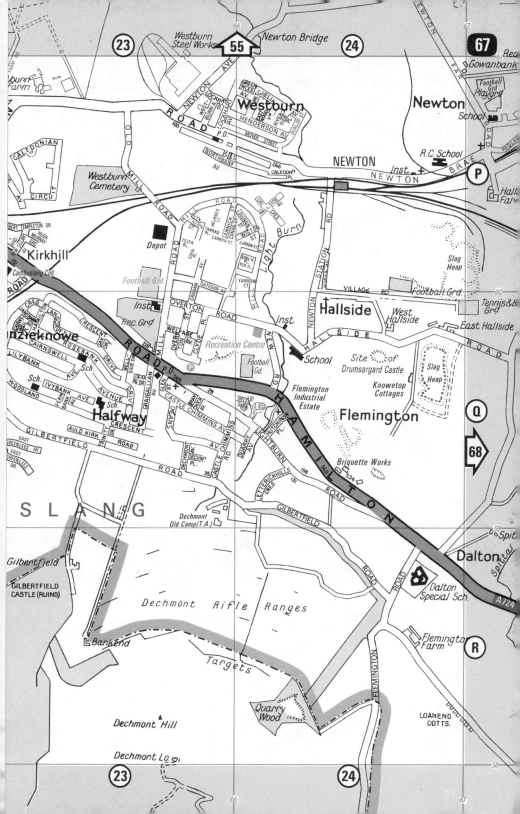

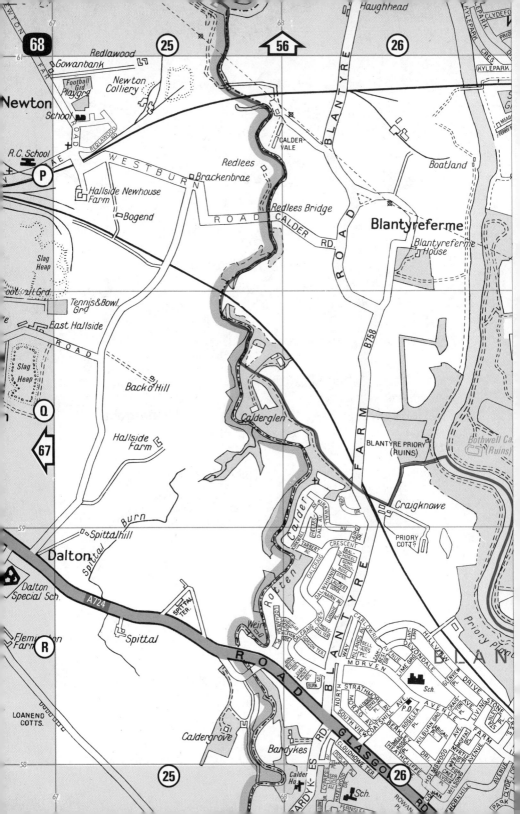

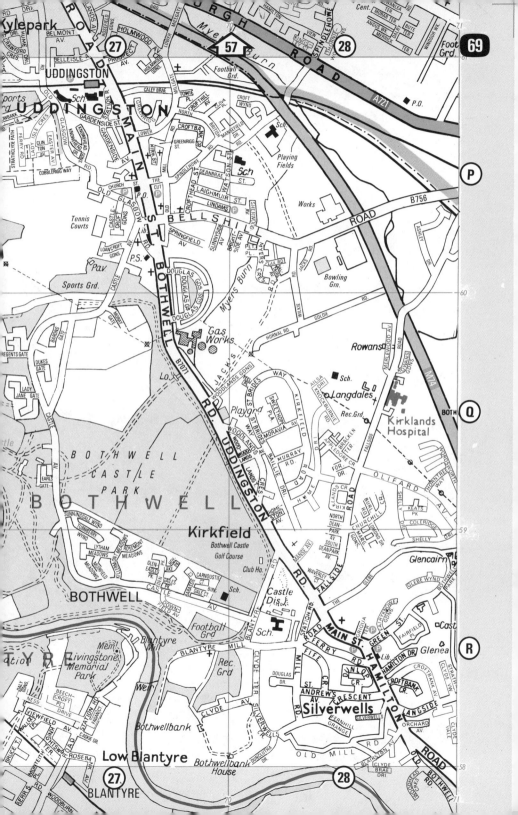

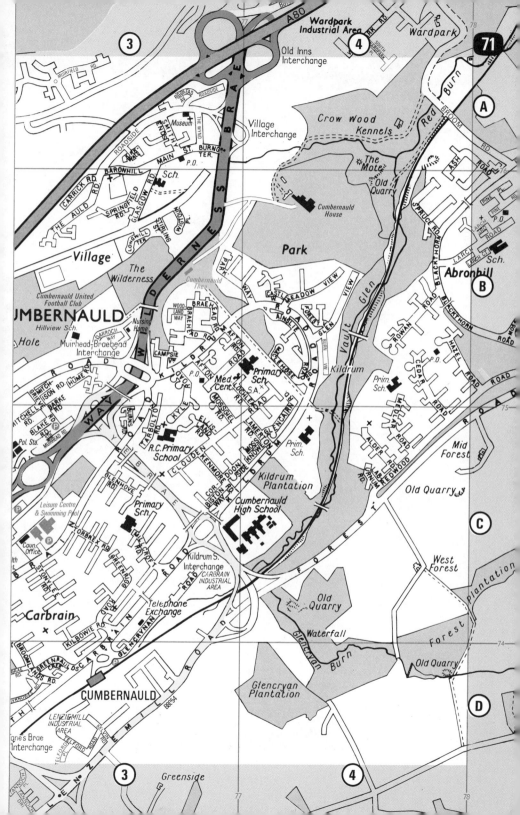

Glasgow

Local Information Guide

Contents

City of Glasgow Local Information Guide

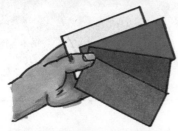

Useful information

Area of City 79 sq. miles (approx)

Population (Glasgow City)
(1989 estimate) 696,577

Early Closing Days
Tuesday with alternative of Saturday.
Most of the shops in the central area
operate six-day trading.

Electricity 240 volts A.C.

Emergency Services
Police, Fire and Ambulance. Dial 999
on any telephone.

Licensing Hours
Public Houses
Daily (except Sundays) 11 a.m. to
2.30 p.m. and 5 to 11 p.m. (many
open continuously 11 a.m. to
11 p.m.)
Sundays, 12.30 to 2.30 p.m. and 6.30
to 10.30 p.m.
Restaurants, Hotels and Public
Houses with catering facilities, same
as above but can be extended for
drinks with meals.

Information Bureau

Tourist Information Centres:
35–39 St. Vincent Place
Glasgow. 041-227 4880

Town Hall, Abbey Close
Paisley. 041-889 0711

Glasgow Airport 041-848 4440

Strathclyde Transport Travel Centre
St. Enoch Square
Open Monday–Saturday 9.30 a.m.
to 5.30 p.m. 041-226 4826 (Monday
to Saturday 7 a.m. to 9 p.m.,
Sunday 9 a.m.to 7-30 p.m.) for City
services, ferry services, local airlines,
train and express services. Free
timetables are available.

Help & Advice

British Broadcasting Corporation
Queen Margaret Drive, G12.
041-339 8844

British Council
6 Belmont Crescent, G12 8ES
041-339 8651

British Telecom Scotland

Glasgow Area
Westergate Chambers, 11 Hope Street,
Glasgow G2 6AB
All Enquires 041-220 1234 or dial
100 and ask for FREEFONE BT
GLASGOW

Chamber of Commerce
30 George Square, G2.
041-204 2121

Citizens Advice Bureau
212 Bath Street, Glasgow G2 4HW.
041-331 2345/6/7/8
119 Main Street, Glasgow G40 1HA.
041-554 0336

27 Dougrie Drive, Castlemilk,
Glasgow G45 9AD 041-634 0338
139 Main Street (Town Hall)
Rutherglen G73 4HG 041-647 5100
216 Main Streeet, Barrhead
041-881 2032
Civic Centre, East Kilbride
East Kilbride 21295
1143 Maryhill Road, Glasgow G20
041-946 6373/4
46 Township Centre, Easterhouse,
Glasgow G34 9DS 041-771 2328

Consumer Advice Centre
St. Enoch House, 1 St. Enoch Square
Glasgow G1 4BH. 041-204 0262

Customs and Excise
21 India Street, G2 4PZ
041-221 3828

H.M. Immigration Office
Admin Block D, Argyll Avenue
Glasgow Airport
Tel. 041-887 4115

Housing Aid and Advice
Shelter, 53 St. Vincent Crescent
Glasgow G3 8NQ. 041-221 8995/6

Legal Aid and Advice
Castlemilk Advice & Law Centre
27 Dougrie Drive, Glasgow G45.
041-634 0338

Law Centre
30 Dougrie Drive
041-634 0313

Lost Property
Strathclyde Passenger Transport
Executive
St. Enoch Underground Station
Tel. 041-248 6950 (City Buses)
12 West George Street G32
041-332 6811. (Underground)
Other Buses–Office of Bus Company.
Trains–Station of arrival.
Elsewhere in City–Strathclyde Police
Lost Property Department,
173 Pitt Street, G2
041-204 2626

Passport Office
Northgate 96 Milton Street
Glasgow G4. Tel. 041-332 0271

**Registrar of Births, Deaths and
Marriages**
1 Martha Street, G1. 041-227 6343
Hours – Monday to Friday 9.15 a.m.
to 4.00 p.m.

Births must be registered within
twenty-one days, deaths within eight
days, and marriages within three
days. The Registrar should be
consulted at least one month before
intended date of marriage.

**Royal Scottish Society for the
Prevention of Cruelty to Children**
15 Annfield Place, G31.
041-556 1156

**RNID–
Royal National Institute for the
Deaf**
9 Clairmont Gardens, Glasgow
G3 7LW. 041-332 0343

Samaritans
218 West Regent Street, Glasgow
G2 4DQ. 041-248 4488

**Scottish Society for the Mentally
Handicapped**
13 Elmbank Street, Glasgow G2.
041-226 4541

Scottish Television
Cowcaddens. G2. 041-332 9999

**Society for the Prevention of
Cruelty to Animals**
15 Royal Terrace, G3.
(Business Hours)   041-332 0716

Newspapers
Morning Daily
Daily Record
Anderston Quay, G3.   041-248 7000

Glasgow Herald
195 Albion Street, G1. 041-552 6255

Scottish Daily Express
Park Circus Place, G3. 041-332 9600

The Scotsman
181-195 West George St., G2 2LB
                              041-221 6485
Evening Daily
Evening Times
195 Albion Street, G1. 041-552 6255

Weekly
Scottish Sunday Express
Park Circus Place, G3. 041-552 3550

Sunday Mail
Anderston Quay, G3.   041-248 7000

Sunday Post
144 Port Dundas Road, G4.
041-332 9933

Parking

Car parking in the central area of Glasgow is controlled. Parking meters are used extensively and signs indicating restrictions are displayed at kerbsides and on entry to the central area. Traffic Wardens are on duty.

British Rail Car Parks
(Open 24 hours)
Central Station
Queen Street Station

Multi-Storey Car Parks
(Open 24 hours)
Anderston Cross: Cambridge Street:
George Street: Mitchell Street: Port
Dundas Road: Waterloo Street.

(Limited Opening)
Charing Cross
Sauchiehall Street Centre

Surface Car Parks
Carrick Street: Holland Street:
Ingram Street: McAlpine Street:
North Frederick Street: Albion
Street: Oswald Street:
Shuttle Street.

Post Offices

Head Post Office
George Square, G2   041-248 2882
Open Monday to Thursday 9 a.m. to
5.30 p.m. Fridays 9.30 a.m. to
5.30 p.m. Saturdays 9.a.m. to 12.30 p.m.
Closed Sunday.
Branch Offices
85–91 Bothwell Street, G2.
4 Dixon Street, G1.

216 Hope Street, G2.
533 Sauchiehall Street, G3.

Taxis

Glasgow has over 1400 traditional London type taxis, all licensed by the Glasgow District Council and all fitted with meters sealed and approved by the Council. A fare card stating the current tariff is displayed in a prominent position within each taxi. At the time of publishing a three mile journey costs £2.40 and waiting time is charged at 10p per minute the total price of each journey is shown on the meter. Fares are normally revued annually by the council. Each taxi can carry a maximum of five passengers.

The major taxi companies in the city offer City tours at fixed prices, listing the places of interest to be visited, leaflets are available at all major hotel reception areas. Tours vary from 2 to 3 hours and in price between £17 and £24.

Any passenger wishing to travel to a destination outside the Glasgow District Boundary should ascertain from the driver the fare to be charged or the method of calculating the fare PRIOR to making the journey.

Complaints

Any complaints regarding the conduct of a taxi driver should be addressed to the Senior Enforcement Officer, Town Clerk's Office, City Chambers, Glasgow. Tel: 041-227-4535.

Local Government

Strathclyde Regional Council
Strathclyde House, 20 India Street
Glasgow G2 4PF
041-204 2900

District Councils:

Argyll & Bute
District Council Headquarters
Kilmory, Lochgilphead PA31 8RT
0546 2127

Bearsden & Milngavie
Municipal Building, Boclair
Bearsden G61 2TQ
041-942 2262

Clydebank
Council Offices, Rosebery Place
Clydebank G81 1TG
041-941 1331

Clydesdale
Clydesdale District Offices
Lanark ML11 7JT
0555 61331

Cumbernauld & Kilsyth
Council Offices, Bron Way
Cumbernauld G67 1DZ
02367 22131

Cummock & Doon Valley
Council Offices, Lugar
Cumnock KA18 3JQ
0290 22111

Cunninghame
Cunninghame House
Irvine KA12 8EE
0294 74166

Dumbarton
Crosslet House
Dumbarton G82 3NS
0389 65100

East Kilbride
Civic Centre
East Kilbride G74 1AB
035-52 28777

Eastwood
Council Offices
Eastwood Park, Rouken Glen Road
Rouken Glen, Giffnock
Glasgow G46 6UG
041-638 6511
041-638 1101

Glasgow City
City Chambers
Glasgow G2 1DU
041-221 9600

Hamilton
Town House
102 Cadzow Street
Hamilton ML3 6HH
0698 282323

Inverclyde
Municipal Buildings
Greenock PA15 1LY
0475 24400

Kilmarnock & Loudoun
Civic Centre
Kilmarnock KA1 1BY
0563 21140

Kyle & Carrick
Burns House
Burns Statue Square
Ayr KA7 1UT
0292 281511

Monklands
Municipal Buildings
Dunbeth Road
Coatbridge ML5 3LF
0236 41200

Motherwell
PO Box 14
Civic Centre
Motherwell ML1 1TW
0698 66166

Renfrew
Municipal Buildings
Cotton Street
Paisley PA1 1BU
041-889 5400

Strathkelvin
Tom Johnston House
Civic Way
Kirkintilloch
Glasgow G66 4TJ
041-776 7171

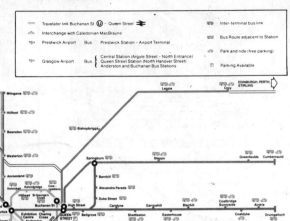

History & Development

The City of Glasgow began life as a makeshift hamlet of huts huddled round a 6thC church, built by St Mungo on the banks of a little salmon river — the Clyde. It was called Gleschow, meaning 'beloved green place' in Celtic. The cathedral was founded in 1136; the university, the second oldest in Scotland, was established in the 15thC; and in 1454 the flourishing mediaeval city wedged between the cathedral and the river was made a Royal burgh. The city's commercial prosperity dates from the 17thC when the lucrative tobacco, sugar and cotton trade with the New World flourished. The River Clyde, Glasgow's gateway to the Americas, was dredged, deepened and widened in the 18thC to make it navigable to the city's heart.

By the 19thC, Glasgow was the greatest shipbuilding centre in the world. From the 1820s onwards, it grew in leaps and bounds westwards along a steep ridge of land running parallel with the river. The hillside became encased in an undulating grid of streets and squares. Gradually the individualism, expressed in one-off set pieces characteristic of the 18thC and early 19thC, gave way to a remarkable coherent series of terraced squares and crescents of epic proportions — making Glasgow one of the finest of Victorian cities. But the price paid for such rapid industrialisation, the tremendous social problems manifest in the squalor of some of the worst of 19thC slums, was high. Today the city is still the commercial and industrial capital of the West of Scotland. The most notorious of the slums have been cleared but the new buildings lack that sparkling clench-fisted Glaswegian character of the 19thC. Ironically, this character was partially destroyed when the slums were cleared for it wasn't the architecture that had failed, only the bureaucrats, who designated such areas as working class ghettos.

Districts
Little remains of mediaeval Glasgow, which stood on the wedge of land squeezed between the cathedral and the River Clyde. Its business centre was The Cross, a space formed by the junction of several streets — the tall, square Tolbooth Steeple, 1626, in the middle. Opposite is Trongate, an arch astride a footpath, complete with tower and steeple salvaged from 17thC St Mary's Church — destroyed by fire in 1793. The centre of 20thC Glasgow is George Square, a tree-lined piazza planned in 1781 and pinned down by more than a dozen statues including an 80-foot-high Doric column built in 1837 to carry a statue of Sir Walter Scott. Buildings of interest: the monumental neo-Baroque City Chambers 1883-88 which take up the east side and the Merchants' House 1874, on the west. To the south of the square, in a huddle of narrow streets, is the old Merchant City. Of interest here is the elegant Trades House, 85 Glassford Street, built by Robert Adam in 1794. An elegant Ionic portico stands on a rusticated ground storey flanked by domed towers. Hutcheson's Hospital, 158 Ingram Street, is a handsome Italianate building designed by David Hamilton in 1805. Nearby is Stirling's Library, originally an 18thC private residence, it became the Royal Exchange in 1827 when the Corinthian portico was added.

To the north west is Kelvingrove, Victorian Glasgow at its best. Built around a steep saddle of land, landscaped by Paxton in 1850 and lined along its edge with handsome terraces.

Last but not least are the banks of the River Clyde. From Clyde Walkway on the north bank you can see: the Suspension Bridge of 1871 with its pylons in the form of triumphal arches; the old clipper ship, C. V. Carrick, a contemporary of the Cutty Sark, moored by Victoria bridge; 17thC Merchants' Steeple; the Gothic Revival St Andrew's R.C. Cathedral of 1816; the church, built 1739, in nearby St Andrew's Square is a typical copy of London's St Martin-in-the-Fields.

Buildings & Shops

Interesting buildings

Victorian Glasgow was extremely eclectic architecturally. Good examples of the Greek Revival style are Royal College of Physicians 1845, by W. H. Playfair and the Custom House 1840, by G. L. Taylor. The Queen's Room 1857, by Charles Wilson, is a handsome temple used now as a Christian Science church. The Gothic style is seen at its most exotic in the Stock Exchange 1877, by J. Burnet. The new Victorian materials and techniques with glass, wrought and cast iron were also ably demonstrated in the buildings of the time. Typical are: Gardener's Stores 1856, by J. Baird; the Buck's Head, Argyle Street, an amalgam of glass and cast iron; and the Egyptian Halls of 1873, in Union Street, which has a masonry framework. Both are by Alexander Thomson. The Templeton Carpet Factory 1889, Glasgow Green, by William Leiper, is a Venetian Gothic building complete with battlemented parapet.

Glasgow University

The great genius of Scottish architecture is Charles Rennie Mackintosh whose major buildings are in Glasgow. In the Scotland Street School 1904-6, he punctuated a 3-storey central block with flanking staircase towers in projecting glazed bays. His most famous building — Glasgow School of Art 1897-9 — is a magnificent Art Nouveau building of taut stone and glass; the handsome library, with its gabled facade, was added later in 1907-9.

Stirling's Library

Galleries & museums

Scotland's largest tourist attraction, The Burrell Collection, is situated in Pollok Country Park, Haggs Road and has more than 8,000 objects, housed in an award-winning gallery. The Museum and Art Gallery , Kelvingrove Park , Argyle Street, a palatial sandstone building with glazed central court, has one of the best municipal collections in Britain; superb Flemish, Dutch and French paintings, drawings, prints, also ceramics, silver, costumes and armour, as well as a natural history section. Provand's Lordship c1471, in Castle Street, is Glasgow's oldest house and now a museum of 17th-18thC furniture and household articles. Pollok House, Pollok Country Park, a handsome house designed by William Adam in 1752, has paintings by William Blake and a notable collection of Spanish paintings, including works by El Greco. The Museum of Transport, housed in Kelvin Hall, Bunhouse Road, has a magnificent collection of trams, cars, ships models, bicycles, horse-drawn carriages and 7 steam locos. The People's Palace, The Green, built 1898 with a huge glazed Winter Garden, has a lively illustrated history of the city. But the oldest museum in Glasgow is the Hunterian Museum, University of Glasgow, University Avenue, opened in 1807, it has a fascinating collection of manuscripts, early printed books, as well as some fine archaeological and geological exhibits. 400-year-old Haggs Castle, St Andrew's Drive, is now a children's museum with practical demonstrations and exhibits showing how everyday life has changed over the centuries.

Streets & shopping

The Oxford Street of Glasgow is Sauchiehall (meaning 'willow meadow') Street. This with Buchanan Street and Argyle Street is the main shopping centre. Here you will find the department stores, boutiques and general shops. All three streets are

Old Sheriff Court

partly pedestrianised, but the most exhilarating is undoubtedly Buchanan Street. Of particular interest is the spatially elegant Argyll Arcade 1828, the Venetian Gothic-style Stock Exchange 1877, the picturesque Dutch gabled Buchanan Street Bank building 1896 and the Glasgow Royal Concert Hall (opened 1990). In Glasgow Green is The Barrows, the city's famous street market, formed by the junction of London Road and Kent Street. The Market is *open weekends*. Some parts of the city have *EC Tue*.

Museum & Art Gallery Kelvingrove

Cathedrals & Churches

Glasgow Cathedral is a perfect example of pre-Reformation Gothic architecture. Begun in 1238, it has a magnificent choir and handsome nave with shallow projecting transepts. On a windy hill to the east is the Necropolis, a cemetery with a spiky skyline of Victoriana consisting of pillars, temples and obelisks, dominated by an 1825 Doric column carrying the statue of John Knox. Other churches of interest: Lansdowne Church built by J. Honeyman in 1863; St George's Tron Church by William Stark 1807; Caledonian Road Church, a temple and tower atop a storey-high base, designed by Alexander Thomson in 1857; a similar design is to be found at the United Presbyterian Church, St Vincent Street, 1858, but on a more highly articulated ground storey; Queen's Cross Church 1897 is an amalgam of Art Nouveau and Gothic Revival by the brilliant Charles Rennie Mackintosh.

Churches within the central area of Glasgow are:

Church of Scotland
Glasgow Cathedral
Castle Street
Renfield St. Stephen's Church
262 Bath Street
St. George's Tron Church
165 Buchanan Street
St. Columba Church (Gaelic)
300 St. Vincent Street

Baptist
Adelaide Place Church
209 Bath Street

Congregational
Hillhead Centre
1 University Avenue

Episcopal Church in Scotland
Cathedral Church of St. Mary
300 Great Western Road, G4.

First Church of Christ Scientist
1 la Bell Place, Clifton Street, G3.
(off Sauchiehall Street)

Free Church of Scotland
265 St. Vincent Street

German Speaking Congregation
Services held at 7 Hughenden
Terrace, G12.

Greek Orthodox Cathedral
St. Luke's, 27 Dundonald Road, G12.

Jewish Orthodox Synagogue
Garnethill, 29 Garnet Street

Methodist
Woodlands Church
229 Woodlands Road

Roman Catholic
St. Andrew's Cathedral
190 Clyde Street
St. Aloysius' Church
25 Rose Street

Unitarian Church
72 Berkeley Street

United Free
Wynd Church,
427 Crown Street, G5.

Glasgow Cathedral

Entertainment

As Scotland's commercial and industrial capital, Glasgow offers a good choice of leisure activities. The city now has 6 theatres where productions ranging from serious drama to pantomime, pop and musicals are performed. The Theatre Royal, Hope Street, is Scotland's only opera house and has been completely restored to its full Victorian splendour. The Royal Scottish National Orchestra gives concerts at the Glasgow Royal Concert Hall, every Sat night in winter and is the venue for the proms in Jun. Cinemas are still thriving in Glasgow, as are the many public houses, some of which provide meals and live entertainment. In the city centre and Byres Road, West End, there is a fair number of restaurants where traditional home cooking, as well as international cuisines, can be sampled. More night life can be found at the city's discos and dance halls — Tiffany's, Sauchiehall Street and the Plaza, Eglinton Toll. Outdoors, apart from the many parks and nature trails, there is Calderpark Zoological Gardens, situated 6 miles from the centre between Mount Vernon and Uddingston. Here you may see white rhinos, black panthers and iguanas among many species. Departing from Stobcross Quay, you can also cruise down the Clyde in 'P.S. Waverley' – the last sea-going paddle-steamer in the world.

Cinemas

Cannon Cinema, 380 Clarkston Rd, G44. 041-637 2641
Cannon Film Centre–
326 Sauchiehall St, G2. 041-332 9513
(Admin Dept), 326 Sauchiehall St, G2
041-332 1592
326 Sauchiehall St, G2. 041-332 1593
Caledonian Associated Cinemas Ltd–
Regent House, 72 Renfield St, G2
041-332 0606
Cannon Grand–
18 Jamaica St, G1. 041-248 4620
Glasgow Film Theatre–
12 Rose St, G3. (Box Off) 041-332 6535

Grosvenor Cinema–
Ashton Lane, G12. 041-339 4298
Kelburne Cinema–
(Manager), Glasgow Rd, Paisley
041-889 3612
Odeon Film Centre, 56 Renfield St, G2.
041-332 8701
Salon Cinema, Vinicombe St, G12.
041-339 4256

Halls

City Halls, Candleriggs, G1.
Couper Institute
86 Clarkston Road, G44.
Dixon Halls, 650 Cathcart Road, G42.
Glasgow Royal Concert Hall
2 Sauchiehall Street, G3
Govan Hall, Summertown Road, G51.
Kelvin Hall, Argyle Street, G3.
Langside Hall, 5 Langside Avenue, G41.
Partick Hall, 9 Burgh Hall Street, G11.
Pollokshaws Hall
2025 Pollokshaws Road, G43.
Woodside Hall, Glenfarg Street, G20.

(More information about the above G.D.C. halls and others from the Director, Halls and Theatres Department, Candleriggs, G1. 041-552 1201).

Theatres

Citizens' Theatre
Gorbals Street. 041-429 0022
King's Theatre, Bath Street.
Mitchell Theatre and Moir Hall
Granville Street.
Pavilion Theatre
Renfield Street. 041-332 1846
Theatre Royal
Hope Street. 041-331 1234
Tron Theatre
38 Parnie Street. 041-552 3748
The Ticket Centre
Glasgow's Central Box Office for King's Theatre, Mitchell Theatre, Kelvin Hall, Citizen's Theatre, Theatre Royal and City Hall at Candleriggs, G1.
Open Monday to Saturday 10.30 a.m. to 6.30 p.m.
041-227 5511

Glasgow *(Abbotsinch)* Airport

Glasgow Airport is located eight miles West of Glasgow alongside the M8 motorway at Junction 28. It is linked by a bus service to Anderston Cross Bus Station, the journey time is 25 minutes and buses leave at 30 minute intervals. There is a frequent coach service linking the Airport with

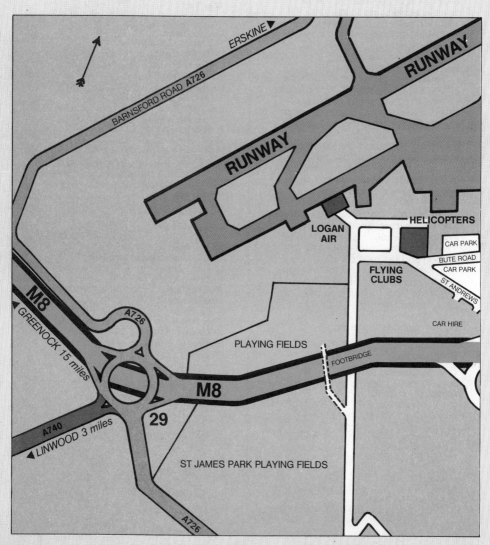

all major bus and rail terminals in the City and a Coach/Air link to and from Prestwick Airport.

The Airport Terminal has a restaurant, grill, buffet, three bars, lounges, shop, post office and banking facilities.

Car parking is available with a graduated scale of charges.

The Airport telephone no is 041-887 1111.

Airlines

(Domestic Routes)
British Airways
66 Gordon Street
Glasgow G1
Reservations Tel: 041-332 9666
British Caledonian Airways
(contact British Airways)
British Midland
Merlin House, Mossland Road,
Hillington, Glasgow
Reservations Tel: 041-204 2436
Loganair Ltd.
Glasgow Airport (administration)
Tel: 041-889 3181.
Trident House, Renfrew Road, Paisley

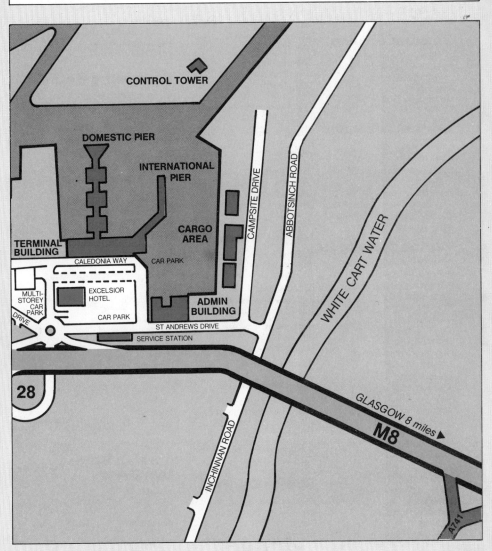

Sport & Recreation

For both spectator and participant, football is Glasgow's favourite sport. Both Celtic and Rangers, Scotland's most famous rival teams, have their grounds within the City. Glasgow houses Scotland's national football stadium at Hampden Park.

Badminton

Scottish Badminton Union's
Cockburn Centre, Bogmoor
Place, G51 4TQ.
041-445 1218

Bowling Greens

There are greens in all the main Parks. Information about clubs from the Scottish Bowling Association:
50 Wellington Street, G2.
041-221 8999.

Cricket Grounds

Cartha Haggs Road, G41.
Clydesdale Beaton Road, G41.
Huntershill Crowhill Road, Bishopbriggs.
Poloc 'Shawholm'
2060 Pollokshaws Road, G43.
West of Scotland Peel Street, G11.

Football Grounds

Celtic Park (Celtic F.C.)
95 Kerrydale St. G40
Firhill Park (Partick Thistle F.C. & Clyde F.C.)
Firhill Rd. G20
Hampden Park (Queen's Park F.C.)
Somerville Dr., G42
Ibrox Park (Rangers F.C.)
Edmiston Dr., G51
Kilbowie Park (Clydebank F.C.)
Argyll Rd., Clydebank
Mertland
Kirkintilloch
St. Mirren Park (St. Mirren F.C.)
Love St., Paisley

Golf Courses

Glasgow District Council
9 holes
Alexandra Park
King's Park.

Knightswood, Lincoln Avenue, G13.
Ruchill, Brassey Street, G20.

18 holes
Lethamhill, Cumbernauld Road,
Littlehill, Auchinairn Road, G64.
Linn Park.

(Charges displayed)
Dougalston Golf Course
Strathblane Road, Milngavie.
(Five miles from Glasgow).
Open to the public daily.
041-956 5750 for charges.

Putting Greens

There are putting greens in some of the main Parks.

Pitch & Putt

Courses at Bellahouston Park,
Queen's Park, Rouken Glen
and several others.

Rugby Grounds

Auldhouse
(Hutchesons'/Aloysians)
Thornliebank

Garscadden
(Glasgow University)
Garscadden Road South, G15.

Hughenden
(Hillhead High School)
Hughenden Road, G12.

New Anniesland
(Glasgow Acad.)
Helensburgh Drive, G13.

Old Anniesland
(Glasgow High School F.P. & Kelvinside Academicals)
Crow Road, G11

Westerlands
(Glasgow University)
Ascot Avenue, G12

Sports Centres

Bellahouston
Bellahouston Drive, G52.
041-427 5454.

Burnhill
Toryglen Road, Rutherglen.
041-643 0327.

James Murray
Caledonia Road, Baillieston.
041-773 0881

Springburn
Springburn Way, Springburn.
041-558 7358.

Helenvale Park
Outdoor Sports Complex
Helenvale Street, G31.
041-554 4109.

Swimming Baths

Glasgow District Council
Castlemilk, 137 Castlemilk Drive, G45.
Drumchapel, 199 Drumry Road East.
Easterhouse, Bogbain Road, G34.
Govan, Harhill Street, G51.
Govanhill, 99 Calder Street, G42.
North Woodside, Braid Square.
Pollokshaws (Dry-Land/Water Sports Complex) Ashtree Road, G43.
Rutherglen, 44 Greenhill Road, G73.
Shettleston, Elvan Street, G32.
Temple, Knightscliffe Avenue, G13.
Whitehill, Onslow Drive, G31.
Whiteinch, Medwyn Street, G14.

Hours
Monday to Friday 9 a.m. to 9 p.m.
Saturday 9 a.m. to 1 p.m.
*Sunday 9 a.m. to 1 p.m.

Charges
Admission charges are minimal.
OAPs free at certain times.

Turkish Baths/ Sun Beds

available at:
Govanhill   041-423 0233
Pollokshaws   041-632 2200
Shettleston   041-778 1346

and Whiteinch,   041-959 2465
Men and women on separate days. Telephone direct to baths for more information.

Hours
(All the year round).
Monday to Friday 9 a.m. to 9 p.m.
Saturday 9 a.m. to 1 p.m.

SAUNA at:

Castlemilk,	041-634 8254
Drumchapel,	041-944 5812
Rutherglen,	041-647 4530
and Whitehill,	041-551 9969

Tennis

There are courts in some of the main parks. Information about clubs from the Secretary of the West of Scotland Lawn Tennis Association:
Mr. N. Floyd, 1 Boclair Road
Bearsden   041-942 0162

Weather

The City of Glasgow is on the same latitude as the City of Moscow, but because of its close proximity to the warm Atlantic Shores, and the prevailing westerly winds, it enjoys a more moderate climate. Summers are generally cool and winters mostly mild, this gives Glasgow fairly consistent summer and winter temperatures. Despite considerable cloud the City is sheltered by hills to the south-west and north and the average rainfall for Glasgow is usually less than 40 inches per year.

The following table shows the approximate average figures for sunshine, rainfall and temperatures to be expected in Glasgow throughout the year:

Weather Forecasts
For the Glasgow Area including Loch Lomond and the Clyde Coast:
Weatherline
0898 500421 (Recording)
The Glasgow Weather Centre
(Meteorological Office)
33 Bothwell Street, G2
041-248 3451

Month	Hours of Sunshine	Inches of Rainfall	Temperature °C		
			Ave. Max.	Ave. Min.	High/Low
Jan	36	3.8	5.5	0.8	−18
Feb	62	2.8	6.3	0.8	−15
Mar	94	2.4	8.8	2.2	21
Apr	147	2.4	11.9	3.9	22
May	185	2.7	15.1	6.2	26
June	181	2.4	17.9	9.3	30
July	159	2.9	18.6	10.8	29
Aug	143	3.5	18.5	10.6	31
Sept	106	4.1	16.3	9.1	−4
Oct	76	4.1	13.0	6.8	−8
Nov	47	3.7	8.7	3.3	−11
Dec	30	4.2	6.5	1.9	−12

Renfrew District

A selection of leisure, recreational and cultural attractions in Renfrew District:

Barrhead Sports' Centre

The Centre contains swimming-pools, sports halls, activity rooms and sauna suite. Bar and restaurant facilities add to the wide range of sporting and leisure activities available.

Barshaw Park, Glasgow Road, Paisley

The park is extensive with formal and informal areas. It adjoins the public golf course and incorporates a boating-pond, playgrounds, model "ride-on" railway and a nature corner.

Castle Semple Country Park, Lochwinnoch

Castle Semple Loch is a popular feature for sailing and fishing. Canoes, rowing boats and sailing boards for hire. Fishing permits available. Tel: Lochwinnoch 842882.

Coats Observatory

The Observatory has traditionally recorded astronomical and meteorological information since 1882. Now installed with a satellite picture receiver, it is one of the best equipped Observatories in the country. Monday, Tuesday, Thursday 2 p.m.-8 p.m., Wednesday, Friday, Saturday 10 a.m.-5 p.m, October to end March 7-15 p.m.-9.45 p.m. Tel: 041 889 3151

Erskine Bridge

The bridge is an impressive high level structure opened by HRH Princess Anne in 1971 and provides a direct link from Renfrew District to Loch Lomond and the Trossachs. The bridge replaced the Erskine Ferry and affords extensive views up and down river to pedestrian users.

Finlayston Estate

Off the A8 at Langbank. The Estate is now a garden centre with woodland walks. The house has connections with John Knox and Robert Burns and is open April to August on Sundays from 2.30–4.30pm. At other times groups by appointment. Tel: Langbank 285.

Formakin Estate, By Bishopton

A group of buildings and landscaped grounds designed in the Arts and Crafts style at the turn of the century. Currently being restored, the estate has a visitor centre, tea room and guided tours. Open Saturday and Sunday 11 a.m.-6 p.m. Tel: 0505 863400

Gleniffer Braes Country Park, Glenfield Road, Paisley

1,000 breathtaking acres including Glen Park nature trail, picnic and children's play areas. Open dawn till dusk, the park affords extensive walks and spectacular views from this elevated moorland area, and contains an area reserved for model aero flying. Tel: 041-884 3794

Houston Village

Houston was developed in the 18th century as an estate village. The traditional smiddy building, village pubs and terraced houses combine to create a quiet, sleepy atmosphere which has successfully survived the development of extensive modern housing on its periphery.

Inchinnan Bridges

Early 19th century stone bridges over the White Cart and Black Cart rivers close to St Conval's stone, and the site of the Inchinnan Church which houses the graves of the Knights Templar, whose order was introduced to Scotland in 1153 by King David I.

Johnstone Castle

The remnants of a 1700 building formerly a much larger structure but largely demolished in the 1950's. The castle has significant historical links with the Cochrane and Houston families, major landowners who were instrumental in the development of the Burgh of Johnstone.

Kilbarchan Village

A good example of an 18 Century weaving village with many original buildings still fronting the narrow streets. A focal point is the steeple building in the square, orginally a school and meal market and now used as public meeting rooms. A cycle route/footpath system links it to Glasgow and the Clyde Coast.

Laigh Kirk, Paisley

Originally built in 1738, the Laigh Kirk has been converted to an Arts Centre, with a theatre, workshop, bistro and bar open daily 10 a.m.-11 p.m. For further information telephone 041-887 1010

Linwood Sports Centre

A wide range of indoor and outdoor sporting activities include football and Rugby pitches, games hall, squash courts, BMX track, fitness trail, tennis courts and conditioning suite.

Lochwinnoch Village

An attractive rural village close to the Castle Semple Water Park, Muirshiel Country Park and the R.S.P.B. nature reserve, Lochwinnoch contains a small local museum with displays reflecting agricultural, social and industrial aspects of village life. Museum open Monday, Wednesday and Friday 10am–1pm, 2–5pm and 6–8pm. Tuesday and Saturday 10am–1pm and 2–5pm. Open most days throughout the year, visitors should telephone Lochwinnoch 842615.

Muirshiel Country Park

Four miles north of Lochwinnoch, the park features trails of varying length radiating from the Information Centre. open daily 9 a.m.-4-30 p.m. (Winter), 9 a m.-7-30 p.m. (Summer). Tel: Lochwinnoch 842803

Paisley Town Trail

An easy-to-follow route taking in the town's historic and architecturally significant buildings. Visitors can spend an hour or two walking round the trail and referring to a printed guide and wall plaques on the main buildings.

Paisley, Lagoon Leisure Centre

Ultra-modern complex with extensive "fun" pool featuring artificial wave machine and water slides. Also has cafe/bar facilities. Unique within the area, the complex is easily reached by public trasport and has ample parking. Monday-Friday 10 a.m.-10 p.m., Saturday and Sunday 10 a.m.-5.00 p.m. Tel: 041-889 4000.

Paisley Abbey

Birthplace of the Stewart Dynasty, the Abbey dates, in part, to the 12th century and features regimental flags, relics, the Barochan Cross and beautiful stained glass windows. Monday-Saturday 10.00 a.m.-12.00 p.m., 1.00-3.00p.m. Tel: 041-889 3630.

Paisley Town Hall

A Renaissance style building by the River Cart in the heart of Paisley, it features a slim clock tower and houses a Tourist Information Centre. It accommodates many exhibitions during the year and is also available for conferences and functions. Monday–Saturday 9am–5pm. Tel: 041-887 1007.

Paisley Museum and Art Gallery, High Street, Paisley

In addition to the world famous collection of Paisley shawls, the Museum traces the history of the Paisley pattern, the development of weaving techniques and houses collections of local and natural history, ceramics and paintings. Monday-Saturday 10 a.m.-5 p.m. Tel: 041-889 3151.

Renfrew Town Hall

The Town Hall has a ''fairy-tale'' style to its 105 feet high spire and was the administrative centre of the Royal Burgh of Renfrew. Originally the principal town in the area, Renfrew was strategically placed on the River Clyde, and a passenger ferry continues to operate daily.

Robert Tannahill, Weaver Poet

The works of Tannahill ranks with those of Burns. Born 1774 he took his own life in 1810 and is buried in a nearby graveyard. Visitors can visit his early home, site of his death, and his grave, and read his works in Paisley Library.

Royal Society for Protection of Birds, Lochwinnoch

An interesting visitor centre with observation tower, hides, displays and gift shop. Thursday, Friday, Saturday and Sunday 10 a.m.-5.15 p.m. Shop open 7 days. Tel: Lochwinnoch 842663

Sma' Shot Cottages, Paisley

Fully restored and furnished artisan's house of the Victorian era; exhibition room displaying photographs plus artefacts of local interest. 18th century weaver's loomshop with combined living quarters. Open May-September 1-5 p.m. Group visits arranged by appointment. Tel: 041-812 2513 or 041-889 0530.

The Clyde Estuary

Visitors travelling along the rural route of the Old Greenock Road above Langbank village at the western end of the District are able to take advantage of extensive views of the upper and lower Clyde Estuary, the Gareloch and the mountains beyond.

Thomas Coats Memorial Church

Open Monday-Friday 9 a.m.-12 noon. Visitors should check in advance. Another gift from the Coats family to Paisley, the church was built in 1894 and constructed of red sandstone, is one of the finest Bapist Churches in the country. Tel: 041 889 9980.

Wallace Monument, Elderslie

The monument was erected in 1912 and marks the birthplace of the Scottish Patriot, Sir William Wallace. It stands adjacent to the reconstructed foundation plan of the adjacent Wallace Buildings which dated from the 17th century.

Weaver's Cottage, Kilbarchan

This cottage, built in 1723, houses the last of the village's 800 looms and demonstrations are still given. It contains displays of weaving and domestic utensils, with Cottage garden and refreshments. Open April 1–May 31 and September 1–October 31 on Tuesdays, Thursdays, Saturdays and Sundays 2–5pm, June 1–August 31 from 2–5pm daily.

Public Transport

The City of Glasgow has one of the most advanced, fully integrated public transport systems in the whole of Europe. The Strathclyde Transport network consists of; the local British Rail network, the local bus services and the fully modernised Glasgow Underground, with links to Glasgow Airport and the Steamer and Car Ferry Services.
Note: Although the information in this section is correct at the time of printing it should be checked before use.

Bus Services and Tours

Long Distance Coach Service
Scottish Citylink Coaches Ltd
041-332 9191

Shorter Journeys
Tel: 041-226 4826(0630-2300 Daily) for City Services and buses to Airdrie, Clydebank, Cumbernauld, Dumbarton, East Kilbride, Erskine, Hamilton, Johnstone, Kirkintilloch, Paisley, Wishaw
Buses leave from Anderston Cross Bus Station 041-248 7432.
for Ayr, Bearsden, Bellshill, Blantyre, Cumbernauld, Edinburgh, Glasgow Airport, Gourock, Hamilton, Kilmarnock, Lanark, Motherwell, Prestwick, Renfrew, Newmains, Wishaw etc.

Buses leave from Buchanan Bus Station 041-332 7133.
for Aberfoyle, Airdrie, Bishopbriggs Callander, Coatbridge, Cumbernauld, Dundee, Dunfermline, Edinburgh, Glasgow Airport, Glencoe, Kirkintilloch,

Kilsyth, Leven, Milngavie, Perth, St.Andrews, Stirling etc.

Day and Half Day Tours
Scottish City Link
Buchanan Bus Station.
041-332 8055

Haldane's of Cathcart, Delvin Road, G44. 041-637 2234.

Strathclyde Buses Ltd.
197 Victoria Road, G42 7AD
041-636 3190
(Glasgow City Bus Tour and Glimpses of Charles R. Mackintosh Architecture with C.R.M. Society) 041-636 3195

British Rail

Passenger enquiries: 041-204 2844.
Sleeper reservations: 041-221 2305.

Central Station
Inter-City electric services for English destinations, including Carlisle, Preston, Liverpool, Manchester (3 hours 35 minutes), Leeds, Nottingham, Crewe, Birmingham (4 hours 20 minutes), London (Euston) (5 hours). Also connections for Wales and West of England.
Scottish destinations in South and West include Ayr (for Burns country), Kilmarnock, Dumfries, Stranraer (for Ireland via Larne), Ardrossan and Largs. Electric trains include Gourock and Wemyss Bay (for Clyde steamers).

Queen Street Station
Trains for scenic West Highland Line to Oban, Fort William and Mallaig. Steamer connections to the Islands. Inter-City expresses for Edinburgh, connecting with trains to England including Newcastle, York, London (King's Cross). Services for North and East Scotland, including Fife, Stirling, Perth, Dundee, Aberdeen, Inverness, Wick, Thurso, Kyle of Lochalsh.
Electric trains: Dumbarton, Balloch (for Loch Lomond), Helensburgh. City Rail Link Service bus connects Queen Street Station and Central Station.

Parks & Gardens

There are over 70 public parks within the city. The most famous is Glasgow Green. Abutting the north bank of the River Clyde, it was acquired in 1662. Of interest are the Winter Gardens attached to the People's Palace. Kelvingrove Park is an 85-acre park laid out by Sir Joseph Paxton in 1852. On the south side of the city is the 148-acre Queen's Park, Victoria Road, established 1857-94. Also of interest: Rouken Glen, Thornliebank, with a spectacular waterfall, walled garden, nature trail and boating facilities; Victoria Park, Victoria Park Drive, with its famous Fossil Grove flower gardens and yachting pond. In Great Western Road are the Botanic Gardens. Founded in 1817, the gardens' 42 acres are crammed with natural attractions, including the celebrated Kibble Palace glasshouse with its fabulous tree ferns, exotic plants and white marble Victorian statues.

The main public parks in Glasgow are:

Alexandra
671 Alexandra Parade, G31.

Bellahouston
Paisley Road West, G52.

Botanic Gardens
730 Gt. Western Road, G12.

Hogganfield Loch
Cumbernauld Road, G33.

Kelvingrove
Sauchiehall Street, G3.

King's
325 Carmunnock Road, G44.

Linn
Clarkston Road at Netherlee Road, G44.

Queen's
Victoria Road, G42.

Rouken Glen
Rouken Glen Road, G46.

Springburn
Broomfield Road, G21.

Tollcross
461 Tollcross Road, G32.

Victoria
Victoria Park Drive North, G14.

Kibble Palace

Strathclyde Further Education

Anniesland College
Hatfield Drive, Glasgow, G12 0YE.
041-357 3969

Ayr College
Dam Park, Ayr, KA8 0EU.
Ayr (0292) 265184

Barmulloch College
186 Rye Road, Glasgow, G21 3JY.
041-558 9071

Bell College of Technology
Almada Street, Hamilton,
Lanarkshire, ML3 0JB.
Hamilton (0698) 283100

Cambuslang College
Hamilton Road,
Cambuslang, Glasgow, G72 7BS.
041-641 6197

**Cardonald College of Further
Education**
690 Mosspark Drive, Glasgow,
G52 3AY.
041-883 6151

Central College of Commerce
300 Cathedral Street, G1 2TA.
041-552 3941

Clydebank College
Kilbowie Road, Clydebank,
Dunbartonshire, G81 2AA.
041-952 7771

Coatbridge College
Kildonan Street, Coatbridge,
Lanarkshire, ML5 3LS.
Coatbridge (0236) 22316

Cumbernauld College
Town Centre, Cumbernauld,
Glasgow, G67 1HU.
Cumbernauld (0236) 731811

**Glasgow College of Building and
Printing**
60 North Hanover Street, Glasgow,
G1 2BP.
041-332 9969

**Glasgow College of Food
Technology**
230 Cathedral Street, Glasgow,
G1 2TG.
041-552 3751

**Glasgow College of Nautical
Studies**
21 Thistle Street, Glasgow, G5 9XB.
041-429 3201

Glasgow College of Technology
Cowcaddens Road, Glasgow,
G4 0BA.
041-332 7090

James Watt College
Finnart Street, Greenock,
Renfrewshire, PA16 8HF.
Greenock (0475) 24433

John Wheatley College
1346-1364 Shettleston Road,
Glasgow G32 9AT
041-778 2426

Kilmarnock College
Holehouse Road, Kilmarnock,
Ayrshire, KA3 7AT.
Kilmarnock (0563) 23501

Langside College
50 Prospecthill Road, Glasgow,
G42 9LB.
041-649 4991

Motherwell College
Dalzell Drive, Motherwell,
Lanarkshire, ML4 2DD.
Motherwell (0698) 59641

Reid Kerr College, The
Renfrew Road, Paisley, Renfrewshire,
PA13 4DR
041-889 4225

Springburn College
110 Flemington Street, Glasgow,
G21 4BX.
041-558 9001

Stow College
43 Shamrock Street, Glasgow,
G4 9LD.
041-332 1786

University of Glasgow
University Avenue, Glasgow
041-339 8855

University of Strathclyde,
George Street, Glasgow
G11XQ
041 552 4400

Hospitals

**Greater Glasgow Health Board
(Adminstration)
112 Ingram St., Glasgow G1 1ET
041-552-6222**

Acorn Street Psychiatric Day Hospital
23 Acorn Street, Bridgeton,
Glasgow G40 4AA
041-556 4789

Baillieston Health Centre
20 Muirside Road,
Glasgow G69 7AD
041-771 0871

Belvidere Hospital
London Road, Glasgow G31 4PG
041-554 1855

Birdston Hospital, Milton of Campsie
Glasgow G65 8BY
041-776 6114

Blawarthill Hospital,
129 Holehouse Drive,
Knightswood.Glasgow G13 3TG
041-954 9547

Bridgeton Health Centre
201 Abercromby Street
Glasgow G40 2EA
041-554 1866

Broomhill & Lanfine Hospitals
Kirkintilloch, Glasgow G66 1RR
041-776 5141

Carsewell House (Psychiatric
Outpatient)
5 Oakley Terrace, Glasgow G31 2HX
041-554 6267

Castlemilk Health Centre
Dougrie Drive, Castlemilk,
Glasgow G45
041-634 3434

Canniesburn Hospital
Switchback Road, Bearsden,
Glasgow G61 1QL
041-942 2255

Charing Cross (Alcohol and Drug)
Day Centre, 8 Woodside Crescent,
Glasgow G3 7UL
041-332 5463

Children's Home Hospital
Strathblane, Glasgow G63 9EP
0360 70203

Clydebank Health Centre
Kilbowie Road, Clydebank G81 2TQ
041-952 2080

Cowglen Hospital
Boydstone Road, Glasgow G53 6XJ
041-632 9106

Darnley Hospital
755 Nitshill Road, Glasgow G53 7RR
041-881 1005

David Elder Infirmary
503 Langlands Road, Glasgow G51 4DY
041-445 2466

Douglas Inch Centre
2 Woodside Terrace,
Glasgow G3 7UY
041-332 3844

Drumchapel Hospital
129 Drumchapel Road,
Glasgow G15 6PX
041-944 2344

Duke Street Hospital
253 Duke Street, Glasgow G31 1HY
041-556 5222

Duntocher Hospital
Duntocher, Clydebank G81 5QU
Duntocher 74294

Easterhouse Health Centre
9 Auchinlea Road, Glasgow G34 9QU
041-771 0781

Gartloch Hospital, Gartloch Road,
Gartcosh, Glasgow G69 8EJ
041-771 0771

Gartnavel General Hospital
1053 Great Western Road,
Glasgow G12 0YN
041-334 8122

Gartnavel Royal Hospital
1055 Great Western Road,
Glasgow G12 0XH
041-334 6241

Glasgow Dental Hospital and School
378 Sauchiehall Street
Glasgow G2 3JZ
041-332 7020

Glasgow Eye Infirmary
3 Sandyford Place, Glasgow G3 7NB
041-204 0721

Glasgow Homeopathic Hospital
1000 Great Western Road,
Glasgow G12 0AA
041-339 0382

Glasgow Royal Infirmary
84 Castle Street, Glasgow G4 0SF
041-552 3535

Glasgow Royal Maternity Hospital
Rottenrow, Glasgow G4 0NA
041-552 3400

Glasgow School of Chiropody
757 Crookston Road,
Glasgow G53 7UA
041-883 0418

Glasgow School of Occupational
Therapy, 29 Sherbrooke Avenue,
Glasgow G41 4ER
041-427 3032

Gorbals Health Centre
45 Pine Place, Glasgow G5 0BQ
041-429 6291

Govan Health Centre
5 Drumoyne Road,
Glasgow G51 4BJ
041-440 1212

Govanhill Health Centre
233 Calder Street
Glasgow G42 7DR
041-424 3003

Knightswood Hospital
125 Knightswood Road,
Glasgow G12 2XG
041-954 9641

Lennox Castle Hospital
Lennoxtown, Glasgow G65 7LB
Lennoxtown 313000

Lenzie Hospital
Auchinloch Road, Kirkintilloch,
Glasgow G66 5DF
041-776 1208

Leverndale Hospital
510 Crookston Road
Glasgow G53 7TU
041-882 6255

Lightburn Hospital
Carntyne Road, Glasgow G32 6ND
041-774 5102

Maryhill Health Centre
41 Shawpark Street,
Glasgow G20 9DR
041-946 7151

Mearnskirk Hospital
Newton Mearns, Glasgow G77 5RZ
041-639 2251

Parkhead Health Centre
101 Salamanca Street,
Glasgow G31 5BA
041-556 5232

Parkhead Hospital
81 Salamanca Street,
Glasgow
041-554 7951

Philipshill Hospital
East Kilbride Road, Busby,
Glasgow G76 9HW
041-644 1144

Pollock Health Centre
21 Cowglen Road
Glasgow G53 6EQ
041-880 8899

Possilpark Health Centre
85 Denmark Street,
Glasgow G22 5EG
041-336 5311

Queen Mother's Hospital
Yorkhill, Glasgow G3 8SH
041-339 8888

Royal Hospital for Sick Children
129 Drumchapel Road
Glasgow G15 6PX
041-944 2344

Royal Hospital for Sick Children
Yorkhill, Glasgow G3 8SJ
041-339 8888

Royal Samaritan Hospital for Women
69 Coplaw Street, Glasgow G42 7JF
041-423 3033

Ruchill Hospital
Bilsland Drive, Glasgow G20 9NB
041-946 7120

Rutherglen Health Centre
130 Stonelaw Road, Rutherglen,
Glasgow G73 2PQ
041-647 7171

Rutherglen Maternity Hospital
120 Stonelaw Road, Rutherglen,
Glasgow G73 2PG
041-647 0011

Shettleston Health Centre
420 Old Shettleston Road,
Glasgow G32 7JZ
041-778 9191

Southern General Hospital
1345 Govan Road, Glasgow G51 4TF
041-445 2466

Springburn Health Centre
200 Springburn Way,
Glasgow G21 1TR
041-558 0101

Stobhill General Hospital
133 Balornock Road,
Glasgow G21 3UW
041-558 0111

Stoneyetts Hospital
Chryston, Glasgow G69 0JG
041-776 1026

Thornliebank Health Centre
20 Kennishead Road
Glasgow G46 8NY
041-620 2222

Townhead Health Centre
16 Alexandra Parade
Glasgow G31 2ES
041-552 3477

Victoria Geriatric Unit
Mansionhouse Road,
Glasgow G41 3DX
041-649 4511

Victoria Infirmary
Langside Road, Glasgow G42 9TY
041-649 4545

Waverley Park Hospital
Kirkintilloch, Glasgow G66 2HE
041-776 2461

Western Infirmary
Dumbarton Road, Glasgow G11 6NT
041-339 8822

Woodilee Hospital
Kirkintilloch, Glasgow G66 3UG
041-776 2451

Woodside Health Centre
Barr Street, Glasgow G20 7LR
041-332 9977

INDEX TO STREETS

General Abbreviations

All.	Alley	Ct.	Court	Mans.	Mansions	S.	South
App.	Approach	Dr.	Drive	Mkt.	Market	Sq.	Square
Arc.	Arcade	E.	East	Ms.	Mews	Sta.	Station
Av.	Avenue	Est.	Estate	Mt.	Mount	St.	Street
Bldgs.	Buildings	Esp.	Esplanade	N.	North	Ter.	Terrace
Boul.	Boulevard	Gdns.	Gardens	Par.	Parade	Trd.	Trading
Bri.	Bridge	Gra.	Grange	Pass.	Passage	Vills.	Villas
Circ.	Circus	Grn.	Green	Pk.	Park	Vw.	View
Cft.	Croft	Gro.	Grove	Pl.	Place	W.	West
Clo.	Close	Ho.	House	Prom.	Promenade	Wf.	Wharf
Cor.	Corner	Ind.	Industrial	Quad.	Quadrant	Wk.	Walk
Cotts.	Cottages	La.	Lane	Ri.	Rise	Yd.	Yard
Cres.	Crescent	Lo.	Lodge	Rd.	Road		

District Abbreviations

Bail.	Baillieston	Clark.	Clarkston	Giff.	Giffnock	Old K.	Old Kilpatrick
Barr.	Barrhead	Clyde.	Clydebank	John.	Johnstone	Pais.	Paisley
Bear.	Bearsden	Coat.	Coatbridge	Kilb.	Kilbarchan	Renf.	Renfrew
Bish.	Bishopbriggs	Cumb.	Cumbernauld	Kirk.	Kirkintilloch	Step.	Stepps
Blan.	Blantyre	Dalm.	Dalmuir	Lenz.	Lenzie	Thorn.	Thornliebank
Both.	Bothwell	E.K.	East Kilbride	Linw.	Linwood	Udd.	Uddingston
Chr.	Chryston	Gart.	Gartcosh	Neil.	Neilston		

NOTES

The figures and letters following a street name indicate the postal district for that street with the square and page number where it will be found in the atlas. Thus the postal district for Abbey Drive is G14, and it will be found in square H12 on page 19.

A street name followed by the name of another street in italics does not appear on the map, but will be found adjoining or near the latter.

Abbey Clo., Pais.	M 6 46	Abington St. G20	H16 21	Aikenhead Rd. G42	M16 51
Abbey Dr. G14	H12 19	Aboukir St. G51	K12 33	Ailean Dr. G32	M24 55
Abbey Rd., John.	N 2 44	Aboyne Dr., Pais.	N 6 46	Ailean Gdns. G32	M24 55
Abbeycraig Rd. G34	J26 40	Aboyne St. G51	L12 33	Ailort Av. G44	P16 63
Abbeydale Way G73	Q20 65	Acacia Av. G78	P 7 59	*Lochinver Dr.*	
Neilvaig Dr.		Acacia Dr., Pais.	N 4 45	Ailsa Dr. G42	O15 51
Abbeyhill St. G32	K21 38	Acacia Pl., John.	O 1 44	Ailsa Dr. G73	P18 64
Abbeylands Rd., Clyde.	B 8 5	Academy Rd., Giff.	R14 62	Ailsa Dr., Clyde.	C 8 5
Abbot St. G41	N15 51	Academy St. G32	M22 54	Ailsa Dr., Pais.	O 5 46
Frankfort St.		Acer Cres. G78	N 4 45	Ailsa Dr., Udd.	Q28 69
Abbot St., Pais.	L 6 30	Achamore Pl. G15	D 9 6	Ailsa Rd., Bish.	E19 11
Abbotsburn Way, Pais.	K 5 30	*Achamore Rd.*		Ailsa Rd., Renf.	J 8 31
Abbotsford Av. G73	O19 53	Achamore Rd. G15	D 9 6	Ainslie Rd. G52	K10 32
Abbotsford Cres., Pais.	O 2 44	Achray Dr., Pais.	N 4 45	Ainslie Rd., Cumb.	B 4 71
Abbotsford Ct., Cumb.	D 2 70	Acorn Ct. G4	M18 52	Airdale Rd., Giff.	R14 62
Abbotsford La. G5	M16 51	*Acorn St.*		Airgold Dr. G15	D 9 6
Cumberland St.		Acorn St. G40	M18 52	Airgold Pl. G15	D 9 6
Abbotsford Pl. G5	M16 51	Acre Dr. G20	E14 8	Airlie Av., Bear.	C12 7
Abbotsford Pl., Cumb.	D 2 70	Acre Rd. G20	E13 8	*Tweedsmuir Dr.*	
Abbotsford Rd., Bear.	C11 7	Acredyke Cres. G21	F20 23	Airlie Gdns. G73	Q20 65
Abbotsford Rd., Clyde.	E 7 5	Acredyke Pl. G21	G20 23	Airlie Rd., Bail.	M25 56
Abbotsford Rd., Cumb.	D 2 70	Acredyke Rd. G21	F19 23	Airlie St. G12	H13 20
Abbotsford, Bish.	E20 11	Acredyke Rd. G73	O18 52	Airlour Rd. G43	P15 63
Abbotshall Av. G15	D 9 6	Acrehill St. G33	J20 37	Airth Dr. G52	M12 49
Abbotsinch Rd.,	J 6 30	Adams Court La. G2	K16 35	Airth La. G51	M12 49
Pais. & Renf.		*Howard St.*		Airth Pl. G51	M12 49
Abbott Cres., Clyde.	F 8 17	Adamswell St. G21	H18 22	Airthrey Av. G14	H12 19
Aberconway St., Clyde.	F 8 17	Adamswell Ter., Chr.	E28 15	Aitken St. G31	K20 37
Abercorn Av. G52	K 9 32	Addiewell St. G32	K22 38	Aitkenhead Av., Coat.	M28 57
Abercorn Pl. G23	E15 9	Addison Gro., Thorn.	Q12 61	Aitkenhead Rd., Udd.	O28 57
Abercorn St., Pais.	L 6 30	Addison Pl., Thorn.	Q12 61	Alasdair Ct., Barr.	R 8 59
Abercrombie Cres., Bail.	L27 41	Addison Rd. G12	H14 20	Albany Av. G32	L23 39
Abercromby Dr. G40	L18 36	Addison Rd., Thorn.	Q12 61	Albany Cotts. G13	G12 19
Abercromby Sq. G40	L18 36	Adelphi St. G5	L17 36	*Crow Rd.*	
Abercromby St. G40	L18 36	Admiral St. G41	L15 35	Albany Dr. G73	P19 65
Aberdalgie Path G34	K25 40	Advie Pl. G42	O16 51	Albany Pl., Both.	R28 69
Aberdalgie Rd. G34	K25 40	*Prospecthill Rd.*		*Marguerite Gdns.*	
Aberdour St. G31	K20 37	Affric Dr., Pais.	N 7 47	Albany Quad. G32	L23 39
Aberfeldy St. G31	K20 37	Afton Cres., Bear.	D13 8	*Mansionhouse Dr.*	
Aberfoyle St. G31	K20 37	Afton Dr., Renf.	H 9 18	Albany St. G40	M19 53
Aberlady Rd. G51	K12 33	Afton Rd., Cumb.	B 3 71	Albany Ter. G72	Q21 66
Abernethy Dr., Linw.	L 1 28	Afton St. G41	O15 51	Albany Way, Pais.	K 6 30
Abernethy St. G31	K20 37	Agamemnon St., Dalm.	E 6 4	*Abbotsburn Way*	
Aberuthven Dr. G32	M22 54	Aigas Cotts. G13	G12 19	Albert Av. G42	N15 51
Abiegail Pl., Blan.	R26 68	*Crow Rd.*		Albert Cross G41	M15 51

Name	Grid	Page
Albert Ct. G41	M15	51
Albert Dr.		
Albert Dr. G41	N14	50
Albert Dr. G73	P19	65
Albert Dr., Bear.	E13	8
Albert Rd. G42	N16	51
Albert Rd., Clyde.	D 7	5
Albert Rd., Lenz.	D23	13
Albert Rd., Renf.	H 8	17
Alberta Ter. G12	H14	20
Saltoun St.		
Albion St. G1	K17	36
Albion St., Bail.	M24	55
Albion St., Pais.	L 6	30
Alcaig Rd. G52	N12	49
Alder Av., Lenz.	C22	12
Alder Ct., Barr.	R 8	59
Alder Pl. G43	P14	62
Alder Pl., John.	N 1	44
Alder Rd. G43	P14	62
Alder Rd., Cumb.	C 4	71
Alder Rd., Dalm.	C 6	4
Alderman Pl. G13	G11	19
Alderman Rd. G13	F 9	18
Aldersdyke Pl., Blan.	R26	68
Alderside Dr., Udd.	O27	57
Alexander St., Clyde.	E 7	5
Alexandra Av. G33	G23	25
Alexandra Av., Lenz.	D23	13
Alexandra Cross G31	K19	37
Duke St.		
Alexandra Ct. G31	K19	37
Roebank St.		
Alexandra Dr., Pais.	M 4	45
Alexandra Dr., Renf.	H 8	17
Alexandra Gdns., Lenz.	D23	13
Alexandra Par. G31	K19	37
Alexandra Park St. G31	K19	37
Alexandra Rd., Lenz.	D23	13
Alford St. G21	H17	22
Alfred Ter. G52	H14	20
Great Western Rd.		
Algie St. G41	O15	51
Alice St. G5	M17	52
Alice St., Pais.	N 6	46
Aline Ct., Barr.	Q 7	59
Allan Av., Renf.	J 9	32
Allan Pl. G40	M19	53
Allan St. G40	N19	53
Allander Gdns., Bish.	D18	10
Allander Rd., Bear.	D11	7
Allander St. G22	H17	22
Allands Av., Renf.	G 5	16
Allanfauld Rd., Cumb.	B 2	70
Allanton Av., Pais.	M 9	48
Allanton Dr. G52	L10	32
Allerton Gdns., Bail.	M24	55
Alleysbank Rd. G73	N19	53
Allison Dr. G72	P22	66
Allison Pl. G42	N16	51
Prince Edward St.		
Allison Pl. Gart.	H27	27
Allison St. G42	N16	51
Allnach Pl. G34	K27	41
Alloway Cres. G73	P18	64
Alloway Dr. G73	P18	64
Alloway Dr., Clyde.	D 8	5
Alloway Rd. G43	P14	62
Alma St. G40	L19	37
Almond Av., Renf.	J 9	32
Almond Cres., Pais.	N 3	45
Almond Dr., Lenz.	C22	12
Almond Rd. G33	G23	25
Almond Rd., Bear.	E11	7
Almond St. G33	J20	37
Almond Vale, Udd.	O28	57
Hamilton Vw.		
Alness Cres. G52	M12	49
Alpatrick Gdns., John.	M 1	44
Alpine Gro., Udd.	O27	57
Alsatian Av., Clyde	E 8	5
Alston La. G40	L18	36
Claythorn St.		
Altnacreag Gdns., Chr.	D28	15
Alton Gdns. G12	H14	20
Great George St.		
Alton Rd., Pais.	M 8	47
Altyre St. G32	M21	54
Alva Gate. G52	N12	49
Alva Gdns. G52	N12	49
Alva Pl., Lenz.	D24	13
Alyth Cres., Clark.	S16	63
Alyth Gdns. G52	M12	49
Alyth Gdns., Clark.	S16	63
Ambassador Way, Renf.	J 8	31
Cockels Loan		
Amisfield St. G20	G15	21
Amochrie Dr., Pais.	O 4	45
Amochrie Rd., Pais.	N 3	45
Amulree Pl. G32	M22	54
Amulree St. G32	L22	38
Ancaster Dr. G13	G12	19
Ancaster La. G13	F11	19
Great Western Rd.		
Anchor Av., Pais.	M 7	47
Anchor Cres., Pais.	M 7	47
Anchor Dr., Pais.	M 7	47
Anchor Wynd, Pais.	M 7	47
Ancroft St. G20	H16	21
Anderson Dr., Renf.	H 8	17
Anderson Gdns., Blan.	R27	69
Station Rd.		
Anderson Quay G3	L15	35
Anderson St. G11	J13	34
Andrew Av., Lenz.	D23	13
Andrew Av., Renf.	H 9	18
Andrew Dr., Clyde.	F 8	17
Andrew Sillars Av. G72	P23	67
Andrews St., Pais.	L 6	30
Anglegate G14	H11	19
Angus Av. G52	M11	49
Angus Av., Bish.	F20	23
Angus Gdns., Udd.	O27	57
Angus La. G64	E20	11
Angus Oval G52	M10	48
Angus Pl. G52	M10	48
Angus St. G21	H18	22
Angus St., Clyde.	F 9	18
Angus Wk., Udd.	O28	57
Annan Dr. G73	O20	53
Annan Dr., Bear.	D11	7
Annan Dr., Pais.	N 3	45
Annan Pl., John.	O08	43
Annan St. G42	O16	51
Annandale St. G42	M16	51
Annbank St. G31	L18	36
Anne Av., Renf.	H 8	17
Anne Cres., Lenz.	D23	13
Annette St. G42	N16	51
Annfield Gdns., Blan.	R26	68
Annfield Pl. G31	K18	36
Annick Dr., Bear.	E11	7
Annick St. G32	L22	38
Annick St. G72	P23	67
Anniesdale Av. G33	G23	25
Anniesland Cres. G14	G10	18
Anniesland Mansions G13	G12	19
Ancaster Dr.		
Anniesland Rd. G13	G11	19
Anniesland Rd. G14	G10	18
Anson St. G40	M18	52
Anson Way, Renf.	J 8	31
Britannia Way		
Anstruther St. G32	L21	38
Antonine Gdns., Clyde.	C 7	5
Antonine Rd., Bear.	C10	6
Anworth St. G32	M22	54
Appin Rd. G31	K19	37
Appin Ter. G73	Q20	65
Lochaber Dr.		
Appin Way, Udd.	Q28	69
Bracken Ter.		
Appleby St. G22	H16	21
Applecross Gdns., Chr.	D27	15
Applecross St. G22	H16	21
Appledore Cres., Udd.	Q28	69
Apsley La. G11	J13	34
Apsley St. G11	J13	34
Aray St. G20	G14	20
Arbroath Av. G52	M10	48
Arcadia St. G40	L18	36
Arcadia St. G40	L18	36
Drake St.		
Arcan Cres. G15	E10	6
Archerfield Av. G32	N22	54
Archerfield Cres. G32	N22	54
Archerfield Dr. G32	N22	54
Archerfield Gro. G32	N22	54
Archerhill Av. G13	F 9	18
Archerhill Cotts. G13	F10	18
Archerhill Rd.		
Archerhill Cres. G13	F10	18
Archerhill Gdns. G13	F10	18
Archerhill Rd.		
Archerhill Rd. G13	F10	18
Archerhill Sq. G13	F10	18
Kelso St.		
Archerhill St. G13	F10	18
Archerhill Rd.		
Archerhill Ter. G13	F10	18
Archerhill Rd.		
Ard Pl. G42	O18	52
Ard Rd., Renf.	H 7	17
Ard St. G32	M22	54
Ardagie Dr. G32	O23	55
Ardagie Pl. G32	O23	55
Ardbeg Av. G73	Q21	66
Ardbeg Av., Bish.	E20	11
Ardbeg St. G42	N16	51
Ardconnel St. G46	Q12	61
Arden Av. G46	R12	61
Arden Dr., Giff.	R13	62
Arden Pl. G46	R12	61
Stewarton Rd.		
Ardencraig Cres. G44	R17	64
Ardencraig Dr. G45	R18	64
Ardencraig La. G45	R17	64
Ardencraig Rd.		
Ardencraig Quad. G45	R18	64
Ardencraig Rd. G45	R17	64
Ardencraig St. G45	R19	65
Ardencraig Ter. G45	R18	64
Ardenlea Rd., Udd.	O27	57
Ardenlea St. G40	M19	53
Ardery St. G11	J13	34
Apsley St.		
Ardessie Pl. G20	G14	20
Ardessie St. G23	E14	8
Torrin Rd.		
Ardfern St. G32	M22	54
Ardgay Pl. G32	M22	54
Ardgay St. G32	M22	54
Ardgay Way G73	Q19	65
Ardgour Dr., Linw.	L 1	28
Ardgowan Av., Pais.	M 6	46
Ardgowan Dr., Udd.	O27	57
Ardgowan St., Pais.	N 6	46
Ardholm St. G32	L22	38
Ardhu Pl. G15	D 9	6
Ardlamont Sq., Linw.	L 2	28
Ardlaw St. G51	L12	33
Ardle Rd. G43	P15	63
Ardlui St. G32	M21	54
Ardmaleish Cres. G45	R18	64
Ardmaleish Rd. G45	R17	64
Ardmaleish St. G45	R18	64
Ardmaleish Ter. G45	R18	64
Ardmay Cres. G44	O17	52
Ardmillan St. G33	K21	38
Ardmore Oval, Pais.	L 4	29
Ardmore St. G31	K19	37
Ardmory Av. G42	O17	52
Ardmory La. G42	O18	52
Ardnacross Dr. G33	J23	39
Ardnahoe Av. G42	O17	52
Ardnahoe Pl. G42	O17	52
Ardneil Rd. G51	L12	33
Ardnish St. G51	K12	33
Ardo Gdns. G51	L13	34
Ardoch Gro. G72	P21	66
Ardoch Rd., Bear.	C13	8
Ardoch St. G22	H17	22
Ardoch Way, Chr.	E27	15
Braeside Av.		
Ardshiel Rd. G51	K12	33
Ardsloy La. G14	H10	18
Ardsloy Pl.		
Ardsloy Pl. G14	H10	18
Ardtoe Cres. G33	G24	25
Ardtoe Pl. G33	G24	25
Arduthie Rd. G51	K12	33
Ardwell Rd. G52	M12	49
Argosy Way, Renf.	J 8	31
Britannia Way		
Argyle St. G3	J14	34
Argyle St., Pais.	M 5	46
Argyll Arc. G2	K16	35
Argyll Av., Renf.	H 7	17
Argyll Rd., Bear.	B12	7

Street	Grid		
Argyll Rd., Clyde.	E	8	5
Arisaig Dr. G52	M12	49	
Arisaig Dr., Bear.	D13	8	
Arisaig Pl. G52	M12	49	
Ark La. G31	K18	36	
Arkleston Cres., Pais.	K	7	31
Arkleston Rd., Pais.	K	7	31
Arklet Rd. G51	L12	33	
Arklie Av., Bear.	B12	7	
Tweedsmuir Cres.			
Arlington St. G3	J15	35	
Armadale Ct. G31	K19	37	
Armadale Path G31	K19	37	
Armadale Pl. G31	K19	37	
Armadale St. G31	K19	37	
Armour Pl., John.	M	1	44
Armour St. G31	L18	36	
Armour St., John.	M	1	44
Arngask Rd. G51	K12	33	
Arnhall Pl. G52	M12	49	
Arnholm Pl. G52	M12	49	
Arnisdale Pl. G34	K25	40	
Arnisdale Rd. G34	K25	40	
Arnisdale Way G73	Q19	65	
Shieldaig Dr.			
Arniston St. G32	K21	38	
Arnol Pl. G33	K24	39	
Arnold Av., Bish.	E19	11	
Arnold St. G20	G16	21	
Arnott Way G72	P22	66	
Arnprior Gdns., Chr.	E27	15	
Braeside Av.			
Arnprior Quad. G45	Q17	64	
Arnprior Rd. G45	Q17	64	
Arnprior St. G45	Q17	64	
Arnside Av., Giff.	Q14	62	
Arnthern St. G72	P23	67	
Arnwood Dr. G12	G13	20	
Aron Ter. G72	Q21	66	
Aros Dr. G52	N12	49	
Arran Dr. G52	M12	49	
Arran Dr., Cumb.	D	1	70
Arran Dr., Giff.	R13	62	
Arran Dr., John.	N08	43	
Arran Dr., Pais.	O	6	46
Arran La., Chr.	E28	15	
Burnbrae Av.			
Arran Pl., Clyde.	E	8	5
Arran Pl., Linw.	L	1	28
Arran Rd., Renf.	J	8	31
Arran Ter. G73	P18	64	
Arranthrue Cres., Renf.	H	8	17
Arranthrue Dr., Renf.	H	8	17
Arriochmill Rd. G20	H14	20	
Kelvin Dr.			
Arrochar Ct. G23	F15	21	
Sunningdale Rd.			
Arrochar Dr. G23	E14	8	
Arrochar St. G23	F14	20	
Arrol Pl. G40	M19	53	
Arrol St. G52	K	9	32
Arrowchar Ct. G23	F15	21	
Arrowchar St.			
Arrowchar St. G23	F14	20	
Arrowsmith Av. G13	F11	19	
Arthur Av., Barr.	R	7	59
Arthur Rd., Pais.	O	6	46
Arthur St. G3	J14	34	
Arthur St., Pais.	L	5	30
Arthurlie Av., Barr.	R	8	59
Arthurlie Dr., Giff.	R14	62	
Arthurlie St. G51	K12	33	
Arthurlie St., Barr.	R	8	59
Arundel Dr. G42	O16	51	
Arundel Dr., Bish.	D19	11	
Asbury Ct., Linw.	L	2	28
Ascaig Cres. G52	N12	49	
Ascog Rd., Bear.	E12	7	
Ascog St. G42	N16	51	
Ascot Av. G12	G12	19	
Ascot Ct. G12	G13	20	
Ash Gro., Bish.	E19	11	
Ash Gro., Lenz.	C22	12	
Ash Gro., Udd.	O28	57	
Douglas Cres.			
Ash Pl., John.	N	1	44
Ash Rd., Bail.	M25	40	
Ash Rd., Cumb.	A	4	71
Ash Rd., Dalm.	C	6	4
Ash Wk. G73	Q20	65	
Ashburton Rd. G12	G13	20	
Ashby Cres. G13	E12	7	
Ashcroft Dr. G44	P18	64	
Ashdale Dr. G52	M12	49	
Ashdene Rd. G22	F16	21	
Ashfield St. G22	H17	22	
Ashfield, Bish.	D19	11	
Ashgill Pl. G22	G17	22	
Ashgill Rd. G22	G16	21	
Ashgrove St. G40	N19	53	
Ashgrove, Bail.	L27	41	
Ashkirk Dr. G52	M12	49	
Ashlea Dr., Giff.	Q14	62	
Ashley La. G3	J15	35	
Woodlands Rd.			
Ashley St. G3	J15	35	
Ashmore Rd. G43	P15	63	
Ashton Gdns. G12	J14	34	
Ashton Rd.			
Ashton La. G12	J14	34	
University Av.			
Ashton Pl. G12	H14	20	
Byres Rd.			
Ashton Rd. G12	J14	34	
University Av.			
Ashton Rd. G73	N19	53	
Ashton Ter. G12	J14	34	
Ashton Rd.			
Ashton Way G78	O	3	45
Ashtree Rd. G43	O14	50	
Ashvale Cres. G21	H18	22	
Ashvale Row E. G21	H18	22	
Ashvale Row			
Ashvale Row W. G21	H18	22	
Ashvale Row			
Aspen Pl., John.	N	1	44
Athelstane Dr., Cumb.	D	1	70
Athelstane Rd. G13	F11	19	
Athena Way, Udd.	O28	57	
Athol Av. G52	K	9	32
Athol Gdns., Bear.	B12	7	
Athol Ter., Udd.	N27	57	
Lomond Rd.			
Athole Gdns. G12	H14	20	
Athole La. G12	H14	20	
Saltoun St.			
Atholl Cres., Pais.	L	9	32
Atholl Dr., Giff.	S14	62	
Atholl Gdns. G73	Q21	66	
Atholl Gdns., Bish.	D19	11	
Atholl La., Chr.	E28	15	
Atholl Pl., Linw.	L	1	28
Atlas Pl. G21	H18	22	
Atlas Rd. G21	H18	22	
Atlas St., Clyde.	F	7	17
Attlee Av., Clyde.	E	8	5
Attlee Pl., Clyde.	E	8	5
Attlee Av.			
Attow Rd. G43	P13	62	
Auburn Dr., Barr.	R	8	59
Auburn Pl. G78	L20	37	
Auchans Rd., Linw.	J	1	28
Auchencrow St. G34	K26	40	
Auchendale, Lenz.	C24	13	
Auchengeich Rd., Chr.	D26	14	
Auchengill Path G34	J26	40	
Auchengill Rd.			
Auchengill Pl. G34	J26	40	
Auchengill Rd. G34	J26	40	
Auchenglen Dr., Chr.	E27	15	
Auchenlodment Rd., John.	N	1	44
Auchentorlie Quad., Pais.	M	7	47
Auchentorlie St. G11	J12	33	
Auchentoshan Av., Clyde.	C	6	4
Auchentoshan Ter. G21	J18	36	
Auchentoshen Cotts., Old K.	C	5	4
Auchinairn Rd., Bish.	F18	22	
Auchinbee Loop Rd., Cumb.	B	1	70
Auchinlea Rd. G34	J24	39	
Auchinleck Av. G33	G21	24	
Auchinleck Cres. G33	G21	24	
Auchinleck Dr. G33	G21	24	
Auchinleck Gdns. G33	G21	24	
Auchinleck Rd. G33	F21	24	
Auchinleck Rd., Clyde,	B	7	5
Auchinleck Ter., Clyde.	B	7	5
Auchinleck Rd.			
Auchinloch Rd., Lenz.	D23	13	
Auchinloch St. G21	H18	22	
Auchmannoch Av., Pais.	L	9	32
Auckengreoch Av., John.	O08	43	
Auckengreoch Rd., John.	O08	43	
Auckland Pl., Dalm.	D	5	4
Auckland St. G22	H16	21	
Auld Kirk Rd. G72	Q23	67	
Auld Rd., The, Cumb.	B	3	71
Auld St., Dalm.	D	6	4
Auldbar Rd. G52	M12	49	
Auldbar Ter., Pais.	N	7	47
Auldburn Rd. G43	P13	62	
Auldearn Rd. G21	F20	23	
Auldgirth Rd. G52	M12	49	
Auldhouse Av. G42	P13	62	
Harriet St.			
Auldhouse Rd. G43	P13	62	
Auldhouse Ter. G43	P14	62	
Auldhouse Rd.			
Aultbea St. G22	F16	21	
Aultmore Rd. G33	K24	39	
Aurs Cres., Barr.	R	8	59
Aurs Dr., Barr.	R	8	59
Aurs Pl., Barr.	R	8	59
Aurs Rd., Barr.	Q	8	59
Aursbridge Dr., Barr.	R	8	59
Austen La. G13	G12	19	
Skaterig La.			
Austen La. G13	G12	19	
Woodend Dr.			
Austen Rd. G13	G12	19	
Avenel Rd. G13	E12	7	
Avenue End Rd. G33	H22	24	
Avenue St. G40	L19	37	
Avenue St. G73	N19	53	
Avenue, The, Kilb.	N07	42	
Low Barholm			
Avenuehead Rd., Chr.	D27	15	
Avenuehead Rd., Gart.	F28	27	
Avenuepark St. G20	H15	21	
Aviemore Gdns., Bear.	C13	8	
Aviemore Rd. G52	N12	49	
Avoch Dr. G46	Q12	61	
Avoch St. G34	J25	40	
Avon Av., Bear.	D13	8	
Avon Dr., Linw.	L	1	28
Avon Dr., Bish.	F19	23	
Avon Rd., Bish.	F19	23	
Avon Rd., Giff.	R13	62	
Avon St. G5	L15	35	
Avonbank Rd. G73	O18	52	
Avondale Dr., Pais.	L	7	31
Avondale St. G33	J22	38	
Avonhead Av. G67	D	1	70
Avonhead Gdns. G67	D	1	70
Avonhead Pl. G67	D	1	70
Avonhead Rd. G67	D	1	70
Avonspark St. G21	H19	23	
Aylmer Rd. G43	P15	63	
Ayr Rd., Giff.	R13	62	
Ayr St. G21	H18	22	
Aytoun Rd. G41	M14	50	
Back Causeway G31	L20	37	
Back Sneddon St., Pais.	L	6	30
Backmuir Rd. G15	D10	6	
Bagnell St. G21	G18	22	
Bailie Dr., Bear.	B11	7	
Baillie Dr., Both.	O28	69	
Baillieston Rd. G32	M23	55	
Baillieston Rd., Udd.	N25	56	
Bain Sq. G40	L18	36	
Bain St.			
Bain St. G40	L18	36	
Bainsford St. G32	L21	38	
Baird Av. G52	K	9	32
Baird Dr., Bear.	C11	7	
Baird St. G4	J17	36	
Bairdsbrae G4	H16	21	
Possil Rd.			
Baker Pl. G41	N15	51	
Baker St.			
Baker St. G41	N15	51	
Bakewell Rd., Bail.	L25	40	

Name	Ref	Page
Bedford St. G5	L16	35
Bedlay Ct., Chr.	D28	15
Bedlay St. G21	H18	22
Linsburn St.		
Bedlay St. G21	H18	22
Petershill Rd.		
Bedlay St., Chr.	D28	15
Beech Av. G41	M13	50
Beech Av. G72	P21	66
Beech Av. G73	Q20	65
Beech Av., Bail.	L25	40
Beech Av., Bear.	C13	8
Beech Av., John.	N 2	44
Beech Av., Pais.	N 7	47
Beech Av. North Av.	P21	66
G72		
Beech Dr., Dalm.	C 7	5
Beech Gdns., Bail.	L25	40
Beech Gro., Barr.	R 8	59
Arthurlie Av.		
Beech Pl., Bish.	F19	23
Beech Rd., Bish.	F19	23
Beech Rd., John.	N08	43
Beech Rd., Lenz.	C23	13
Beechcroft Pl., Blan.	R27	69
Beeches Av., Clyde.	C 6	4
Beeches Rd., Clyde.	C 6	4
Beeches Ter., Clyde.	C 7	4
Beechgrove St. G40	N19	53
Beechlands Av., Giff.	R15	63
Beechmount Cotts. G14	G 9	18
Dumbarton Rd,		
Beechmount Rd., Lenz.	D23	13
Beechwood Av. G11	H12	19
Beechwood Dr.		
Beechwood Av. G73	P20	65
Beechwood Ct., Bear.	D12	7
Beechwood Dr. G11	H12	19
Beechwood Dr., Renf.	J 7	31
Beechwood La., Bear.	D12	7
Beechwood Ct.		
Beechwood Pl. G11	H12	19
Beechwood Dr.		
Beechwood Rd., Cumb.	C 2	70
Beil Dr. G13	F 9	18
Beith Rd., John.	O07	42
Beith St. G11	J13	34
Belgrave La. G12	H15	21
Belgrave Rd.		
Belgrave Ter. G12	H15	21
Belhaven Cres. La. G12	H14	20
Lorraine Rd.		
Belhaven Ter. G12	H14	20
Belhaven Ter. W. G12	H14	20
Bell St. G1	L17	36
Bell St., Clyde.	F 8	17
Bell St., Renf.	H 8	17
Bellahouston Dr. G52	M12	49
Bellahouston La. G52	M12	49
Bellairs Pl., Blan.	R26	68
Belleisle Av., Udd.	O27	57
Belleisle St. G42	N16	51
Bellevue Pl. G21	J18	36
Bellfield Cres., Barr.	Q 7	59
Bellfield St. G31	L19	37
Bellfield St., Barr.	Q 7	59
Bellgrove St. G31	L18	36
Bellrock Cres. G33	K22	38
Bellrock St. G33	K22	38
Bellscroft Av. G73	O18	52
Bellshaugh La. G12	G14	20
Bellshaugh Pl. G12	G14	20
Bellshaugh Rd. G12	G14	20
Bellshill Rd., Both.	R28	69
Bellshill Rd., Udd.	P27	69
Belltrees Cres., Pais.	M 4	45
Bellwood St. G41	O15	51
Belmar Ct., Linw.	L 2	28
Belmont Av., Udd.	O27	57
Belmont Cres. G12	H15	21
Belmont Dr. G73	O19	53
Belmont Dr., Barr.	R 8	59
Belmont Dr., Giff.	Q13	62
Belmont La. G12	H14	20
Great Western Rd.		
Belmont Rd. G21	G18	22
Belmont Rd. G72	Q21	66
Belmont Rd., Pais.	L 7	31
Belmont St. G12	H15	21
Belmont St., Clyde.	F 7	17
Belses Dr. G52	L11	33
Belstane Pl., Udd.	Q28	69
Appledore Cres.		
Belsyde Av. G15	E10	6
Beltane St. G3	K15	35
Beltrees Av. G53	N10	48
Beltrees Cres. G53	N10	48
Beltrees Rd. G53	N10	48
Belvidere Cres., Bish.	D19	11
Belvoir Pl., Bish.	S26	68
Bemersyde Av. G43	P13	62
Bemersyde Rd. G78	O 3	45
Bemersyde, Bish.	E20	11
Ben Alder Dr., Pais.	N 8	47
Ben Buie Way, Pais.	N 8	47
Ben Ledi Av., Pais.	N 8	47
Ben Lui Dr., Pais.	N 8	47
Ben More Dr., Pais.	N 8	47
Ben Nevis Rd., Pais.	N 8	47
Ben Venue Way, Pais.	N 8	47
Ben Wyvis Dr., Pais.	N 8	47
Benalder St. G11	J14	34
Benarty Gdns., Bish.	E19	11
Bencroft Dr. G44	P18	64
Bengairn St. G31	K20	37
Bengal Pl. G43	O14	50
Christian St.		
Bengal St. G43	O14	50
Benhar Pl. G33	K21	38
Benholme St. G32	M21	54
Benhope Av., Pais.	N 8	47
Benlawers Dr., Pais.	N 8	47
Benloyal Av., Pais.	N 8	47
Benmore St. G21	G18	22
Bennan Sq. G42	N17	52
Benston Pl., John.	N09	43
Benston Rd., John.	N09	43
Bentall St. G5	M17	52
Bentinck St. G3	J15	35
Bents Rd., Bail.	L25	40
Benvane Av., Pais.	N 8	47
Benvie Gdns., Bish.	E19	11
Benview St. G20	H15	21
Benview Ter., Pais.	N 7	47
Berelands Cres. G73	O18	52
Berelands Pl. G73	O18	52
Beresford Av. G14	H12	19
Berkeley St. G3	K15	35
Berkeley Terrace La. G3	J15	35
Elderslie St.		
Berkley Dr., Blan.	R26	68
Bernard Path G40	M19	53
Bernard St. G40	M19	53
Bernard Ter. G40	M19	53
Berneray St. G22	F17	22
Berridale Av. G44	P16	63
Berriedale Av., Bail.	M25	56
Berryburn Rd. G21	H20	23
Berryhill Dr., Giff.	R13	62
Berryhill Rd., Cumb.	C 2	70
Berryhill Rd., Giff.	R13	62
Berryknowes Av. G52	L11	33
Berryknowes La. G52	L11	33
Berryknowes Rd. G52	M11	49
Berryknowes Rd., Chr.	F26	26
Bertram St. G41	N15	51
Bertrohill Ter. G33	K23	39
Stepps Rd.		
Bervie St. G51	L12	33
Berwick Cres., Linw.	K 1	28
Berwick Dr. G52	M10	48
Berwick Dr. G73	O20	53
Betula Dr., Dalm.	C 7	5
Bevan Gro., John.	O08	43
Beverley Rd. G43	P14	62
Bevin Av., Clyde.	E 8	5
Bideford Cres. G32	M23	55
Biggar Pl. G31	L19	37
Biggar St. G31	L19	37
Bigton St. G33	J22	38
Bilbao St. G45	M17	52
Bilsland Dr. G20	G15	21
Binend Rd. G53	O11	49
Binnie Pl. G40	L18	36
Binniehill Rd., Cumb.	B 1	70
Binns Rd. G33	J23	39
Birch Cres., John.	N 1	44
Birch Dr., Lenz.	C23	13
Birch Gro., Udd.	O28	57
Burnhead St.		
Birch Knowle, Bish.	F19	23
Birch Rd., Dalm.	C 7	5
Birch Vw., Bear.	C13	8
Birchfield Dr. G14	H10	18
Birchlea Dr., Giff.	Q14	62
Birchwood Av. G32	M24	55
Birchwood Dr., Pais.	N 4	45
Birchwood Pl. G32	M24	55
Birdston Rd. G21	G20	23
Birgidale Av. G45	R17	64
Birgidale Rd. G45	R17	64
Birgidale Ter. G45	R17	64
Birkdale Ct., Both.	R27	69
Birken Rd., Lenz.	D24	13
Birkenshaw St. G31	K19	37
Birkenshaw Way, Pais.	K 6	30
Abbotsburn Way		
Birkhall Av. G52	M 9	48
Birkhall Av., Renf.	F 5	16
Birkhall Dr., Bear.	E12	7
Birkhill Av., Bish.	D19	11
Birkhill Gdns., Bish.	D20	11
Birkmyre Rd. G51	L12	33
Birks Rd., Renf.	J 7	31
Tower Dr.		
Birkwood St. G40	N19	53
Birmingham Rd., Renf.	J 7	31
Birnam Av., Bish.	D19	11
Birnam Cres., Bear.	C13	8
Birnam Gdns., Bish.	E19	11
Birnam Rd. G31	M20	53
Birness Dr. G43	O14	50
Birness St. G43	O14	50
Birnie Ct. G21	H20	23
Birnie Rd. G21	H20	23
Birnock Av., Renf.	J 9	32
Birsay Rd. G22	F16	21
Bishop Gdns., Bish.	E18	10
Bishop St. G2	K16	35
Bishopmill Pl. G21	H20	23
Bishopmill Rd. G21	H20	23
Bisset Cres., Clyde.	C 6	4
Black St. G4	J17	36
Blackburn Sq., Barr.	R 8	59
Blackburn St. G51	L14	34
Blackburn St. G51	L15	35
Blackbyres Rd., Barr.	P 8	59
Blackcraig Av. G15	D10	6
Blackcroft Gdns. G32	M23	55
Blackcroft Rd. G32	M23	55
Blackfaulds Rd. G73	O18	52
Blackford Cres. G32	M23	55
Blackford Pl. G32	M23	55
Blackford Rd., Pais.	M 7	47
Blackfriars St. G1	K17	36
Blackhall La., Pais.	M 6	46
Blackhall St., Pais.	M 6	46
Blackhill Cotts. G23	E16	9
Blackhill Pl. G33	J20	37
Blackhill Rd. G23	E14	8
Blackie St. G3	J14	34
Blacklands Pl., Lenz.	D24	13
Blacklaw La., Pais.	L 6	30
Blackstone Av. G53	O11	49
Blackstone Cres. G53	N11	49
Blackstone Rd., Candren	K 3	29
Blackstoun Av., Linw.	L 1	28
Blackstoun Oval, Pais.	L 4	29
Blackstoun Rd., Pais.	L 4	29
Blackthorn Av., Lenz.	C22	12
Blackthorn Gro., Lenz.	C22	12
Blackthorn Rd., Cumb.	B 4	71
Blackthorn St. G22	G18	22
Blackwood Av., Linw.	L 1	28
Blackwood St. G13	F12	19
Blackwood St., Barr.	R 7	59
Blackwoods Cres., Chr.	E27	15
Blacurvie Rd. G34	J25	40
Bladda La., Pais.	M 6	46
Blades Ct., Gart.	G28	27
Bladnoch Dr. G15	E11	7
Moraine Av.		
Blaeloch Av. G45	R17	64
Blaeloch Dr. G45	R17	64
Blaeloch Ter. G45	R17	64
Blair Cres., Bail.	M25	56
Blair Rd., Pais.	L 9	32
Blair St. G32	L21	38
Blairatholl Av. G11	H13	20
Blairatholl Gdns. G11	H13	20

Blairbeth Dr. G44	O16	51
Blairbeth Rd. G73	P19	65
Blairbeth Ter. G73	Q19	65
Blairdardie Rd. G15	E10	6
Blairdenan Av., Chr.	D28	15
Blairgowrie Rd. G52	M11	49
Blairhall Av. G41	O15	51
Blairhill Av., Chr. & Waterside	C25	14
Blairlogie St. G33	J22	38
Blairston Av., Both.	R28	69
Blairston Gdns., Both.	R28	69
Blairston Av.		
Blairtum Dr. G73	P19	65
Blairtummock Rd. G32	K23	39
Blake Rd., Cumb.	C 3	71
Blane St. G4	J17	36
Blantyre Cres., Clyde.	B 6	4
Blantyre Farm Rd., Blan. & Udd.	R26	68
Blantyre Mill Rd., Both.	R27	69
Blantyre Rd., Both.	R28	69
Blantyre St. G3	J14	34
Blaven Ct., Bail.	M26	56
Bracadale Rd.		
Blawarthill St. G14	G 9	18
Blenheim Av. G33	G23	25
Blenheim Ct. G33	G24	25
Blenheim Av.		
Blenheim La. G33	G24	25
Blesdale Ct., Clyde.	E 7	5
Blochairn Rd. G21	J19	37
Bluevale St. G31	L19	37
Blyth Pl. G32	L23	39
Blyth Rd., G33	L24	39
Blythswood Av., Renf.	H 8	17
Blythswood Dr., Pais.	L 6	30
Blythswood Rd., Renf.	G 8	17
Blythswood Sq. G2	K16	35
Blythswood St. G2	K16	35
Boclair Av., Bear.	D12	7
Boclair Cres., Bear.	D13	8
Boclair Cres., Bish.	E19	11
Boclair Rd., Bear.	D13	8
Boclair Rd., Bish.	E19	11
Boclair St. G13	F12	19
Boden St. G40	M19	53
Bodmin Gdns., Chr.	D27	15
Gartferry Rd.		
Bogany Ter. G45	R18	64
Bogbain Rd. G34	K25	40
Boghall Rd., Udd.	N25	56
Boghall St. G33	J22	38
Boghead Rd. G21	H19	23
Boghead Rd., Lenz.	D22	12
Bogleshole Rd. G72	O21	54
Bogmoor Rd. G51	K11	33
Bogside Pl., Bail.	K26	40
Whamflet Av.		
Bogside Rd. G33	G22	24
Bogside St. G40	M19	53
Bogton Av. G44	Q15	63
Bogton Avenue La. G44	Q15	63
Bogton Av.		
Boleyn Rd. G41	N15	51
Bolivar Ter. G42	O17	52
Bolton Dr. G42	O16	51
Bon Accord St., Clyde.	F 7	17
Bonawe St. G20	H15	21
Kirkland St.		
Boness St. G40	M19	53
Bonhill St. G22	H16	21
Bonnar St. G40	M19	53
Bonnaughton Rd., Bear.	C10	6
Bonnyholm Av. G53	M10	48
Bonnyrigg Dr. G43	P13	62
Bonyton Av. G13	G 9	18
Boon Dr. G15	E10	6
Boquhanran Pl., Clyde.	D 7	5
Albert Rd.		
Boquhanran Rd., Clyde	E 6	4
Borden La. G13	G12	19
Borden Rd. G13	G12	19
Boreland Dr. G13	F10	18
Boreland Pl. G13	G10	18
Borgie Cres. G72	P22	66
Borland Rd., Bear.	D13	8
Borron St. G4	H17	22
Borthwick St. G33	J22	38
Boswell Sq. G52	K 9	32

Botanic Cres. G20	H14	20
Bothlyn Cres., Gart.	F27	27
Bothlynn Dr. G33	G23	25
Bothlynn Rd., Chr.	F26	26
Bothwell La. G2	K16	35
West Campbell St.		
Bothwell Park Rd. G71	R28	69
Bothwell Rd., Udd. & Both.	P27	69
Bothwell St. G72	P21	66
Bothwell Ter. G12	J15	35
Bank St.		
Bothwick Way, Pais.	O 3	45
Crosbie Dr.		
Boundary Rd. G73	N18	52
Bourne Cres., Renf.	F 5	16
Bourne Ct., Renf.	F 5	16
Bourock Sq., Barr.	R 9	60
Bourtree Dr. G73	Q20	65
Bouverie St. G14	G 9	18
Bouverie St. G73	O18	52
Bowden Dr. G52	L10	32
Bower St. G12	H15	21
Bowerwalls St., Barr.	Q 9	60
Bowes Cres., Bail.	M24	55
Bowfield Av. G52	L 9	32
Bowfield Cres. G52	L 9	32
Bowfield Dr. G52	L 9	32
Bowfield Pl. G52	L 9	32
Bowfield Ter. G52	L 9	32
Bowfield Cres.		
Bowhouse Way G73	Q19	65
Bowling Green La. G14	H11	19
Westland Dr.		
Bowling Green Rd. G14	H11	19
Bowling Green Rd. G32	M23	55
Bowling Green Rd. G44	P16	63
Bowman St. G42	N16	51
Bowmont Gdns. G12	H14	20
Bowmont Hill, Bish.	D19	11
Bowmont Ter. G12	H14	20
Bowmore Gdns. G73	Q21	66
Bowmore Gdns., Udd.	O27	57
Bowmore Rd. G52	L12	33
Boyd St. G42	N16	51
Boydstone Pl. G46	P12	61
Boydstone Rd. G43	P12	61
Boyle St., Clyde.	F 8	17
Boyleston Rd., Barr.	Q 7	59
Boyndie Path G34	K25	40
Boyndie St. G34	K25	40
Brabloch Cres., Pais.	L 6	30
Bracadale Dr., Bail.	M26	56
Bracadale Gdns., Bail.	M26	56
Bracadale Gro., Bail.	M26	56
Bracadale Rd., Bail.	M26	56
Bracken Rd., Barr.	P 7	59
Bracken St. G22	G16	21
Bracken Ter., Udd.	Q28	69
Brackenbrae Av., Bish.	E18	10
Brackenbrae Rd., Bish.	E18	10
Brackenrig Rd. G46	R12	61
Brackla Av. G13	F 9	18
Bracora Pl. G20	G14	20
Glenfinnan Dr.		
Bradan Av. G13	F 9	18
Bradda Av. G73	Q20	65
Bradfield Av. G12	G14	20
Braeface Rd., Cumb.	C 2	70
Braefield Dr., Thorn.	Q13	62
Braefoot Cres., Pais.	O 6	46
Braehead Rd., Clyde.	B 7	5
Braehead Rd., Cumb.	B 3	71
Braehead Rd., Pais.	P 5	58
Braehead St. G5	M17	52
Braemar Av., Dalm.	D 6	4
Braemar Cres., Bear.	E12	7
Braemar Dr., John.	N 1	44
Braemar Rd. G73	Q21	66
Braemar Rd., Renf.	G 5	16
Braemar St., G42	O15	51
Braemar Vw., Dalm.	C 6	4
Braemount Av., Pais.	P 5	58
Braes Av., Clyde.	F 8	17
Braeside Av. G73	O20	53
Braeside Av., Chr.	E27	15
Braeside Cres., Bail.	L27	41
Braeside Cres., Barr.	R 9	60

Braeside Dr., Barr.	R 8	59
Braeside Pl. G72	Q22	66
Braeside St. G20	H15	21
Braid Sq. G4	J16	35
Braid St. G4	J16	35
Braidbar Farm Rd., Giff.	Q14	62
Braidbar Rd., Giff.	Q14	62
Braidcraft Rd. G53	N11	49
Braidfauld Gdns. G32	M21	54
Braidfauld Pl. G32	N21	54
Braidfauld St. G32	N21	54
Braidfield Rd., Clyde.	C 7	5
Braidholm Cres., Giff.	Q14	62
Braidholm Rd., Giff.	Q14	62
Braidpark Cres., Giff.	Q14	62
Braidpark Dr., Giff.	Q14	62
Braids Rd., Pais.	N 6	46
Bramley Pl., Lenz.	D24	13
Branchock Av. G72	Q23	67
Brand St. G51	L14	34
Brandon Gdns. G72	P21	66
Brandon St. G31	L18	36
Branscroft G78	M07	42
Brassey St. G20	G15	21
Breadalbane Gdns. G73	Q20	65
Breadalbane St. G3	K15	35
Brech Av., Bail.	L27	41
Brechin Rd., Bish.	E20	11
Brechin St. G3	K15	35
Breck Av. G78	O 2	44
Brediland Rd., Linw.	L 1	28
Brediland Rd., Pais.	N 3	45
Bredisholm Dr., Bail.	M26	56
Bredisholm Rd., Bail.	M27	57
Bredisholm Ter., Bail.	M26	56
Brenfield Av. G44	Q15	63
Brenfield Dr. G44	Q15	63
Brentwood Av. G53	Q10	60
Brentwood Dr. G53	Q10	60
Brentwood Sq. G53	Q10	60
Brentwood Sq. G53	Q10	60
Brentwood Dr.		
Brereton St. G42	N17	52
Bressey Rd. G33	L24	39
Breval Cres., Clyde.	B 7	5
Brewery St., John.	M09	43
Brewster Av., Pais.	K 7	31
Briar Dr., Clyde.	D 7	5
Briar Neuk, Bish.	F19	23
Briar Rd. G43	P14	62
Briarlea Dr., Giff.	Q14	62
Briarwood Ct. G32	N24	55
Brick La., Pais.	L 6	30
Bridge of Weir Rd. Kilb. & Linw.	L08	43
Bridge St., Dalm.	D 6	4
Bridge St., G72	P22	66
Bridge St., Linw.	L 2	28
Bridge St., Pais.	M 6	46
Bridgebar St., Barr.	Q 9	60
Bridgeburn Dr., Chr.	E27	15
Bridgegate G1	L17	36
Bridgend Rd. G53	O11	49
Bridgeton Cross G40	L18	36
Brigham Pl. G23	F15	21
Broughton Rd.		
Brighton Pl. G51	L13	34
Brighton St. G51	L13	34
Brightside Av., Udd.	P28	69
Brisbane St. G42	O16	51
Brisbane St., Dalm.	D 5	4
Britannia Way, Clyde.	E 7	5
Britannia Way, Renf.	J 8	31
Briton St. G51	L13	34
Broad Pl. G40	L18	36
Broad St.		
Broad St. G40	L18	36
Broadford St. G4	J17	36
Harvey St.		
Broadholm St. G22	G16	21
Broadleys Av., Bish.	D18	10
Broadlie Dr. G13	G10	18
Broadloan, Renf.	J 8	31
Broadwood Dr. G44	P16	63
Brock Oval G53	P11	61
Brock Pl. G53	O11	49
Brock Rd. G53	O11	49
Brock Ter. G53	P11	61
Brock Way G67	C 3	71
North Carbrain Rd.		

Street	Map	Pg
Brockburn Rd. G53	N10	48
Brockburn Ter. G53	O11	49
Brockville St. G32	L21	38
Brodick Sq. G64	F19	23
Brodick St. G21	J19	37
Brodie Park Av., Pais.	N 6	46
Brodie Pl., Renf.	J 7	31
Brodie Rd. G21	F20	23
Brogknowe, Udd.	O26	56
Glasgow Rd.		
Brook St. G40	L18	36
Brooklands Av., Udd.	O27	57
Brooklea Dr., Giff.	P14	62
Brookside St. G40	L19	37
Broom Cres., Barr.	P 7	59
Broom Dr., Clyde.	D 7	5
Broom Gdns., Lenz.	C22	12
Broom Rd. G43	P14	62
Broom Rd. G67	A 4	71
Broom Ter., John.	N 1	44
Broomdyke Way, Pais.	K 5	30
Broomfield Av. G21	H19	23
Broomfield Rd.		
Broomfield Av. G72	O20	53
Broomfield Pl. G21	G18	22
Broomfield Rd.		
Broomfield Rd. G21	G18	22
Broomfield Ter., Udd.	N27	57
Broomhill Av. G11	J12	33
Broomhill Av. G32	O22	54
Broomhill Cres. G11	H12	19
Broomhill Dr. G11	H12	19
Broomhill Dr. G73	P19	65
Broomhill Gdns. G11	H12	19
Broomhill La. G11	H12	19
Broomhill Path G11	J12	33
Broomhill Pl. G11	H12	19
Broomhill Pl. G11	J12	33
Broomhill Ter. G11	J12	33
Broomieknowe Dr. G73	P19	65
Broomieknowe Rd. G73	P19	65
Broomielaw G1	L16	35
Broomknowe Pl. G66	D24	13
Broomknowe, Cumb.	B 1	70
Broomknowes Rd. G21	H19	23
Broomlands Av., Renf.	F 5	16
Broomlands Cres., Renf.	F 5	16
Broomlands Gdns., Renf.	F 5	16
Broomlands Rd., Cumb.	D 3	71
Broomlands St., Pais.	M 5	46
Broomlands Way, Renf.	F 6	16
Broomlea Cres., Renf.	F 5	16
Broomley Dr. G46	R14	62
Broomley La., Giff.	R14	62
Broomloan Ct. G51	L13	34
Broomloan Pl. G51	L13	34
Broomloan Rd. G51	L13	34
Broompark Circus G31	K18	36
Broompark Dr. G31	K18	36
Broompark Dr., Renf.	F 5	16
Broompark St. G31	K18	36
Broomton Rd. G21	F20	23
Broomward Dr., John.	M 1	44
Brora Dr., Bear.	D13	8
Brora Dr., Giff.	R14	62
Brora Dr., Renf.	H 9	18
Brora Gdns., Bish.	E19	11
Brora La. G31	J20	37
Brora St.		
Brora Rd., Bish.	E19	11
Brora St. G33	J20	37
Broughton Dr. G23	F15	21
Broughton Gdns. G23	E15	9
Broughton Rd. G23	F15	21
Brown Av., Clyde.	F 8	17
Brown Rd., Cumb.	C 2	70
Brown St. G2	K16	35
Brown St., Pais.	L 5	30
Brown St., Renf.	J 7	31
Brownhill Rd. G43	Q13	62
Brownlie St. G42	O16	51
Browns La., Pais.	M 6	46
Brownsdale Rd. G73	O18	52
Brownside Av. G72	P21	66
Brownside Av., Barr.	P 7	59
Brownside Av., Barr.	O 5	46
Brownside Cres., Barr.	P 7	59
Brownside Dr. G13	G 9	18
Brownside Dr., Barr.	P 7	59
Brownside Gro., Barr.	P 7	59
Brownside Rd. G72 & G73	P20	65
Bruce Av., John.	O09	43
Bruce Av., Pais.	K 7	31
Bruce Rd. G41	M15	51
Bruce Rd., Pais.	L 7	31
Bruce Rd., Renf.	J 7	31
Bruce St., Clyde.	E 7	5
Bruce Ter., Blan.	R27	69
Brucefield Pl. G34	K26	40
Brunstance Rd. G34	J25	40
Brunswick Ho., Dalm.	C 5	4
Perth Cres.		
Brunswick St. G1	K17	36
Brunton St. G44	P16	63
Brunton Ter. G44	Q15	63
Bruntsfield Av. G53	Q10	48
Bruntsfield Gdns. G53	Q10	60
Brydson Pl., Linw.	L 1	28
Fulwood Av.		
Buccleuch Av. G52	K 9	32
Buccleuch La. G3	J16	35
Scott St.		
Buccleuch St. G3	J16	35
Buchan St. G5	L16	35
Norfolk St.		
Buchan Ter., G72	Q21	66
Buchanan Cres. G64	F20	23
Buchanan Dr. G64	F20	23
Buchanan Dr. G72	P21	66
Buchanan Dr. G73	P19	65
Buchanan Dr., Bear.	D13	8
Buchanan Dr., Bish.	F20	23
Buchanan Dr., Lenz.	D23	13
Buchanan Gdns. G32	N24	55
Buchanan St. G1	K16	35
Buchanan St., Bail.	M25	56
Buchanan St., John.	N09	43
Buchlyvie Path G34	K25	40
Buchlyvie Rd., Pais.	L 9	32
Buchlyvie St. G34	K25	40
Buckingham Bldgs. G12	H14	20
Great Western Rd.		
Buckingham Dr. G32	O22	54
Buckingham Dr. G73	O20	53
Buckingham St. G12	H14	20
Buckingham Ter. G12	H14	20
Great Western Rd.		
Bucklaw Gdns. G52	M11	49
Bucklaw Pl. G52	M11	49
Bucklaw Ter. G52	M11	49
Buckley St. G22	G17	22
Bucksburn Rd. G21	H20	23
Buddon St. G40	M20	53
Budhill Av. G32	L22	38
Bulldale St. G14	G 9	18
Bullionslaw Dr. G73	P20	65
Bulloch Av., Giff.	R14	62
Bullwood Av. G53	N 9	48
Bullwood Ct. G53	N 9	48
Bullwood Dr. G53	N 9	48
Bullwood Gdns. G53	N 9	48
Bullwood Pl. G53	N 9	48
Bunessan St. G52	L12	33
Bunhouse Rd. G3	J14	34
Burgh Hall La. G11	J13	34
Fortrose St.		
Burgh Hall St. G11	J13	34
Burgh La. G12	H14	20
Vinicombe St.		
Burghead Dr. G51	K12	33
Burghead Pl. G51	K12	33
Burgher St. G31	L20	37
Burleigh Rd., Udd.	O28	69
Burleigh St. G51	K13	34
Burlington Av. G12	G13	20
Burmola St. G22	H16	21
Burmouth Rd. G33	L24	39
Burn Gdns., Blan.	R26	68
Burn Ter. G72	O21	54
Burn Vw., Cumb.	B 4	71
Burnacre Gdns., Udd.	O27	57
Burnbank Dr., Barr.	R 8	59
Burnbank Gdns. G20	J15	35
Burnbank Pl. G4	K18	36
Drygate		
Burnbank Ter. G20	J15	35
Burnbrae Av., Bear.	B13	8
Burnbrae Av., Chr.	E28	15
Burnbrae Av., Linw.	L 2	28
Bridge St.		
Burnbrae Ct., Lenz.	D23	13
Auchinloch Rd.		
Burnbrae Dr. G73	P20	65
East Kilbride Rd.		
Burnbrae Rd., John.	M 2	44
Burnbrae Rd., Lenz.	E24	13
Burnbrae St. G21	H19	23
Burnbrae, Clyde.	C 7	5
Burncleuch Av., G72	Q22	66
Burncrooks Ct., Clyde.	C 6	4
Burndyke Ct. G51	K14	34
Burndyke Sq. G51	K14	34
Burndyke St. G51	K13	34
Burnett Rd. G33	K24	39
Burnfield Av., Giff.	Q13	62
Burnfield Cotts., Giff.	Q13	62
Burnfield Dr. G43	Q13	62
Burnfield Gdns., Giff.	Q14	62
Burnfield Rd.		
Burnfield Rd., Giff.	P13	62
Burnfoot Cres. G73	P20	65
Burnfoot Cres., Pais.	O 5	46
Burnfoot Dr. G52	L10	32
Burngreen Ter., Cumb.	A 3	71
Burnham Rd. G14	H10	18
Burnham Ter. G14	H10	18
Burnham Rd.		
Burnhead Rd. G43	P15	63
Burnhead Rd., Cumb.	C 1	70
Burnhead St., Udd.	O28	57
Burnhill Quadrant G73	O18	52
Burnhill St. G73	O18	52
Burnhouse St. G20	G14	20
Burnmouth Ct. G33	L24	39
Pendeen Rd.		
Burnpark Av., Udd.	O26	56
Burns Dr., John.	O09	43
Burns Gro., Thorn.	R13	62
Burns Rd., Cumb.	C 3	71
Burns St. G4	J16	35
Burns St., Dalm.	D 6	4
Burnside Av., Barr.	Q 7	59
Burnside Cres., Clyde.	B 7	5
Burnside Ct., Dalm.	D 6	4
Scott St.		
Burnside Gate G73	P20	65
Burnside Gdns., Kilb.	N 7	42
Burnside Rd. G73	P20	65
Burnside Rd., John.	N 2	44
Burnside Ter. G72	Q24	67
Burntbroom Dr., Bail.	M24	55
Burntbroom Gdns., Bail.	M24	55
Burntbroom Rd., Udd. & Bail.	M24	55
Burntbroom St. G33	K23	39
Burntshields Rd., Kilb.	N06	42
Burr Gdns., Bish.	E20	11
Solway Rd.		
Burrells La. G4	K18	36
High St.		
Burrelton Rd. G43	P15	63
Burton La. G43	N16	51
Langside Rd.		
Bushes Av., Pais.	N 5	46
Busheyhill St. G72	P22	66
Bute Av., Renf.	J 8	31
Bute Cres., Bear.	E12	7
Bute Cres., Pais.	O 5	46
Bute Dr., John.	N08	43
Bute Gdns. G12	J14	34
Bute Gdns. G44	Q16	53
Bute Ter. G73	P19	65
Bute Ter., Udd.	O28	57
Butterbiggins Rd. G42	M16	51
Butterfield Pl. G41	N15	51
Pollokshaws Rd.		
Byrebush Rd. G53	N11	49
Byres Av., Pais.	L 7	31
Byres Cres.		
Byres Cres., Pais.	L 7	31
Byres Rd. G11	J14	34
Byres Rd., John.	N 2	44
Byron Ct., Udd.	R28	69
Shelly Dr.		
Byron La. G11	J12	33
Sandeman St.		

Street	Ref	Page
Byron St. G11	J12	33
Byron St., Clyde.	D 6	4
Byshot St. G22	H17	22
Cable Depot Rd., Dalm.	E 6	4
Cadder Ct., Bish.	C19	11
Cadder Gro. G20	F15	21
Cadder Rd.		
Cadder Pl. G20	F15	21
Cadder Rd. G20	F15	21
Cadder Rd., Bish.	C19	11
Cadder Way, Bish.	C19	11
Cadoc St., G72	P22	66
Cadogan St. G2	K16	35
Cadzow Av., Giff.	S13	62
Cadzow Dr., G72	P21	66
Caird Dr. G11	J13	34
Cairn Av., Renf.	J 9	32
Cairn Dr., Linw.	L 1	28
Cairn La., Pais.	K 5	30
Mosslands Rd.		
Cairn St. G21	G18	22
Cairnban St. G51	L11	33
Cairnbrook Rd. G34	K26	40
Cairncraig St. G31	M20	53
Cairndow Av. G44	Q15	63
Cairndow Ct. G44	Q15	63
Cairngorm Cres., Barr.	R 8	59
Cairngorm Cres., Bear.	C10	6
Cairngorm Cres., Pais.	N 6	46
Cairngorm Rd. G43	P14	62
Cairnhill Circus G52	M 9	48
Cairnhill Dr. G52	M 9	48
Cairnhill Pl. G52	M 9	48
Cairnhill Circus		
Cairnhill Rd. G61	E12	7
Cairnlea Dr. G51	L13	34
Cairnmuir Rd. G72	R21	66
Cairns Av. G72	P22	66
Cairns Rd. G72	Q22	66
Cairnsmore Pl. G15	E 9	6
Cairnsmore Rd. G15	E 9	6
Cairnswell Av. G72	Q23	67
Cairnswell Pl. G72	Q23	67
Cairntoul Dr. G14	G10	18
Cairntoul Pl. G14	G10	18
Calcots Path G34	J26	40
Auchengill Rd.		
Calcots Pl. G34	J26	40
Caldarvan St. G22	H16	21
Calder Av., Barr.	R 8	59
Calder Dr. G72	P22	66
Calder Gate, Bish.	D18	10
Calder Pl., Bail.	M25	56
Calder Rd., Pais.	L 4	29
Calder Rd., Udd.	P26	68
Calder St. G42	N16	51
Calderbank Vw., Bail.	M26	56
Calderbraes Av., Udd.	O27	57
Caldercuilt Rd. G20	F14	20
Caldercuilt St. G20	F14	20
Calderpark Av., Udd.	N25	56
Calderpark Cres., Udd.	N25	56
Caldervale, Udd.	P26	68
Calderwood Av., Bail.	M25	56
Calderwood Dr., Bail.	M25	56
Calderwood Gdns., Bail.	M25	56
Calderwood Rd. G20	O20	53
Calderwood Rd., G43	P14	62
Caldwell Av. G13	G10	18
Caldwell Av., Linw.	L 1	28
Caledon La. G12	J14	34
Highburgh Rd.		
Caledon St. G12	J14	34
Caledonia Av. G5	M17	52
Caledonia Av. G73	O19	53
Caledonia Dr., Bail.	M25	56
Caledonia Rd. G5	M17	52
Caledonia Rd., Bail.	M25	56
Caledonia St. G5	M17	52
Caledonia St., Dalm.	E 6	4
Caledonia St., Pais.	L 5	30
Caledonian Circuit G72	P23	67
Caledonian Cotts., Both.	R28	69
Caledonian Cres. G12	H14	20
Great Western Rd.		
Caledonian Cres. G12	J15	35
Caledonian Mans. G12	H14	20
Great Western Rd.		
Caledonian Pl. G72	P24	67
Caley Brae, Udd.	P27	69
Calfhill Rd. G53	M10	48
Calfmuir Rd., Chr. & Waterside	C25	14
Calgary St. G4	J17	36
Callander St. G20	H16	21
Callieburn Rd., Bish.	F19	23
Cally Av. G15	D10	6
Calside Av., Pais.	M 5	46
Calside, Pais.	N 6	46
Calton Entry G40	L18	36
Gallowgate		
Calvay Cres. G33	K23	39
Calvay Pl. G33	L24	39
Calvay Rd. G33	K23	39
Cambourne Rd., Chr.	D27	15
Cambridge Av., Clyde.	D 7	5
Cambridge Dr. G20	G14	20
Glenfinnan Dr.		
Cambridge La. G3	J16	35
Cambridge St.		
Cambridge Rd., Renf.	J 8	31
Cambridge St.	K16	35
Camburn St. G32	L21	38
Cambus Pl. G32	J23	39
Cambusdoon Rd. G32	J23	39
Cambuskenneth Gdns.	L24	39
Cambuskenneth Pl. G32	J23	39
Cambuslang Rd. G32	O21	54
Cambuslang Rd. G72 & G73	N19	53
Cambusmore Pl. G32	J23	39
Camden St. G5	M17	52
Camelon St. G32	L21	38
Cameron Dr., Bear.	D13	8
Cameron Dr., Udd.	O28	57
Cameron Sq., Clyde.	C 8	5
Glasgow Rd.		
Cameron St. G20	H16	21
Cameron St. G52	K 9	32
Cameron St., Clyde.	F 8	17
Camlachie St. G31	L19	37
Camp Rd. G73	N18	52
Camp Rd., Bail.	L25	40
Campbell Dr., Barr.	R 8	59
Campbell Dr., Bear.	C11	7
Campbell St. G20	F14	21
Campbell St., John.	N09	43
Campbell St., Renf.	H 8	17
Camperdown St. G20	H16	21
Garscube Rd.		
Camphill Av. G41	O15	51
Camphill, Pais.	M 5	46
Camps Cres., Renf.	J 9	32
Campsie Av., Barr.	R 8	59
Campsie Dr., Bear.	B12	7
Campsie Dr., Pais.	K 7	31
Campsie Dr., Pais.	O 5	46
Campsie Pl., Chr.	F26	26
Campsie St. G21	G18	22
Campsie Vw., Bail.	L27	41
Campsie Vw., Chr.	F26	26
Campsie Vw., Cumb.	B 3	71
Campsie Vw.G33	H23	25
Campston Pl. G33	J22	38
Camstradden Dr. E., Bear.	D11	7
Camstradden Dr. W., Bear.	D11	7
Camus Pl. G15	D 9	6
Canal Av., John.	M 1	44
Canal Rd., John.	N09	43
Canal St. G4	J17	36
Canal St., Clyde.	F 7	17
Canal St., John.	M 2	44
Canal St., Pais.	M 5	46
Canal St., Renf.	H 8	17
Canal Ter., Pais.	M 6	46
Canberra Av., Dalm.	D 5	4
Cander Rigg, Bish.	D19	11
Candleriggs G1	L17	36
Candren Rd., Linw.	L 2	28
Candren Rd., Pais.	M 4	45
Canmore Pl. G31	M20	53
Canmore St. G31	M20	53
Cannich Dr., Pais.	N 7	47
Canniesburn Rd., Bear.	D11	7
Canniesburn Sq., Bear.	E12	7
Macfarlane Rd.		
Canniesburn Toll, Bear.	D12	7
Canonbie St. G34	J26	40
Canting Way G51	K14	34
Capelrig St. G46	Q12	61
Caplaw Rd., Pais.	P 5	58
Caplethill Rd., Pais. & Barr.	O 6	46
Caprington St. G33	J22	38
Cara Dr. G51	K12	33
Caravelle Way, Renf.	J 8	31
Friendship Way		
Carberry Rd. G41	N14	50
Carbeth St. G22	H16	21
Carbisdale St. G22	G18	22
Carbost St. G23	E14	8
Torgyle St.		
Carbrook St. G21	J19	37
Carbrook St., Pais.	M 5	46
Cardarrach St. G21	H19	23
Cardell Dr., Pais.	M 4	45
Cardell Rd., Pais.	M 4	45
Carding La. G3	K15	35
Argyle St.		
Cardonald Dr. G52	M10	48
Cardonald Gdns. G52	M10	48
Cardonald Place Rd. G52	M10	48
Cardow Rd. G21	H20	23
Cardowan Dr. G33	G23	25
Cardowan Rd. G33	G24	25
Cardowan Rd. G33	L21	38
Cardrona St. G33	H22	24
Cardross Ct. G31	K18	36
Cardross St. G31	K18	36
Cardwell St. G41	M16	51
Cardyke St. G21	H19	23
Careston Pl., Bish.	E20	11
Carfin St. G42	N16	51
Carfrae St. G3	K14	34
Cargill St. G31	M21	54
Cargill St. G64	F19	23
Carham Cres. G52	L11	33
Carham Dr. G52	L11	33
Carillon Rd. G51	L14	34
Carisbrooke Cres., Bish.	D19	11
Carlaverock Rd. G43	P14	62
Carleith Av., Clyde.	C 6	4
Carleith Quad. G51	K11	33
Carleith Ter., Clyde.	C 6	4
Carleith Av.		
Carleston St. G21	H18	22
Carleton Dr., Giff.	Q14	62
Carleton Gate, Giff.	Q14	62
Carlibar Av. G13	G 9	18
Carlibar Dr., Barr.	Q 8	59
Carlibar Gdns., Barr.	Q 8	59
Commercial Rd.		
Carlibar Rd., Barr.	Q 7	59
Carlile La., Pais.	L 6	30
New Sneddon St.		
Carlile Pl., Pais.	L 6	30
Carlisle St. G21	H17	22
Carlowrie Av., Blan.	R26	68
Carlton Ct. G5	L16	35
Carlton Pl. G5	L16	35
Carlton Ter. G20	H15	21
Wilton St.		
Carlyle Av. G52	K 9	32
Carlyle Rd., Pais.	L 6	30
Carlyle Ter. G73	N19	53
Carmaben Rd. G33	K24	39
Carment Dr. G41	O14	50
Carment La. G41	O14	50
Carmichael Pl. G42	O15	51
Carmichael St. G51	L13	34
Carmunnock By-pass G44	R17	64
Carmunnock La. G44	P16	63
Madison Av.		
Carmunnock Rd. G44	O16	51
Carmyle Av. G32	N22	54
Carna Dr. G44	P17	64
Carnarvon St. G3	J15	35
Carnbooth Ct. G42	R18	64
Carnbroe St. G20	J16	35
Carnegie Rd. G52	L10	32
Carnock Cres., Barr.	R 7	59
Carnock Rd. G53	O11	49
Carnoustie Cres., Bish.	E20	11
Carnoustie St., Both.	R27	69
Carnoustie St. G5	L15	35

Street	Grid
Carntyne Pl. G32	K20 37
Carntyne Rd. G31	L20 37
Carntynehall Rd. G32	K21 38
Carnwadric Rd. G46	Q12 61
Carnwath Av. G43	P15 63
Caroline St. G31	L21 38
Carolside Dr. G15	D10 6
Carradale Gdns., Bish.	E20 11
Thrums Av.	
Carradale Pl., Linw.	L 1 28
Carrbridge Dr. G20	G14 20
Glenfinnan Dr.	
Carriagehill Dr., Pais.	N 6 46
Carrick Cres., Giff.	R14 62
Carrick Dr. G32	M24 55
Carrick Dr. G73	P19 65
Carrick Gro. G32	M24 55
Carrick Rd. G73	P18 64
Carrick Rd., Bish.	E20 11
Carrick Rd., Cumb.	B 3 71
Carrick St. G2	K16 35
Carrickarden Rd., Bear.	D12 7
Carrickstone Vw., Cumb.	A 2 70
Carriden Pl. G33	K24 39
Carrington St. G4	J15 35
Carroglen Gdns. G32	L23 39
Carroglen Gro. G32	L23 39
Carron Cres. G22	G17 22
Carron Cres. G66	D24 13
Carron Cres., Bear.	D11 7
Carron Cres., Bish.	E19 11
Carron Ct. G72	P23 67
Carron La., Pais.	K 7 31
Kilearn Rd.	
Carron Pl. G22	G18 22
Carron St., G22	G18 22
Carrour Gdns., Bish.	E18 10
Carsaig Dr. G52	L12 33
Carse View Dr., Bear.	C13 8
Carsebrook Av., Chr. & Waterside	C25 14
Chryston Rd.	
Carsegreen Av., Pais.	O 4 45
Carstairs St. G40	N19 53
Carswell Gdns. G41	N15 51
Cart St., Clyde.	F 7 17
Cartartan Rd., Pais.	L 9 32
Cartcraigs Rd. G43	P13 62
Cartha Cres., Pais.	M 7 47
Cartha St. G41	O15 51
Cartside Av., John.	N08 43
Cartside Quad. G42	O16 51
Cartside St. G42	O15 51
Cartside Ter., Kilb.	N08 43
Kilbarchan Rd.	
Cartvale La., Pais.	L 6 30
Cartvale Rd. G42	O15 51
Caskie Dr., Blan.	R27 69
Cassley Av., Renf.	J 9 32
Castle Av., Both.	R27 69
Castle Av., John.	N 1 44
Castle Av., Udd.	P27 69
Castle Chimmins Av. G72	Q23 67
Castle Chimmins Rd. G72	Q23 67
Castle Crescent North Ct. G1	K17 36
Royal Exchange Sq.	
Castle Gait, Pais.	M 6 46
Castle Gdns., Chr.	E27 15
Castle Pl., Udd.	P27 69
Ferry Rd.	
Castle Rd. G78	M 2 44
Main Rd.	
Castle Rd., John.	M 2 44
Castle Sq., Dalm.	D 6 4
Castle St. G4	K18 36
Castle St. G73	O19 53
Castle St., Bail.	M25 56
Castle St., Dalm.	D 6 4
Castle St., Pais.	M 5 46
Castle Vw., Clyde.	D 7 5
Granville St.	
Castle Way, Cumb.	B 4 71
Castlebank Cres., G11	J13 34
Meadowside Rd.	
Castlebank Ct. G13	G12 19
Castlebank Gdns. G13	G12 19
Castlebank St. G11	J12 33
Castlebank Vill. G13	G12 19
Castlebay Dr. G22	E17 10
Castlebay Pl. G22	F17 22
Castlebay St. G22	F17 22
Castlecroft Gdns., Udd.	P27 69
Castlefern Rd. G73	Q19 65
Castlehill Cres., Renf.	H 8 17
Ferry Rd.	
Castlehill Rd., Bear.	C10 6
Castlelaw Gdns. G32	L22 38
Castlelaw Pl. G32	L22 38
Castlelaw St. G32	L22 38
Castlemilk Cres. G44	P18 64
Castlemilk Dr. G45	Q18 64
Castlemilk Mews G44	P18 64
Castlemilk Rd.	
Castlemilk Rd. G44	O18 52
Castleton Av. G21	F18 22
Colston Rd.	
Castleton Ct. G42	R18 64
Cathay St. G22	F17 22
Cathcart Cres., Pais.	M 7 47
Cathcart Pl.	O18 52
Cathcart Rd. G42	O16 51
Cathcart Rd. G73	O18 52
Cathedral Ct. G4	K17 36
Rottenrow East	
Cathedral La. G4	K17 36
Cathedral St.	
Cathedral Sq. G4	K18 36
Cathedral St. G1	K17 36
Cathedral St. G4	K18 36
Catherine Pl. G3	K15 35
Hydepark St.	
Cathkin Av. G72	P21 66
Cathkin Av. G73	O20 53
Cathkin By-pass G73	Q20 65
Cathkin Ct. G42	R18 64
Cathkin Gdns., Udd.	N27 57
Cathkin Pl., G72	P21 66
Cathkin Rd. G42	O15 51
Cathkin Rd., E.K.	R19 65
Cathkin Rd., Udd.	N27 57
Cathkin Vw. G32	O22 54
Cathkinview Rd. G42	O16 51
Catrine Av., Clyde.	D 8 5
Causewayside St. G32	N22 54
Causeyside St., Pais.	M 6 46
Cavendish Pl. G5	M16 51
Cavendish St. G5	M16 51
Cavin Dr. G45	Q18 64
Cavin Rd. G45	Q18 64
Caxton St. G13	G12 19
Cayton Gdns., Bail.	M24 55
Cecil Pl. G11	L15 35
Paisley Rd. W.	
Cecil St. G12	H14 20
Cedar Av. G78	O 1 44
Cedar Av., Dalm.	D 5 4
Cedar Ct. G20	J16 35
Cedar Ct. G78	M07 42
Cedar Dr., Lenz.	C23 13
Cedar Gdns. G73	Q20 65
Cedar Pl., Barr.	R 8 59
Cedar Pl., Blan.	R26 68
Cedar Rd., Bish.	F19 23
Cedar Rd., Cumb.	B 4 71
Cedar St. G20	J16 35
Cedar Wk., Bish.	F19 23
Cedric Pl. G13	F11 19
Cedric Rd. G13	F11 19
Celtic Pl. G20	F14 20
Maryhill Rd.	
Cemetery Rd. G32	L23 39
Cemetery Rd. G52	M11 49
Paisley Rd. W.	
Central Av. G11	J12 33
Broomhill Ter.	
Central Av. G32	M23 55
Central Av. G72	P21 66
Central Av., Udd.	P29 69
Central Chambers G2	K16 35
Hope St.	
Central Path G32	M24 55
Central Way, Cumb.	D 2 70
Central Way, Pais.	L 6 30
Centre St. G5	L16 35
Centre, The, Barr.	R 7 59
Ceres Gdns. G64	E20 11
Cessnock Rd. G33	G22 24
Cessnock St. G51	L14 34
Cessnock St., Clyde.	D 8 5
Chachan Dr. G51	K12 33
Skipness Dr.	
Chalmers Ct. G40	L18 36
Chalmers Gate G40	L18 36
Chalmers Pl. G40	L18 36
Claythorn St.	
Chalmers St. G40	L18 36
Chalmers St., Clyde.	E 7 5
Chamberlain La. G13	G12 19
Chamberlain Rd. G13	G12 19
Chancellor St. G11	J13 34
Chapel Rd., Clyde.	C 7 5
Chapel St. G20	G15 21
Chapel St. G73	O18 52
Chapelhill Rd., Pais.	N 7 47
Chapelton Av., Bear.	D12 7
Chapelton Gdns., Bear.	D12 7
Chapelton St., G22	G16 21
Chaplet Av., G13	F11 19
Chapman St. G42	N16 51
Allison St.	
Chappel St., Barr.	Q 7 59
Charing Cross G2	J15 35
Charing Cross La. G3	K15 35
Granville St.	
Charles Av., Renf.	H 8 17
Charles Cres., Lenz.	D23 13
Charles St. G21	J18 36
Charlotte La. G1	L17 36
London Rd.	
Charlotte La. S. G1	L17 36
Charlotte St.	
Charlotte Pl., Pais.	N 6 46
Charlotte St., G1	L17 36
Chatelherault Av. G72	P21 66
Chatton St. G23	E14 8
Cheapside St. G3	K15 35
Chelmsford Dr. G12	G13 20
Cherry Bank, Lenz.	C22 12
Cherry Cres., Clyde.	D 7 5
Cherry Pl., Bish.	F19 23
Cherry Pl., John.	N 1 44
Cherrybank Rd. G43	P15 63
Chester St. G32	L22 38
Chesterfield Av. G12	G13 20
Chesters Pl. G73	O19 53
Chesters Rd., Bear.	D11 7
Chestnut Dr., Dalm.	C 7 5
Chestnut Dr., Lenz.	C22 12
Chestnut Pl., John.	O 1 44
Chestnut St. G22	G17 22
Cheviot Av., Barr.	R 8 59
Cheviot Rd., G43	P14 62
Cheviot Rd., Pais.	O 6 46
Chirnside Pl. G52	L10 32
Chirnside Rd. G52	L10 32
Chisholm St. G1	L17 36
Christian St. G43	O14 50
Christie La., Pais.	L 6 30
New Sneddon St.	
Christie Pl. G72	P22 66
Christie St., Pais.	L 6 30
Christopher St. G21	J19 37
Chryston Rd.	C25 14
Waterside & Chr.	
Chryston Rd., Chr.	F26 26
Church Av. G33	G23 25
Church Av. G73	P20 65
Church Dr., Lenz.	C23 13
Church Hill, Pais.	L 6 30
Church La. G42	N16 51
Victoria Rd.	
Church Rd., Chr.	F26 26
Church Rd., Giff.	R14 62
Church St. G11	J14 34
Church St., Bail.	M26 56
Church St., Clyde.	D 7 5
Church St., John.	M09 43
Church St., Kilb.	M07 42
Church St., Udd.	P27 69
Churchill Av., John.	O08 43
Churchill Cres., Udd.	Q28 69
Churchill Dr. G11	H12 19
Churchill Pl., Kilb.	M07 42
Churchill Way, Bish.	E18 10
Kirkintilloch Rd.	

Street	Grid	Page
Churchill Way, Bish.	E18	10
Kirkintilloch Rd.		
Circus Dr. G31	K18	36
Circus Pl. G31	K18	36
Circus Place La. G31	K18	36
Circus Pl.		
Civic Way, Lenz.	B23	13
Kirkintilloch Rd.		
Clachan Dr. G51	K12	33
Skipness Dr.		
Claddens Pl., Lenz.	D24	13
Claddens Quad. G22	G17	22
Claddens St. G22	G16	21
Claddens Wynd G66	D24	13
Claddon Vw., Clyde.	D 8	5
Kirkoswald Dr.		
Clair Rd., Bish.	E20	11
Clairmont Gdns. G3	J15	35
Clare St. G21	J19	37
Claremont Av., Giff.	R14	62
Claremont Pl. G3	J15	35
Claremont Ter.		
Claremont St. G3	K15	35
Claremont Ter. G3	J15	35
Claremont Terrace La.	J15	35
G3		
Clifton St.		
Clarence Dr. G11	H13	20
Clarence Gdns. G11	H13	20
Clarence St., Clyde.	D 8	5
Clarence St., Pais.	L 7	31
Clarendon La., G20	J16	35
Clarendon St.		
Clarendon Pl. G20	J16	35
Clarendon St. G20	J16	35
Clarion Cres. G13	F10	18
Clarion Rd. G13	F10	18
Clark St. G41	L15	35
Tower St.		
Clark St., Dalm.	D 6	4
Clark St., John.	M09	43
Clark St., Pais.	L 5	30
Clark St., Renf.	H 7	17
Clarkston Av. G44	Q15	63
Clarkston Rd. G44	R15	63
Clathic Av., Bear.	D13	8
Claude Av. G72	Q24	67
Claude Rd., Pais.	L 7	31
Claudhall Av., Gart.	F27	27
Clavens Rd. G52	L 9	32
Claverhouse Pl., Pais.	M 7	47
Claverhouse Rd. G52	K 9	32
Clavering St. E., Pais.	L 5	30
Well St.		
Clavering St. W., Pais.	L 5	30
King St.		
Clayhouse Rd. G33	G24	25
Claypotts Pl. G33	J22	38
Claypotts Rd. G33	J22	38
Clayslaps Rd. G3	J14	34
Argyle St.		
Claythorn Av. G40	L18	36
Claythorn Circus G40	L18	36
Claythorn Av.		
Claythorn Ct. G40	L18	36
Claythorn Pk.		
Claythorn Pk. G40	L18	36
Claythorn Ter. G40	L18	36
Claythorn Pk.		
Clayton Ter. G31	K18	36
Cleddans Cres., Clyde.	C 8	5
Cleddans Rd., Clyde.	C 8	5
Cleddens Ct., Bish.	E10	11
Cleeves Pl. G53	P10	60
Cleeves Quadrant G53	P10	60
Cleeves Rd. G53	P10	60
Cleghorn St. G22	H16	21
Cleland La. G5	L17	36
Cleland St.		
Cleland St. G5	L17	36
Clelland Av., Bish.	F19	23
Clerwood St. G32	L20	37
Cleveden Cres. G12	G13	20
Cleveden Cres. La. G12	G13	20
Cleveden Dr.		
Cleveden Dr. G12	G13	20
Cleveden Dr. G73	P20	65
Cleveden Gardens G12	G14	20
Cleveden Pl. G12	G13	20
Cleveden Rd. G12	G13	20
Cleveland St. G3	K15	35
Cliff Rd. G3	J15	35
Clifford Gdns. G51	L13	34
Clifford La. G51	L14	34
Gower St.		
Clifford Pl. G51	L14	34
Clifford St.		
Clifford St. G51	L13	34
Clifton Pl. G3	J15	35
Clifton St.		
Clifton Rd., Giff.	Q13	62
Clifton St. G3	J15	35
Clifton Ter. G72	Q21	66
Clifton Ter., John.	N 1	44
Clincarthill Rd. G73	O19	53
Clincart Rd. G42	O16	51
Clinton Av., Udd.	P27	69
Clippens Rd., Linw.	L 1	28
Cloan Av. G15	E10	6
Cloan Cres., Bish.	D19	11
Cloberhill Rd. G13	E11	7
Cloch St. G33	K22	38
Clochoderick Av., Kilb.	N07	42
Mackenzie Dr.		
Clonbeith St. G33	J24	39
Closeburn St. G22	G17	22
Cloth St., Barr.	R 8	59
Clouden Rd., Cumb.	C 3	71
Cloudhowe Ter., Blan.	R26	68
Clouston Ct. G20	H15	21
Clouston La. G20	H14	20
Clouston St.		
Clouston St. G20	H14	20
Clova Pl., Udd.	P27	69
Clova St. G46	Q12	61
Clover Av., Bish.	E18	10
Cloverbank St. G21	J19	37
Clovergate, Bish.	E18	10
Clunie Rd. G52	M12	49
Cluny Av., Bear.	E13	8
Cluny Dr., Bear.	E13	8
Cluny Dr., Pais.	L 7	31
Cluny Gdns. G14	H12	19
Cluny Gdns., Bail.	M25	56
Cluny Vill. G14	H11	19
Westland Dr.		
Clutha St. G51	L15	35
Paisley Rd. W.		
Clyde Av., Barr.	R 8	59
Clyde Av., Both.	R27	69
Clyde Cres., Blan.	S26	68
Clyde Ct., Dalm.	D 6	4
Little Holm		
Clyde Pl. G5	L16	35
Clyde Pl. G72	Q23	67
Clyde Pl., John.	O08	43
Clyde Rd., Pais.	K 7	31
Clyde St. G1	L16	35
Clyde St., Clyde.	F 8	17
Clyde St., Renf.	G 8	17
Clyde Ter., Both.	R28	69
Clyde Vale G71	R28	69
Clyde Vw. G71	R28	69
Clyde Vw., Pais.	N 7	47
Clydebrae Dr. G71	R28	69
Clydebrae St. G51	K13	34
Clydeford Dr. G32	M21	54
Clydeford Dr., Udd.	O26	56
Clydeford Rd. G72	O22	54
Clydeham Ter., Clyde.	F 8	17
Clydeholm Rd. G14	J11	33
Clydeneuk Dr., Udd.	O26	56
Clydesdale Av.,	J 7	31
Pais. & Renf.		
Clydeside Expressway	H11	19
G14		
Clydeside Rd. G73	N18	52
Clydesmill Dr. G32	O22	54
Clydesmill Gro. G32	O22	54
Clydesmill Pl. G32	O22	54
Clydesmill Rd. G32	O22	54
Clydeview G11	J13	34
Dumbarton Rd.		
Clydeview La. G11	J12	33
Broomhill Ter.		
Clydeview Ter. G32	O23	55
Clydeview Ter. G40	M18	52
Newhall St.		
Clynder St. G51	L13	34
Clyth Dr., Giff.	R14	62
Coalhill St. G31	L19	37
Coatbridge Rd., Bail.	L27	41
Coatbridge Rd., Gart.	H27	27
Coates Cres. G53	O11	49
Coats Cres., Bail.	L25	40
Coats Dr., Pais.	M 4	45
Coatshill Av., Blan.	R26	68
Cobbleriggs Way, Udd.	P27	69
Cobinshaw St. G32	L22	38
Cobinton Pl. G38	J22	38
Coburg St. G5	L16	35
Coburg St. G5	L16	35
Bedford St.		
Cochno Rd., Clyde.	B 7	5
Cochno St., Clyde.	F 8	17
Cochran St., Pais.	M 6	46
Cochrane St. G1	K17	36
Cochrane St., Barr.	R 7	59
Cochranemill Rd., John.	N08	43
Cockels Loan, Renf.	J 7	31
Cockenzie St. G32	L22	38
Cockmuir St. G21	H19	23
Cogan Rd. G43	P14	62
Cogan St. G43	O14	50
Cogan St., Barr.	R 7	59
Colbert St. G40	M18	52
Colbreggan Ct., Clyde.	C 8	5
St. Helena Cres.		
Colbreggan Gdns.,	C 8	5
Clyde.		
Colchester Dr. G12	G13	20
Coldingham Av. G14	G 9	18
Coldstream Dr. G73	P20	65
Coldstream Dr., Pais.	N 4	45
Coldstream Pl. G21	H17	22
Keppochhill Rd.		
Coldstream Rd., Clyde.	E 7	5
Colebrook St. G72	P22	66
Colebrook Ter. G12	H15	21
Colebrooke St.		
Colebrooke La. G12	H15	21
Colebrooke St.		
Colebrooke Pl. G12	H15	21
Belmont St.		
Colebrooke St. G12	H15	21
Coleridge, Udd.	Q28	69
Colfin St. G34	J26	40
Colgrain St. G20	G16	21
Colinbar Circle, Barr.	R 7	59
Colinslee Av., Pais.	N 6	46
Colinslee Cres., Pais.	N 6	46
Colinslee Dr., Pais.	N 6	46
Colinslie Rd. G53	O11	49
Colinton Pl. G32	K22	38
Colintraive Av. G33	H21	24
Coll Av., Renf.	J 8	31
Coll Pl. G21	J19	37
Coll St. G21	J19	37
Colla Gdns., Bish.	E20	11
College La. G1	L17	36
High St.		
College St. G1	K17	36
Collessie Dr. G33	J23	39
Collier St., John.	M09	43
Collina St. G20	G14	20
Collins St. G4	K18	36
Collins St., Clyde.	C 8	5
Collylin Rd., Bear.	D12	7
Colmonell Av. G13	F 9	18
Colonsay Av., Renf.	J 8	31
Colonsay Rd. G52	L12	33
Colonsay Rd., Pais.	O 5	46
Colquhoun Av. G52	K10	32
Colquhoun Dr., Bear.	C11	7
Colston Av., Bish.	F18	22
Colston Dr., Bish.	F18	22
Colston Gdns., Bish.	F18	22
Colston Path, Bish.	F18	22
Colston Gdns.		
Colston Pl., Bish.	F18	22
Colston Rd., Bish.	F18	22
Coltmuir St. G22	G16	21
Coltness La. G33	K23	39
Coltness St. G33	K23	39
Coltpark Av., Bish.	F18	22
Coltpark La., Bish.	F18	22
Coltsfoot Dr. G53	Q10	60
Columba Path, Clyde.	E 8	5
Onslow Rd.		
Columba St. G51	K13	34

Colvend Dr. G73 — Q19 65
Colvend St. G40 — M18 52
Colville Dr. G73 — P20 65
Colwood Av. G53 — Q10 60
Colwood Gdns. G53 — Q10 60
Colwood Av.
Colwood Path G53 — Q10 60
Parkhouse Rd.
Colwood Pl. G53 — Q10 60
Colwood Sq. G53 — Q10 60
Colwood Av.
Comedie Rd. G33 — H24 25
Comely Park St. G31 — L19 37
Comley Pl. G31 — L19 37
Gallowgate
Commerce St. G5 — L16 35
Commercial Ct. G5 — L17 36
Commercial Rd. G5 — M17 52
Commercial Rd., Barr. — Q 8 59
Commonhead Rd. G34 — K26 40
Commonhead Rd., Bail. — K27 41
Commore Av., Barr. — R 8 59
Commore Dr. G13 — F10 18
Comrie Rd. G33 — G23 25
Comrie St. G32 — M22 54
Cona St. G46 — Q12 61
Conan Ct. G72 — P23 67
Condorrat Ring Rd., Cumb. — D 1 70
Congleton St. G53 — P 9 60
Nitshill Rd.
Congress Rd. G3 — K15 35
Conifer Pl., Lenz. — C22 12
Conisborough Path G34 — J24 39
Balfluig St.
Conisborough Rd. G34 — J24 39
Connal St. G40 — M19 53
Conniston St. G32 — K21 38
Conon Av., Bear. — D11 7
Consett St. G33 — K23 39
Consett St. G33 — K23 39
Consett La.
Contin Pl. G12 — G14 20
Convair Way, Renf. — J 8 31
Lismore Av.
Conval Way, Pais. — K 5 30
Abbotsburn Way
Cook St. G5 — L16 35
Coopers Well La. G11 — J14 34
Dumbarton Rd.
Coopers Well St. G11 — J14 34
Dumbarton Rd.
Copland Pl. G51 — L13 34
Copland Quad. G51 — L13 34
Copland Rd. G51 — L13 34
Coplaw St. G42 — M16 51
Copperfield La., Udd. — O28 57
Hamilton Vw.
Corbett St. G32 — M22 54
Corbiston Way, Cumb. — C 3 71
Cordiner St. G44 — O16 51
Corkerhill Gdns. G52 — M12 49
Corkerhill Pl. G52 — N11 49
Corkerhill Rd. G52 — N11 49
Corlaich Av. G42 — O18 52
Corlaich Dr. G42 — O18 52
Corn St. G4 — J16 35
Cornaig Rd. G53 — O10 48
Cornalee Gdns. G53 — O10 48
Cornalee Pl. G53 — O10 48
Cornalee Rd. G53 — O10 48
Cornhill St. G21 — G19 23
Cornoch St. G23 — E14 8
Torrin Rd.
Cornock Cres., Clyde. — D 7 5
Cornock St., Clyde. — D 7 5
Cornwall Av. G73 — P20 65
Cornwall St. G41 — L14 34
Coronation Pl., Gart. — F27 27
Coronation Way, Bear. — E13 8
Corpach Pl. G34 — J26 40
Corran St. G33 — K21 38
Corrie Dr., Pais. — M 9 48
Corrie Gro. G44 — Q15 63
Corrie Pl., Lenz. — D24 13
Corrour Rd. G43 — O14 50
Corse Rd. G52 — L 9 32
Corsebar Av., Pais. — N 5 46
Corsebar Cres, Pais. — N 5 46
Corsebar Dr., Pais. — N 5 46

Corsebar La. G78 — N 4 45
Balgonie Av.
Corsebar Rd., Pais. — N 5 46
Corseford Av., John. — O08 43
Corsehill Pl. G34 — K26 40
Corsehill St. G34 — K26 40
Corselet Rd. G53 — Q10 60
Corsewall Av. G32 — M24 55
Corsford Dr. G53 — P11 61
Corsock St. G31 — K20 37
Corston St. G33 — K20 37
Cortachy Pl., Bish. — E20 11
Coruisk Way — O 3 45
Spencer Dr.
Coruisk Way, Pais. — O 3 45
Spencer Dr.
Corunna St. G3 — K15 35
Coshneuk Rd. G33 — G22 24
Cottar St. G20 — F15 21
Cotton Av., Linw. — L 1 28
Cotton St. G40 — N19 53
Cotton St., Pais. — M 6 46
Coulters La. G40 — L18 36
Countess Wk., Bail. — L28 41
County Av. G72 — O20 53
County Pl., Pais. — L 6 30
Moss St.
County Sq., Pais. — L 6 30
Couper St. G4 — J17 36
Courthill Av. G44 — P16 63
Coustonhill St. G43 — O14 50
Pleasance St.
Coustonholm Rd. G43 — O14 50
Coventry Dr. G31 — K19 37
Cowal Dr., Linw. — L 1 28
Cowal Rd. G20 — F14 20
Cowal St. G20 — F14 20
Cowan Clo., Barr. — Q 8 59
Cowan Cres. — R 8 59
Cowan La. G12 — J15 35
Cowan St.
Cowan Rd., Cumb. — A 1 70
Cowan St. G12 — J15 35
Cowan Wilson Av., Blan. — S26 68
Cowcaddens Rd. G2 — J16 35
Cowden Dr., Bish. — D19 11
Cowden St. G51 — K11 33
Cowdenhill Circus G13 — F11 19
Cowdenhill Pl. G13 — F11 19
Cowdenhill Rd. G13 — F11 19
Cowdie St., Pais. — K 5 30
Cowdray Cres., Renf. — H 8 17
Cowell Vw., Clyde. — D 7 5
Granville St.
Cowglen Pl. G53 — O11 49
Cowglen Rd.
Cowglen Rd. G53 — O11 49
Cowglen Ter. G53 — O11 49
Cowie St. G41 — L15 35
Cowlairs Rd. G21 — H18 22
Coxhill St. G21 — H17 22
Coxton Pl. G33 — J23 39
Coylton Rd. G43 — P15 63
Craggan Dr. G14 — G 9 18
Cragielea St. G31 — K19 37
Crags Av., Pais. — N 6 46
Crags Cres., Pais. — N 6 46
Crags Rd., Pais. — N 6 46
Craig Rd. G44 — P16 63
Craig Rd., Linw. — K 1 28
Craigallian Av. G72 — Q23 67
Craiganour La. G43 — P14 62
Craiganour Pl. G43 — P14 62
Craigard Pl. G73 — Q21 66
Inverclyde Gdns.
Craigbank Dr. G53 — P10 60
Craigbank St. G22 — H17 22
Craigbarnet Cres. G33 — H22 24
Craigbo Av. G23 — E14 8
Craigbo Ct. G23 — F14 20
Craigbo Dr. G23 — F14 20
Craigbo Pl. G23 — F14 20
Craigbo Rd. G23 — F14 20
Craigbo St. G23 — E14 8
Craigbog Av., John. — N08 43
Craigdonald Pl., John. — M09 43
Craigellan Rd. G43 — P14 62
Craigenbay Cres., Lenz. — C23 13
Craigenbay Rd., Lenz. — D23 13
Craigenbay St. G21 — H19 23

Craigencart Ct., Clyde. — C 6 4
Gentle Row
Craigend Dr., Coat. — M29 57
Craigend Pl. G13 — G12 19
Craigend St. G13 — G12 19
Craigendmuir Rd. G33 — H24 25
Craigendmuir St. G33 — J20 37
Craigendon Oval, Pais. — P 5 58
Craigendon Rd., Pais. — P 5 58
Craigends Dr., Kilb. — M07 42
High Barholm
Craigenfeoch Av., John. — N08 43
Craigfaulds Av., Pais. — N04 45
Craigflower Gdns. G53 — Q10 60
Craigflower Rd. G53 — Q10 60
Craighalbert Rd. G68 — B 1 70
Craighall Rd. G4 — J16 35
Craighead Av. G33 — H20 23
Craighead St., Barr. — R 7 59
Craighead Way, Barr. — R 7 59
Craighouse St. G33 — J22 38
Craigie Pk. G66 — C24 13
Craigie St. G42 — N16 51
Craigiebar Dr., Pais. — O 5 46
Craigieburn Gdns. G20 — F13 20
Craigieburn Rd., Cumb. — C 2 70
Craigiehall Pl. G51 — L14 34
Craigielea Dr., Pais. — L 5 30
Craigielea Rd. G81 — B 6 4
Craigielea Rd., Renf. — H 8 17
Craigielinn Av., Pais. — P 5 58
Craigievar St. G33 — J24 39
Craigleith St. G32 — L21 38
Craiglockhart St. G33 — J23 39
Craigmaddie Ter. La. G3 — K15 35
Derby St.
Craigmillar Rd. G42 — O16 51
Craigmont Dr. G20 — G15 21
Craigmont St. G20 — G15 21
Craigmore Rd., Bear. — B10 6
Craigmore St. G31 — L20 37
Craigmount Av., Pais. — P 5 58
Craigmuir Cres. G52 — L 9 32
Craigmuir Pl. G52 — L 9 32
Craigmuir Rd.
Craigmuir Rd. G52 — L 9 32
Craigneil St. G33 — J24 39
Craignestock St. G40 — L18 36
Craignethan Gdns. G11 — J13 34
Lawrie St.
Craignure Rd. G73 — Q19 65
Craigpark Dr. G31 — K19 37
Craigpark G31 — K19 37
Craigpark Ter. G31 — K19 37
Craigpark
Craigpark Way, Udd. — O28 57
Newton Dr.
Craigs Av., Clyde. — C 8 5
Craigston Pl., John. — N09 43
Craigston Rd., John. — N09 43
Craigton Av., Barr. — R 9 60
Craigton Dr. G51 — L12 33
Craigton Dr., Barr. — R 9 60
Craigton Pl. G51 — L12 33
Craigton Dr.
Craigton Pl., Blan. — R26 68
Craigton Rd. G51 — L12 33
Craigvicar Gdns. G32 — L23 39
Hailes Av.
Craigview Av., John. — O08 43
Craigwell Av. G73 — P20 65
Crail St. G31 — L20 37
Cramond Av., Renf. — J 9 32
Cramond St. G5 — N17 52
Cramond Ter. G32 — L22 38
Cranborne Rd. G12 — G13 20
Cranbrooke Dr. G20 — F14 20
Cranhill St. G33 — J20 37
Cranston St. G3 — K15 35
Cranworth La. G12 — H14 20
Great George St.
Cranworth St. G12 — H14 20
Crarae Av., Bear. — E12 7
Crathie Dr. G11 — J13 34
Crathie La. G11 — J13 34
Exeter Dr.
Craw Rd., Pais. — M 5 46
Crawford Av., Lenz. — D23 13
Crawford Cres., Blan. — R26 68
Crawford Cres., Udd. — O27 57

Street	Grid	Map
Crawford Ct., Giff.	R13	62
Milverton Rd.		
Crawford Dr. G15	E 9	6
Crawford La. G11	J13	34
Crawford Path G11	J13	34
Crawford St.		
Crawford St. G11	J13	34
Crawfurd Dr., Pais.	L 4	29
Crawfurd Gdns. G73	Q19	65
Crawfurd Rd. G73	Q19	65
Crawriggs Av., Lenz.	C23	13
Crebar Dr., Barr.	R 8	59
Crebar St. G46	Q12	61
Credon Gdns. G73	Q20	65
Cree Av., Bish.	E20	11
Cree Gdns. G32	L21	38
Kilmany Dr.		
Creran St. G40	L18	36
Tobago St.		
Crescent Ct., Dalm.	D 6	4
Swindon St.		
Crescent Rd. G13	G10	18
Cresswell La. G12	H14	20
Great George St.		
Cresswell St. G12	H14	20
Cressy St. G11	K12	33
Crest Av. G13	F10	18
Crestlea Av., Pais.	O 6	46
Creswell Ter., Udd.	O27	57
Kylepark Dr.		
Crichton Ct. G42	R18	64
Crichton St. G21	H18	22
Crieff Ct. G3	K15	35
North St.		
Criffell Gdns. G32	M23	55
Criffell Rd. G32	M23	55
Crimea St. G2	K16	35
Crinan Gdns., Bish.	E19	11
Crinan Rd., Bish.	E19	11
Crinan St. G31	K19	37
Cripps Av., Clyde.	E 8	5
Croft Rd. G73	P22	66
Croft Wynd, Udd.	P28	69
Croftbank Av. G71	R28	69
Croftbank Cres., Both.	R28	69
Croftbank Cres., Udd.	P27	69
Croftbank St. G21	H18	22
Croftbank St., Udd.	P27	69
Croftburn Dr. G44	Q17	64
Croftcroighn Rd. G33	J22	38
Croftend Av. G44	P18	64
Croftfoor Rd. G44	Q17	64
Croftfoot Cotts., Gart.	G28	27
Croftfoot Cres. G45	Q19	65
Croftfoot Dr. G45	Q18	64
Croftfoot Quad. G45	Q18	64
Croftfoot Rd. G45	Q17	64
Croftfoot St. G45	Q19	65
Croftfoot Ter. G45	Q18	64
Crofthead St., Udd.	P27	69
Crofthill Av., Udd.	P27	69
Crofthill Rd. G44	P17	64
Crofthouse Dr. G44	Q18	64
Croftmont Av. G44	Q18	64
Croftmoraig Av., Chr.	D28	15
Crofton Av. G44	Q17	64
Croftpark Av. G44	Q17	64
Croftpark Rd., Clyde.	B 7	5
Croftside Av. G44	Q18	64
Croftspar Av. G32	L23	39
Croftspar Dr. G32	L23	39
Croftspar Pl. G32	L23	39
Croftwood Av. G44	Q17	64
Croftwood, Bish.	D19	11
Cromart Pl., Chr.	E26	14
Cromarty Av. G43	P15	63
Cromarty Av., Bish.	E20	11
Cromarty Gdns., Clark.	R16	63
Crombie Gdns., Bail.	M25	56
Cromdale St. G51	L12	33
Cromer La., Pais.	K 5	30
Abbotsburn Way		
Cromer St. G20	G15	21
Cromer Way, Pais.	K 5	30
Mosslands Rd.		
Crompton Av. G44	P16	63
Cromwell La. G20	J16	35
Cromwell St.		
Cromwell St. G20	J16	35
Cronberry Quad. G52	M 9	48
Cronberry Ter. G52	M 9	48
Crookedshields Rd. G72	R22	66
Crookston Av. G52	M10	48
Crookston Ct. G52	M10	48
Crookston Dr. G52	M 9	48
Crookston Gdns. G52	M 9	48
Crookston Gro. G52	M10	48
Crookston Pl. G52	M 9	48
Crookston Quad. G52	M 9	48
Crookston Rd. G52	N10	48
Crookston Ter. G52	M10	48
Crookston Rd.		
Crosbie Dr. G78	O 3	45
Crosbie St. G20	F14	20
Crosbie Woods, Pais.	N 4	45
Cross Arthurlie St.,	R 7	59
Barr.		
Cross Rd., Pais.	N 4	45
Cross St. G32	N23	55
Cross St., Pais.	M 5	46
Cross, The, G1	L17	36
Cross, The, Pais.	L 6	30
Crossbank Av. G42	N18	52
Crossbank Dr. G42	N18	52
Crossbank Rd. G42	N17	52
Crossbank Ter. G42	N17	52
Crossflat Cres., Pais.	L 7	31
Crossford Dr. G23	E15	9
Crosshill Av. G42	N16	51
Crosshill Av., Lenz.	C23	13
Crosshill Dr. G73	P19	65
Crosshill Rd.,	C20	11
Bish. & Lenz.		
Crosshill Sq., Bail.	M26	56
Crosslee St. G52	L12	33
Crosslees Ct., Thorn.	Q12	61
Main St.		
Crosslees Dr., Thorn.	Q12	61
Crosslees Pk., Thorn.	Q12	61
Crosslees Rd., Thorn.	R12	61
Crossloan Pl. G51	K12	33
Crossloan Rd. G51	K12	33
Crossloan Ter. G51	K12	33
Crossmill Av., Barr.	Q 8	59
Crossmyloof Gdns.	N14	50
G41		
Crosspoint Dr. G23	E15	9
Invershiel Rd.		
Crosstobs Rd. G53	N10	48
Crovie Rd. G53	O10	48
Crow Ct., The, Bish.	E18	10
Kenmure Av.		
Crow La. G13	G12	19
Crow Rd. G11	H12	19
Crow Wood Rd., Chr.	F25	26
Crowflats Rd., Udd.	P27	69
Lady Isle Cres.		
Crowhill Rd. G64	F18	22
Crowhill St. G22	G17	22
Crowlin Cres. G33	K22	38
Crown Av., Clyde.	D 7	5
Crown Circuit G12	H13	20
Crown Rd.		
Crown Circus G12	H13	20
Crown Rd. S.		
Crown Ct. G1	K17	36
Virginia St.		
Crown Gdns. G12	H13	20
Crown Rd. N.		
Crown Mansions G11	H13	20
North Gardner St.		
Crown Pl. N. G12	H13	20
Crown Rd. S. G12	H13	20
Crown St. G5	M17	52
Crown St., Bail.	M24	55
Crown Ter. G12	H13	20
Crown Rd. S.		
Crownpoint Rd. G40	L18	36
Crowpoint Rd. G40	L19	37
Alma St.		
Crowwood Ter., Chr.	F25	26
Croy Pl. G21	G20	23
Rye Rd.		
Croy Pl. G21	G20	23
Croy Rd.		
Croy Rd. G21	G20	23
Cruachan Av., Renf.	J 8	31
Cruachan Cres., Pais.	O 6	46
Cruachan Dr., Barr.	R 8	59
Cruachan Rd. G73	Q20	65
Cruachan Rd., Bear.	B10	6
Ledi Dr.		
Cruachan St. G46	Q12	61
Cruachan Way, Barr.	R 8	59
Cruden St. G51	L12	33
Crum Av., Thorn.	Q13	62
Crusader Av. G13	E11	7
Cubie St. G40	L18	36
Cuilhill Rd., Bail.	K27	41
Cuillin Way, Barr.	R 8	59
Cuillins Rd. G73	Q20	65
Cuillins, The, Udd.	N26	56
Culbin Dr. G13	F 9	18
Cullen St. G32	M22	54
Cullins, The, Chr.	D28	15
Culloden St. G31	K19	37
Culrain Gdns. G32	L22	38
Culrain St. G32	L22	38
Culross La. G32	M23	55
Culross St. G32	M23	55
Cult Rd., Lenz.	D24	13
Cults St. G51	L12	33
Culzean Cres., Bail.	M25	56
Huntingtower Rd.		
Culzean Dr. G32	M23	39
Cumberland Ct. G1	L17	36
Gallowgate		
Cumberland La. G5	M16	51
Cumberland St.		
Cumberland Pl. G5	M17	52
Cumberland Pl., Pais.	M 6	46
Laigh Kirk La.		
Cumberland St. G5	L16	35
Cumberland St. G5	M17	52
Cumbernauld Rd. G31	K20	37
Cumbrae Ct., Clyde.	E 7	5
Montrose St.		
Cumbrae Rd., Pais.	O 6	46
Cumbrae Rd., Renf.	J 8	31
Cumbrae St. G33	K22	38
Cumlodden Dr. G20	F14	20
Cumming Dr. G42	O16	51
Cumnock Dr., Renf.	R 8	59
Cunard St., Clyde.	F 8	17
Cunningham Dr., Clyde.	C 6	4
Cunningham Dr., Giff.	Q15	63
Cunningham Rd. G73	O20	53
Cambuslang Rd.		
Cunningham Rd., G52	K 9	32
Cunninghame Rd., Kilb.	M07	42
Curfew Rd. G13	E11	7
Curle St. G14	J11	33
Curlew Pl., John.	O08	43
Curling Cres. G44	O17	52
Currie St. G20	G15	21
Curtis Av. G44	O17	52
Curzon St. G20	G15	21
Cut, The, Udd.	P27	69
Cuthbert St., Udd.	O28	57
Oakdene Av.		
Cuthbertson St. G42	N16	51
Cuthelton Dr. G31	M21	54
Cuthelton St.		
Cuthelton St. G31	M20	53
Cuthelton Ter. G31	M20	53
Cypress Av., Blan.	S26	68
Cypress Av., Udd.	O28	57
Myrtle Av.		
Cypress Ct., Lenz.	C22	12
Cypress St. G22	G17	22
Cyprus Av., John.	N 1	44
Cyprus St., Clyde.	F 8	17
Cyril St., Pais.	M 7	47
Daer Av., Renf.	J 9	32
Dairsie Gdns., Bish.	F20	23
Dairsie St. G44	Q15	63
Daisy St. G42	N16	51
Dakota Way, Renf.	J 8	31
Friendship Way		
Dalbeth Rd. G32	N21	54
Dalchurn Path G34	K25	40
Dalchurn Pl.		
Dalchurn Pl. G34	K25	40
Dalcraig Cres., Blan.	R26	68
Dalcross La. G11	J14	34
Byres Rd.		
Dalcross St. G11	J14	34
Dalcruin Gdns. G69	D28	15
Daldowie Av. G32	M23	55

Street	Grid	Page
Dale Path G40	M18	52
Dale St. G40	M18	52
Dale Way G73	Q19	65
Daleview Av. G12	G13	20
Dalfoil Ct. G52	M 9	48
Dalgarroch Av. G13	F 9	18
Dalgleish Av., Clyde.	C 6	4
Dalhousie Gdns., Bish.	E18	10
Dalhousie La. G3	J16	35
Scott St.		
Dalhousie La. W. G3	J16	35
Buccleuch St.		
Dalhousie Rd., Kilb.	N07	42
Dalhousie St. G3	J16	35
Dalilea Dr. G34	J26	40
Dalilea Path G34	J26	40
Dalilea Dr.		
Dalilea Pl. G34	J26	40
Dalintober St. G5	L16	35
Dalkeith Av. G41	M13	50
Dalkeith Av., Bish.	D19	11
Dalkeith Rd., Bish.	D19	11
Dalmahoy St. G32	K21	38
Dalmally St. G20	H15	21
Dalmarnock Ct. G40	M19	53
Baltic St.		
Dalmary Dr., Pais.	L 7	31
Dalmeny Av., Giff.	Q14	62
Dalmeny Dr., Barr.	R 7	59
Dalmeny St. G5	N18	52
Dalmuir Ct., Dalm.	D 6	4
Stewart St.		
Dalnair St. G3	J14	34
Dalness Pass. G32	M22	54
Ochil St.		
Dalness St. G32	M22	54
Dalnottar Hill Rd., Old.K.	C 4	4
Dalreoch Av., Bail.	L26	40
Dalriada St. G40	M20	53
Dalry Rd., Udd.	O28	57
Myrtle Rd.		
Dalry St. G32	M22	54
Dalserf Cres., Giff.	R13	62
Dalserf St. G31	L19	37
Dalsetter Av. G15	E 9	6
Dalsetter Pl. G15	E10	6
Dalsholm Rd. G20	F13	20
Dalskeith Av., Pais.	L 4	29
Dalskeith Cres., Pais.	L 4	29
Dalskeith Rd., Pais.	M 4	45
Dalswinton Pl. G34	K26	40
Dalswinton St.		
Dalswinton St. G34	K26	40
Dalton Av., Clyde.	E 9	6
Dalton St. G31	L21	38
Dalveen Av., Udd.	O27	57
Dalveen Ct., Barr.	R 8	59
Dalveen St. G32	L21	38
Dalveen Way G73	Q20	65
Dalwhinnie Av., Blan.	R26	68
Daly Gdns., Blan.	R27	69
Dalziel Dr. G41	M14	50
Dalziel Quadrant G41	M14	50
Dalziel Dr.		
Dalziel Rd. G52	K 9	32
Damshot Cres. G53	N11	49
Damshot Rd. G53	O11	49
Danes Cres. G14	G10	18
Danes Dr. G14	G10	18
Danes La. S. G14	H11	19
Dunglass Av.		
Dargarvel Av. G41	M13	50
Darkwood Cres., Pais.	L 4	29
Darleith St. G32	L21	38
Darluith Rd., Linw.	L 1	28
Darnaway Av. G33	J23	39
Darnaway St. G33	J23	39
Darnick St. G21	H19	23
Hobden St.		
Darnley Cres., Bish.	D18	10
Darnley Gdns. G41	N15	51
Darnley Pl. G41	N15	51
Darnley Rd.		
Darnley Rd. G41	N15	51
Darnley Rd., Barr.	Q 9	60
Darnley St. G41	N15	51
Darroch Way, Cumb.	B 3	71
Dartford St. G22	H16	21
Darvaar Rd., Renf.	J 8	31
Darvel Cres., Pais.	M 8	47
Darvel St. G53	P 9	60
Darwin Pl., Dalm.	D 5	4
Dava St. G51	K13	34
Davaar Rd., Pais.	O 6	46
Davaar St. G40	M19	53
Daventry Dr. G12	G13	20
David Pl., Bail.	M24	55
David Pl., Pais.	K 7	31
Killarn Way		
David St. G40	L19	37
David Way, Pais.	K 7	31
Killarn Way		
Davidson Gdns. G14	H11	19
Westland Dr.		
Davidson Quad., Clyde.	B 6	4
Davidson St. G40	N19	53
Davidson St., Clyde.	F 9	18
Davidston Pl., Lenz.	D24	13
Davieland Rd., Giff.	R13	62
Daviot St. G51	L11	33
Dawes La. N. G14	H11	19
Upland Dr.		
Dawson Pl. G4	H16	21
Dawson Rd.		
Dawson Rd. G4	H16	21
Dealston Rd., Barr.	Q 7	59
Dean Park Dr. G72	Q23	67
Dean Park Rd., Renf.	J 9	32
Dean St., Clyde.	E 8	5
Deanbrae St., Udd.	P27	69
Deanfield Quad. G52	L 9	32
Deanpark Av., Udd.	Q28	69
Deans Av. G72	Q23	67
Deanside La. G4	K17	36
Rotton Row		
Deanside Rd., Renf.	K10	32
Deanston Dr. G41	O15	51
Deanwood Av. G44	Q15	63
Deanwood Rd. G44	Q15	63
Debdale Cotts. G13	G12	19
Whittingehame Dr.		
Dechmont Av. G72	Q23	67
Dechmont Gdns., Blan.	R26	68
Dechmont Gdns., Udd.	N27	57
Dechmont Pl. G72	Q23	67
Dechmont Rd., Udd.	N27	57
Dechmont St. G31	M20	53
Dechmont Vw., Udd.	O28	57
Hamilton Vw.		
Dee Av. G78	N 3	45
Dee Av., Renf.	H 9	18
Dee Dr., Pais.	N 3	45
Dee Pl., John.	O08	43
Dee St. G33	J20	37
Deepdene Rd., Bear.	E11	7
Deepdene Rd., Chr.	E28	15
Delburn St. G31	M20	53
Delhi Av., Dalm.	D 5	4
Delhmont Vw., Udd.	O28	57
Hamilton Vw.		
Delny Pl. G33	K24	39
Delvin Rd., G44	P16	63
Denbeck St. G32	L21	38
Denbrae St. G32	L21	38
Dene Wk., Bish.	F20	23
Denewood Av., Pais.	O 5	46
Denham St. G22	H16	21
Denholme Dr., Giff.	R14	62
Denkenny Sq. G15	D 9	6
Denmark St. G22	H17	22
Denmilne Path G34	K26	40
Denmilne Pl. G34	K26	40
Denmilne St. G34	K26	40
Derby St. G3	K15	35
Derby Terrace La. G3	K15	35
Derby St.		
Derwent St. G22	H16	21
Despard Av. G32	M24	55
Despard Gdns. G32	M24	55
Deveron Av., Giff.	R14	62
Deveron Rd., Bear.	E11	7
Deveron St. G33	J20	37
Devol Cres. G53	O10	48
Devon Gdns. G12	H13	20
Hyndland Rd.		
Devon Gdns., Bish.	D18	10
Devon Pl. G42	M16	51
Devon St. G5	M16	51
Devondale Av., Blan.	R26	68
Devonshire Gdns. G12	H13	20
Devonshire Gdns. La. G12	H13	20
Hyndland Rd.		
Devonshire Ter. G12	H13	20
Devonshire Ter. La. G12	H13	20
Hughenden Rd.		
Diana Av. G13	F10	18
Dick St. G20	H15	21
Henderson St.		
Dickens Av., Clyde.	D 6	4
Dilwara Av. G14	J12	33
Dimity St., John.	N09	43
Dinard Dr., Giff.	Q14	62
Dinart St. G33	J20	37
Dinduff St. G34	J26	40
Dingwall St. G3	K14	34
Kelvinhaugh St.		
Dinmont Pl. G41	N15	51
Norham St.		
Dinmont Rd. G41	N14	50
Dinwiddie St. G21	J20	37
Dipple Pl. G15	E10	6
Dirleton Av. G41	O15	51
Dirleton Dr., Pais.	N 4	45
Dirleton Gate, Bear.	E11	7
Divernia Way, Barr.	S 8	59
Dixon Av. G42	N16	51
Dixon Rd. G42	N17	52
Dixon St. G1	L16	35
Dixon St., Pais.	M 6	46
Dobbies Loan G4	J16	35
Dobbies Loan Pl. G4	K17	36
Dochart Av., Renf.	J 9	32
Dochart St. G33	J21	38
Dock St., Clyde.	F 8	17
Dodhill Pl. G13	G10	18
Dodside Gdns. G32	M23	55
Dodside Pl. G32	M23	55
Dodside St. G32	M23	55
Dolan St., Bail.	L25	40
Dollar Ter. G20	F14	20
Crosbie St.		
Dolphin Rd. G41	N14	50
Don Av., Renf.	J 9	32
Don Dr., Pais.	N 3	45
Don Pl., John.	O08	43
Don St. G33	K20	37
Donald Way, Udd.	O28	57
Donaldson Dr., Renf.	H 8	17
Ferguson St.		
Donaldswood Rd., Pais.	O 5	46
Doncaster St. G20	H16	21
Doon Cres., Bear.	D11	7
Doon Side, Cumb.	C 3	71
Doon St., Clyde.	D 8	5
Doonfoot Rd. G43	P14	62
Dora St. G40	M19	53
Dorchester Av., G12	G13	20
Dorchester Ct. G12	G13	20
Dorchester Av.		
Dorchester Pl. G12	G13	20
Dorian Dr., Clark.	S14	62
Dorlin Rd. G33	G24	25
Dormanside Rd. G53	M10	48
Dornal Av. G13	F 9	18
Dornford Av. G32	N23	55
Dornford Rd. G32	N23	55
Dornie Dr. G32	O23	55
Dornie Dr. G46	Q12	61
Dornoch Av., Giff.	R14	62
Dornoch Pl., Bish.	E20	11
Dornoch Pl., Chr.	E26	14
Dornoch Rd., Bear.	E11	7
Dornoch St. G40	L18	36
Dorset Sq. G3	K15	35
Dorset St.		
Dorset St. G3	K15	35
Dosk Av. G13	F 9	18
Dosk Pl. G13	F 9	18
Douglas Av. G32	N22	54
Douglas Av. G73	P20	65
Douglas Av., Giff.	R14	62
Douglas Av., John.	N 1	44
Douglas Av., Lenz.	C23	13
Douglas Ct., Lenz.	C23	13
Douglas Dr. G15	E 9	6
Douglas Dr. G72	P21	66
Douglas Dr., Bail.	L24	39
Douglas Dr., Both.	R28	69

Street	Grid	Page
Douglas Gdns., Bear.	D12	7
Douglas Gdns., Giff.	R14	62
Douglas Gdns., Lenz.	C23	13
Douglas Gdns., Udd.	P27	69
Douglas La. G2	K16	35
West George St.		
Douglas Park Cres.,	C13	8
Bear.		
Douglas Pl., Bear.	C12	7
Douglas Pl., Lenz.	C23	13
Douglas Rd.,	K 7	31
Pais. & Renf.		
Douglas St. G2	K16	35
Douglas St., Pais.	L 5	30
Douglas St., Udd.	O28	57
Douglas Ter. G41	M15	51
Shields Rd.		
Douglas Ter., Pais.	J 6	30
Douglaston Rd. G23	E15	9
Dougray Pl., Barr.	R 8	59
Dougrie Dr. G45	Q17	64
Dougrie Pl. G45	Q18	64
Dougrie Rd. G45	R17	64
Dougrie St. G45	Q18	64
Dougrie Ter. G45	Q17	64
Doune Cres., Bish.	D19	11
Doune Gdns. G20	H15	21
Doune Quad. G20	H15	21
Dove St. G53	P10	60
Dovecot G43	O14	50
Shawhill Rd.		
Dovecothall St., Barr.	Q 8	59
Dowanfield Rd., Cumb.	C 2	70
Dowanhill Pl. G11	J14	34
Old Dumbarton Rd.		
Dowanhill St. G11	J14	34
Dowanside La. G12	H14	20
Byres Rd.		
Dowanside Rd. G12	H14	20
Dowanvale Ter. G11	J13	34
White St.		
Down St. G21	H18	22
Downcraig Dr. G45	R17	64
Downcraig Rd. G45	R17	64
Downcraig Ter. G45	R17	64
Downfield Gdns., Both.	R27	69
Downfield St. G32	M21	54
Downiebrae Rd. G73	N19	53
Dowrie Cres. G53	N10	48
Dows Pl. G4	H16	21
Possil Rd.		
Drainie St. G34	K25	40
Westerhouse Rd.		
Drake St. G40	L18	36
Drakemire Av. G45	Q17	64
Drakemire Dr. G45	Q17	64
Dreghorn St. G31	K20	37
Drem Pl. G11	J13	34
Merkland St.		
Drimnin Rd. G33	G24	25
Drive Gdns., John.	M 3	45
Drive Rd. G51	K12	33
Drochil St. G34	J25	40
Drumbeg Dr. G53	P10	60
Drumbeg Pl. G53	P10	60
Drumbottie Rd. G21	G19	23
Drumby Cres., Clark.	S14	62
Drumby Dr., Clark.	S14	62
Drumcavel Rd.,	F26	26
Chr. & Gart.		
Drumchapel Gdns. G15	E10	6
Drumchapel Pl. G15	E10	6
Drumchapel Rd. G15	E10	6
Drumclog Gdns. G33	G21	24
Auchinleck Av.		
Drumclutha Dr., Both.	R28	69
Drumcross Rd. G53	N11	49
Drumhead Pl. G32	N21	54
Drumhead Rd. G32	N21	54
Drumilaw Rd. G73	P19	65
Drumilaw Way G73	P19	65
Drumlaken Av. G23	E14	8
Drumlaken Ct. G23	E14	8
Drumlaken St. G23	E14	8
Drumlanrig Av. G34	J26	40
Drumlanrig Pl. G34	J26	40
Drumlanrig Quad. G34	J26	40
Drumlochy Rd. G33	J22	38
Drummond Av. G73	O18	52
Drummond Dr., Pais.	M 8	47
Drummond Gdns. G13	G12	19
Crow Rd.		
Drummore Rd. G15	D10	6
Drummyne Pl. G51	L12	33
Drumoyne Circus		
Drumover Dr. G31	M21	54
Drumoyne Av. G51	K12	33
Drumoyne Circus G51	L12	33
Drumoyne Dr. G51	K12	33
Drumoyne Quad. G51	L12	33
Drumoyne Rd. G51	L12	33
Drumoyne Sq. G51	K12	33
Drumpark St. G46	Q12	61
Drumpark St., Coat.	M28	57
Dunnachie Dr.		
Drumpeller Rd., Bail.	M25	56
Drumpellier Av., Bail.	M25	56
Drumpellier Pl., Bail.	M25	56
Drumpellier St. G33	J20	37
Drumreoch Dr. G42	O18	52
Drumreoch Pl. G42	O18	52
Drumry Pl. G15	E 9	6
Drumry Rd. E. G15	E 9	6
Drumry Rd., Clyde.	D 7	5
Drums Av., Pais.	L 5	30
Drums Cres., Pais.	L 5	30
Drums Rd. G53	M10	48
Drumsack Av., Chr.	F26	26
Drumsargard Rd. G73	P20	65
Drumshaw Dr. G32	O23	55
Drumvale Dr., Chr.	E27	15
Drury St. G2	K16	35
Dryad St. G46	P12	61
Dryborough Av., John.	N 4	45
Dryburgh Av. G73	O19	53
Dryburgh Gdns. G20	H15	21
Dryburgh Rd., Bear.	C11	7
Dryburn Av. G52	L10	32
Drygate G4	K18	36
Drygrange Rd. G33	J23	39
Drymen Pl., Lenz.	D23	13
Drymen Rd., Bear.	C11	7
Drymen St. G52	L12	33
Morven St.		
Drymen Wynd, Bear.	D12	7
Drynoch Pl. G22	F16	21
Duart Dr., John.	N 1	44
Duart St. G20	F14	20
Dubs Rd., Barr.	Q 9	60
Dubton Path G34	J25	40
Dubton St. G34	J25	40
Duchall Pl. G14	H10	18
Duchess Pl. G73	O20	53
Duchess Rd. G73	N20	53
Duchray Dr., Pais.	M 9	48
Duchray La. G31	J20	37
Duchray St.		
Duchray St. G33	J20	37
Ducraig St. G32	L22	38
Dudhope St. G33	J23	39
Dudley Dr. G12	H13	20
Duffus Pl. G32	O23	55
Duffus St. G34	J25	40
Duffus Ter. G32	O23	55
Duisdale Rd. G32	O23	55
Duke St., G4	K18	36
Duke St., Linw.	L 2	28
Duke St., Pais.	N 6	46
Dukes Gate, Both.	Q27	69
Dukes Rd. G72 & G73	P20	65
Dukes Rd., Bail.	L28	41
Dulnain St. G72	P24	67
Dulsie Rd. G21	G20	23
Dumbarton Rd. G11	G 9	18
Dumbarton Rd., Clyde.	C 6	4
Dumbarton Rd., Old.K.	D 5	4
Dalm. & Clyde.		
Dumbreck Av. G41	M13	50
Dumbreck Ct. G41	M13	50
Dumbreck Pl., Lenz.	D24	13
Dumbreck Rd. G41	M13	50
Dumbreck Sq. G41	M13	50
Dumbreck Av.		
Dunagoil Rd. G45	R17	64
Dunagoil St. G45	R18	64
Dunagoil Ter. G45	R18	64
Dunalastair Dr. G33	G22	24
Dunalistair Av. G33	G22	24
Dunan Pl. G33	K24	39
Dunard Rd. G73	O19	53
Dunard St. G20	H15	21
Dunard Way, Pais.	K 5	30
Mosslands Rd.		
Dunaskin St. G11	J14	34
Dunbar Av. G73	O20	53
Dunbar Av., John.	O09	43
Dunbar Rd., Pais.	N 4	45
Dunbeith Pl. G20	G14	20
Dunblane St. G4	J16	35
Dunbrach Rd., Cumb.	B 1	70
Duncan Av. G14	H11	19
Duncan La. G14	H11	19
Duncan Av.		
Duncan La. N. G14	H11	19
Ormiston Av.		
Duncan St., Clyde.	D 7	5
Duncansby Rd. G33	L23	39
Dunchatt St. G31	K18	36
Dunchattan Pl. G31	K18	36
Duke St.		
Dunchurch Rd., Pais.	L 8	31
Dunclutha Dr., Both.	R28	69
Dunclutha St. G40	N19	53
Duncombe St. G20	F14	20
Duncombe Vw., Clyde.	D 8	5
Kirkoswald Dr.		
Duncraig Cres., John.	O08	43
Duncrub Dr., Bish.	E18	10
Duncruin St. G20	F14	20
Duncryne Av. G32	M23	55
Duncryne Gdns. G32	M24	55
Duncryne Pl., Bish.	F18	22
Dundas La. G1	K17	36
Dundas St. G1	K17	36
Dundasvale Ct. G4	J16	35
Maitland St.		
Dundasvale Rd. G4	J16	35
Maitland St.		
Dundee Dr. G52	M10	48
Dundonald Av., John.	N08	43
Dundonald Rd. G12	H14	20
Dundonald Rd., Pais.	K 7	31
Dundrennan Rd. G42	O15	51
Dunearn Pl., Pais.	M 7	47
Dunearn St. G4	J15	35
Dunegoin St. G51	K13	34
Sharp St.		
Dunellan Dr., Clyde.	B 7	5
Dunellan St. G52	L12	33
Dungeonhill Rd. G34	K26	40
Dunglass Av. G14	H11	19
Dunglass La. N. G14	H11	19
Verona Av.		
Dungoil Av., Cumb.	B 1	70
Dungoil Rd., Lenz.	D24	13
Dungoyne St. G20	F14	20
Dunira St. G32	M21	54
Dunivaig St. G33	K24	39
Dunkeld Av. G73	O19	53
Dunkeld Dr., Bear.	D13	8
Dunkeld Gdns., Bish.	E19	11
Dunkeld La., Chr.	E28	15
Burnbrae Av.		
Dunkeld St. G31	M20	53
Dunkenny Pl. G15	D 9	6
Dunkenny Rd. G15	D 9	6
Dunlop Cres., Both.	R28	69
Dunlop Cres., Renf.	H 8	17
Hairst St.		
Dunlop St. G1	L17	36
Dunlop St. G72	P24	67
Dunlop St., Linw.	L 2	28
Dunlop St., Renf.	H 8	17
Hairst St.		
Dunmore La. G5	L16	35
Norfolk St.		
Dunmore St. G5	L16	35
Dunmore St., Clyde.	F 8	17
Dunn St. G40	M19	53
Dunn St., Clyde.	C 6	4
Dunn St., Dalm.	D 6	4
Dunn St., Pais.	M 7	47
Dunnachie Dr., Coat.	M28	57
Dunnichen Pl., Bish.	E20	11
Dunning St. G31	M20	53
Dunolly St. G21	J19	37
Dunottar St. G33	J22	38
Dunottar St., Bish.	E20	11
Dunphail Dr. G34	K26	40
Dunphail Rd. G34	K26	40

Street	Ref	
Dunragit St. G31	K20	37
Dunrobin Av., John.	N 1	44
Dunrobin St. G31	L19	37
Dunrod St. G32	M22	54
Dunside Dr. G53	P10	60
Dunskaith Pl. G34	K26	40
Dunskaith St. G34	K26	40
Dunsmuir St. G51	K13	34
Dunster Gdns., Bish.	D19	11
Dunswin Av., Dalm.	D 6	4
Dunswin Ct., Dalm.	D 6	4
Dunswin Av.		
Dunsyre Pl. G23	E15	9
Dunsyre Pl. G23	F15	21
Broughton Rd.		
Dunsyre St. G33	K21	38
Duntarvie Cres. G34	K26	40
Duntarvie Pl. G34	K25	40
Duntarvie Quad. G34	K26	40
Duntarvie Rd. G34	K25	40
Dunterle Ct., Barr.	Q 8	59
Dunterlie Av. G13	G10	18
Duntiglennan Rd., Clyde.	C 7	5
Duntocher Rd.,	D 6	4
Dalm. & Clyde.		
Duntocher Rd., Bear.	C10	6
Duntocher Rd., Clyde.	C 7	5
Duntocher St. G21	H18	22
Northcroft Rd.		
Duntreath Av. G13	F 9	18
Duntroon St. G31	K19	37
Dunure Dr. G73	P18	64
Dunure St. G20	F14	20
Dunvegan Av., John.	N 2	44
Dunvegan Ct. G13	G10	18
Kintillo Dr.		
Dunvegan Dr., Bish.	D19	11
Dunvegan Quad., Renf.	H 7	17
Kirklandneuk Rd.		
Dunvegan St. G51	K13	34
Sharp Av.		
Dunwan Av. G13	F 9	18
Dunwan Pl. G13	F 9	18
Durban Av., Dalm.	D 5	4
Durness Av., Bear.	C13	8
Durno St. G33	K24	39
Duror St. G32	L22	38
Durris Gdns. G32	M23	55
Durrockstock Cres., Pais.	O 3	45
Durward Av. G41	N14	50
Durward Cres., Pais.	N 3	45
Durwood Ct. G41	N14	50
Duthil St. G51	L11	33
Dyce La. G11	J13	34
Dyers La. G1	L17	36
Turnbull St.		
Dyers Wynd, Pais.	L 6	30
Gilmour St.		
Dyke Pl. G13	F10	18
Dyke Rd. G13	G 9	18
Dyke St., Bail.	L26	40
Dykebar Av. G13	G10	18
Dykebar Cres., Pais.	N 7	47
Dykefoot Dr. G53	O11	49
Dykehead La. G33	K23	39
Dykehead Rd., Bail.	L27	41
Dykehead St. G33	K23	39
Dykemuir Pl. G21	H19	23
Dykemuir Quadrant G21	H19	23
Dykemuir St.		
Dykemuir St. G21	H19	23
Eagle Cres., Bear.	C10	6
Eagle St. G4	J17	36
Eaglesham Ct. G51	L15	35
Blackburn St.		
Eaglesham Pl. G51	L15	35
Earl Haig Rd. G52	K 9	32
Earl Pl. G14	H11	19
Earl St. G14	H10	18
Earlbank Av. G14	H11	19
Earlbank La. N. G14	H11	19
Dunglass Av.		
Earlbank La. N. G14	H11	19
Vancouver Rd.		
Earlbank La. S. G14	H11	19
Verona Av.		
Earls Ct., Chr.	E27	15
Longdale Rd.		
Earls Gate, Both.	Q27	69
Earls Hill G68	B 1	70
Earlsburn Rd., Lenz.	D24	13
Earlspark Av. G43	O15	51
Earn Av., Bear.	D13	8
Earn Av., Renf.	J 9	32
Almond Av.		
Earn St. G33	J21	38
Earnock St. G33	H20	23
Earnside St. G32	L22	38
Easdale Dr. G32	M22	54
East Av., Renf.	H 8	17
East Av., Udd.	P29	69
East Barns St., Clyde.	F 8	17
East Bath La. G2	K16	35
Sauchiehall St.		
East Buchanan St., Pais.	L 6	30
East Campbell St. G1	L18	36
East Fulton Holdings,	K 1	28
Linw.		
East Greenlees Av. G72	Q23	67
East Greenlees Cres.	Q22	66
G72		
East Greenlees Dr. G72	Q22	66
East Greenlees Rd. G72	Q22	66
East Hallhill Rd., Bail.	L25	40
East Kilbride Expressway	R22	66
G72		
East Kilbride Rd. G73	P20	65
East La., Pais.	M 7	47
East Reid St. G73	O20	53
East Springfield Ter.,	F19	23
Bish.		
East St., Kilb.	M07	42
East Thomson St.,	D 7	5
Clyde.		
East Whitby St. G31	M20	53
Eastburn Rd. G21	G19	23
Eastcote Av. G14	H12	19
Eastcroft G73	O19	53
Eastcroft Ter. G21	H19	23
Easter Av., Udd.	P27	69
Easter Garngaber Rd.	C24	13
G66		
Easter Ms., Udd.	P27	69
Church St.		
Easter Queenslie Rd.	K24	39
G33		
Eastercraigs G31	K19	37
Easterhill Pl. G32	M21	54
Easterhill St. G32	M21	54
Easterhouse Path G34	K26	40
Easterhouse Pl. G34	K26	40
Easterhouse Quad. G34	K26	40
Easterhouse Rd. G34	K26	40
Eastfield Av. G72	P21	66
Eastfield Rd. G21	H18	22
Eastgate, Gart.	G28	27
Eastmuir St. G32	L22	38
Eastvale Pl. G3	K14	34
Eastwood Av. G41	O14	50
Eastwood Av., Giff.	R14	62
Eastwood Cres., Thorn.	Q12	61
Eastwood Ct., Thorn.	Q12	61
Main St.		
Eastwood Rd., Chr.	E27	15
Eastwood Vw. G72	P24	67
Eastwoodmains Rd.,	R14	62
Giff. & Clark.		
Easwald Bank, Kilb.	N07	42
Eccles St. G22	G18	22
Eckford St. G32	M22	54
Eday St. G22	G17	22
Edderton Pl. G33	K25	40
Eddleston Pl. G72	P24	67
Eddlewood Path G33	K24	39
Eddlewood Rd. G33	K24	39
Edelweiss Ter. G11	J13	34
Gardner St.		
Eden La. G33	J20	37
Eden Pk., Both.	R27	69
Eden Pl. G72	P23	67
Eden Pl., Renf.	J 9	32
Eden St. G33	J20	37
Edenwood St. G33	L21	38
Edgam Dr. G52	L11	33
Edgefauld Av. G21	H18	22
Edgefauld Dr. G21	H18	22
Edgefauld Pl. G21	G18	22
Balgrayhill Rd.		
Edgefauld Rd. G21	H18	22
Edgehill La. G11	H13	20
Marlborough Av.		
Edgehill Rd. G11	H13	20
Edgehill Rd., Bear.	C12	7
Edgemont St. G41	O15	51
Edina St. G31	K19	37
Edinbeg Av. G42	O18	52
Edinbeg Pl. G42	O18	52
Edington Gdns., Chr.	D27	15
Edington St. G4	J16	35
Edison St. G52	K 9	32
Edmiston Dr. G51	L12	33
Edmiston Dr., Linw.	L 1	28
Edmiston St. G31	M20	53
Edmondstone Ct., Clyde.	F 8	17
Yokerburn Ter.		
Edrom Path G32	L21	38
Edrom St.		
Edrom St. G32	L21	38
Edward Av., Renf.	H 9	18
Edward St. G3	K14	34
Lumsden St.		
Edward St., Bail.	L27	41
Edward St., Clyde.	F 8	17
Edwin St. G51	L14	34
Edzell Ct. G14	J11	33
Edzell St.		
Edzell Dr., John.	N 2	44
Edzell Gdns., Bish.	F20	23
Edzell Pl. G14	J11	33
Edzell St.		
Edzell St. G14	J11	33
Egidia Av., Giff.	R13	62
Egilsay Cres. G22	F17	22
Egilsay Pl. G22	F17	22
Egilsay St. G22	F17	22
Egilsay Ter. G22	F17	22
Eglinton Ct. G5	L16	35
Eglinton Dr., Giff.	R14	62
Eglinton La. G5	M16	51
Eglinton St.		
Eglinton St. G5	M16	51
Egunton Ct. G5	M16	51
Cumberland St.		
Eighth St., Udd.	N27	57
Eildon Dr., Barr.	R 8	59
Eileen Gdns., Bish.	E19	11
Elba La. G31	L20	37
Elcho St. G40	L18	36
Elder Gro., Udd.	O28	57
Burnhead St.		
Elder St. G51	K12	33
Elderpark Gdns. G51	K12	33
Elderpark Gro. G51	K12	33
Elderpark St. G51	K12	33
Elderslie St. G3	J15	35
Eldon Gdns., Bish.	E18	10
Eldon Pl., John.	N 1	44
Eldon St. G3	J15	35
Eldon Ter. G11	J13	34
Caird Dr.		
Elgin Dr., Linw.	L 1	28
Elgin St. G40	L19	37
Elibank St. G33	J22	38
Elie St. G11	J14	34
Elizabeth Cres., Thorn.	Q13	62
Elizabeth St. G51	L14	34
Elizabethan Way, Renf.	J 8	31
Cockels Loan		
Ellangowan Rd. G41	O14	50
Ellergreen Rd., Bear.	D12	7
Ellerslie St., John.	M 1	44
Ellesmere St. G22	H16	21
Ellinger Ct., Dalm.	D 6	4
Scott St.		
Elliot Av. G78	O 3	45
Elliot Av., Giff.	R14	62
Elliot Dr., Giff.	Q14	62
Elliot La. G3	K15	35
Elliot St.		
Elliot Pl. G3	K15	35
Elliot St. G3	K15	35
Ellisland Av., Clyde.	D 8	5
Ellisland Cres. G73	P18	64
Ellisland Rd. G43	P14	62
Ellisland Rd., Cumb.	C 3	71
Ellismuir Farm Rd., Bail.	M26	56
Ellismuir Pl., Bail.	M26	56
Ellismuir Rd., Bail.	M26	56
Elliston Av. G53	P11	61

Name	Ref		
Elliston Dr. G53	P11	61	
Elliston Pl. G53	P11	61	
Ravenscraig Dr.			
Elm Av., Lenz.	C23	13	
Elm Av., Renf.	H 8	17	
Elm Bank, Bish.	E19	11	
Elm Dr., John.	O09	43	
Elm Gdns., Bear.	C12	7	
Elm Rd. G73	Q19	65	
Elm Rd., Dalm.	C 7	5	
Elm Rd., Pais.	N 7	47	
Elm St. G14	H11	19	
Elm Wk., Bear.	C12	7	
Elmbank Av., Udd.	O28	57	
Elmbank Cres. G2	K16	35	
Elmbank La. G3	K15	35	
North St.			
Elmbank St. G2	K16	35	
Elmbank Street La. G3	K15	35	
North St.			
Elmfoot St. G5	N17	52	
Elmore Av. G44	P16	63	
Elmore La. G44	P16	63	
Elmslie Ct., Bail.	M25	56	
Elmvale Row E. G21	H18	22	
Elmvale Row			
Elmvale Row G21	H18	22	
Elmvale Row W. G21	H18	22	
Elmvale Row			
Elmvale St. G21	G18	22	
Elmwood Av. G11	H12	19	
Elmwood Ct., Both.	R28	69	
Blantyre Mill Rd.			
Elmwood Gdns. G11	H12	19	
Randolph Rd.			
Elmwood Gdns., Kirk.	C22	12	
Elmwood La. G11	H11	19	
Elmwood Av.			
Elmwood Ter. G11	H12	19	
Crow Rd.			
Elphin St. G23	E14	8	
Invershiel Rd.			
Elphinstone Pl. G51	K14	34	
Elrig Rd. G44	P16	63	
Elspeth Gdns., Bish.	E19	11	
Eltham St. G22	H16	21	
Elvan Ct. G32	L21	38	
Edrom St.			
Elvan St. G32	L21	38	
Embo Dr. G13	G10	18	
Emerson Rd., Bish.	E19	11	
Emerson St. G20	G16	21	
Emily Pl. G31	L18	36	
Endfield Av. G12	G13	20	
Endrick Bank, Bish.	D19	11	
Endrick Dr., Bear.	D12	7	
Endrick Dr., Pais.	L 7	31	
Endrick St. G21	H17	22	
Endsleigh Gdns. G11	H13	20	
Partickhill Rd.			
Ennerdale St. G32	L21	38	
Ensay St. G22	F17	22	
Enterkin St. G32	M21	54	
Ericht Rd. G43	P14	62	
Eriska Av. G14	G10	18	
Erradale St. G22	F16	21	
Erriboll Pl. G22	F16	21	
Erriboll St. G22	F16	21	
Errogie St. G34	K25	40	
Erskine Av. G41	M13	50	
Erskine Sq. G52	K 9	32	
Erskine Vw., Clyde.	D 7	5	
Singer St.			
Erskinefauld Rd., Linw.	L 1	28	
Ervie St. G34	K26	40	
Esk Av., Renf.	J 9	32	
Esk Dr., Pais.	N 3	45	
Esk St. G14	G 9	18	
Esk Way, Pais.	N 3	45	
Eskbank St. G32	L22	38	
Eskdale Dr. G73	O20	53	
Eskdale Rd., Bear.	E11	7	
Eskdale St. G42	N16	51	
Esmond St. G3	J14	34	
Espedair St., Pais.	M 6	46	
Essenside Av. G15	E11	7	
Essex Dr. G14	H12	19	
Essex La. G14	H12	19	
Esslemont Av. G14	G10	18	
Estate Quad. G32	O23	55	
Estate Rd. G32	O23	55	
Etive Av., Bear.	D13	8	
Etive Cres., Bish.	E19	11	
Etive Ct., Clyde.	C 8	5	
Etive Dr., Giff.	R14	62	
Etive St. G32	L22	38	
Eton Gdns. G12	J15	35	
Eton La. G12	J15	35	
Great George St.			
Eton Pl. G12	J15	35	
Oakfield Av.			
Eton Ter. G12	J15	35	
Oakfield Av.			
Ettrick Av., Renf.	J 9	32	
Ettrick Cres. G73	O20	53	
Ettrick Ct. G72	Q24	67	
Gateside Av.			
Ettrick Oval, Pais.	O 3	45	
Ettrick Pl. G43	O14	50	
Ettrick Ter., John.	O08	43	
Ettrick Way, Renf.	J 9	32	
Evan Cres., Giff.	R14	62	
Evan Dr., Giff.	R14	62	
Evanton Dr. G46	R12	61	
Evanton Pl. G46	Q12	61	
Evanton Dr.			
Everard Dr. G21	F18	22	
Everard Pl. G21	F18	22	
Everard Quad. G21	F18	22	
Everglades, The, Chr.	F25	26	
Eversley St. G32	M22	54	
Everton Rd. G53	N11	49	
Ewart Pl. G3	K14	34	
Kelvinhaugh St.			
Ewing Pl. G31	L20	37	
Ewing St. G73	O19	53	
Ewing St., Kilb.	M07	42	
Exchange Pl. G1	K17	36	
Buchanan St.			
Exeter Dr. G11	J13	34	
Exeter La. G11	J13	34	
Exeter Dr.			
Eynort St. G22	F16	21	
Fagan Ct., Blan.	R27	69	
Faifley Rd., Clyde.	C 7	5	
Fairbairn Cres., Thorn.	R13	62	
Fairbairn Path G40	M19	53	
Ruby St.			
Fairbairn St. G40	M19	53	
Dalmarnock Rd.			
Fairburn St. G32	M21	54	
Fairfax Av. G44	P17	64	
Fairfield Gdns. G51	K12	33	
Fairfield Pl. G51	K12	33	
Fairfield Pl. G71	R28	69	
Fairfield St. G51	K12	33	
Fairhaven Dr. G23	F14	20	
Fairhill Av. G53	O11	49	
Fairholm St. G32	M21	54	
Fairley St. G51	L13	34	
Fairlie Park Dr. G11	J13	34	
Fairway Av., Pais.	O 5	46	
Fairways, Bear.	C10	6	
Fairyknowe Gdns. G71	R28	69	
Falcon Cres., Pais.	L 4	29	
Falcon Rd., John.	O08	43	
Falcon Ter. G20	F14	20	
Falfield St. G5	M16	51	
Falkland Cres., Bish.	F20	23	
Falkland Mansions G12	H13	20	
Clarence Dr.			
Falkland St. G12	H13	20	
Falloch Rd., Bear.	E11	7	
Fallside Rd., Both.	R28	69	
Falside Av., Pais.	N 6	46	
Falside Rd. G32	M22	54	
Falside Rd., Pais.	N 5	46	
Fara St. G23	F15	21	
Farie St. G73	O19	53	
Farm Ct., Both.	Q28	69	
Fallside Rd.			
Farm La., Udd.	P28	69	
Myers Cres.			
Farm Pk., Lenz.	D23	13	
Farm Rd. G41	M13	50	
Farm Rd., Blan.	R26	68	
Farm Rd., Clyde.	C 7	5	
Farm Rd., Dalm.	D 5	4	
Farme Cross G73	N19	53	
Farmeloan Rd. G73	O19	53	
Farmington Av. G32	L23	39	
Farmington Gate G32	L23	39	
Farmington Gdns. G32	L23	39	
Farmington Gro. G32	L23	39	
Farne Dr. G44	Q16	63	
Farnell St. G4	J16	35	
Farrier Ct., John.	M09	43	
Faskally Av., Bish.	D18	10	
Faskin Cres. G53	O 9	48	
Faskin Pl. G53	O 9	48	
Faskin Rd. G53	O 9	48	
Fasque Pl. G15	D 9	6	
Fastnet St. G33	K22	38	
Faulbswood Cres., Pais.	N 4	45	
Fauldhouse St. G5	M17	52	
Faulds Gdns., Bail.	L26	40	
Faulds, Bail.	L26	40	
Fauldshead Rd., Renf.	H 8	17	
Fauldspark Cres., Bail.	L26	40	
Fauldswood Cres., Pais.	N 4	45	
Fauldswood Dr., Pais.	N 4	45	
Fearnmore Rd. G20	F14	20	
Fendoch St. G32	M22	54	
Fenella St. G32	L22	38	
Fennsbank Av. G73	Q20	65	
Fenwick Dr., Barr.	R 8	59	
Fenwick Pl., Giff.	R13	62	
Fenwick Rd., Giff.	R14	62	
Fereneze Av., Barr.	Q 7	59	
Fereneze Av., Pais.	K 7	31	
Ferenze Cres. G13	F10	18	
Ferenze Dr., Pais.	O 5	46	
Fergus Ct. G20	H15	21	
Fergus Dr. G20	H15	21	
Ferguslie Park Av.,	L 4	29	
Pais.			
Ferguslie Park Cres.,	M 4	45	
Pais.			
Ferguslie Pk.	L 3	29	
Ferguslie Wk., Pais.	M 4	45	
Ferguslie, Pais.	M 4	45	
Ferguson Av., Renf.	H 8	17	
Ferguson St., John.	M09	43	
Ferguson St., Renf.	H 8	17	
Fergusson Rd., Cumb.	C 2	70	
Ferguston Rd., Bear.	D12	7	
Fern Av., Bish.	F19	23	
Fern Av., Lenz.	C23	13	
Fern Dr., Barr.	Q 7	59	
Fern Hill Grange G71	R28	69	
Fernan St. G32	L21	38	
Fernbank Av. G72	Q23	67	
Fernbank St. G22	G18	22	
Fernbrae Rd. G46	Q20	65	
Fernbrae Way G73	Q19	65	
Ferncroft Dr. G44	P17	64	
Ferndale Ct. G23	F14	20	
Rothes Dr.			
Ferndale Dr. G23	F14	20	
Ferndale Gdns. G23	F14	20	
Ferndale Pl. G23	F14	20	
Rothes Drive			
Ferness Oval G21	F20	23	
Ferness Pl. G21	F20	23	
Ferness Rd. G21	G20	23	
Ferngrove Av. G12	G13	20	
Fernhill Rd. G73	Q19	65	
Fernleigh Pl., Chr.	E27	15	
Fernleigh Rd. G43	P14	62	
Fernslea Av. G72	S26	68	
Ferry Rd. G3	K13	34	
Ferry Rd., Both.	R28	69	
Ferry Rd., Renf.	H 8	17	
Ferry Rd., Udd.	P26	68	
Ferryden St. G14	J12	33	
Fersit St. G43	P14	62	
Fetlar Dr. G44	P17	64	
Fettercairn Av. G15	D 9	6	
Fettercairn Gdns., Bish.	E20	11	
Fettes St. G33	K21	38	
Fidra St. G33	K21	38	
Fielden Pl. G40	L19	37	
Fielden St. G40	L19	37	
Fieldhead Dr. G43	P13	62	
Fieldhead Sq. G43	P13	62	
Fife Av. G52	M10	48	
Fife Cres., Both.	R28	69	
Fifeway, Bish.	F20	23	

Name	Ref		Name	Ref		Name	Ref	
Fifth Av. G12	G12	19	Florentine Pl. G12	J15	35	Frankfield St. G33	J20	37
Fifth Av. G33	G22	24	*Gibson St.*			Frankfort St. G41	N15	51
Fifth Av., Lenz.	E23	13	Florentine Ter. G12	J15	35	Franklin St. G40	M18	52
Fifth Av., Renf.	J 8	31	*Southpark Av.*			Fraser Av. G73	O20	53
Finart Dr., Pais.	N 7	47	Florida Av. G42	O16	51	Fraser Av., John.	N 1	44
Finch Pl., John.	O08	43	Florida Cres. G66	O16	51	Fraser St. G72	P21	66
Findhorn Av., Renf.	H 9	18	Florida Dr. G42	O16	51	Fraserbank St. G21	H17	22
Findhorn Cres., Pais.	N 3	45	Florida Gdns., Bail.	L25	40	*Keppochhill Rd.*		
Findhorn St. G33	K20	37	Florida Sq. G42	O16	51	Frazer St. G31	L20	37
Findochty St. G33	J23	39	Florida St. G42	O16	51	Freeland Dr. G53	P10	60
Fingal La. G20	F14	20	Fochabers Dr. G52	L11	33	Freeland Dr., Renf.	G 5	16
Fingal St.			Fogo Pl. G20	G14	20	Freelands Cres., Old K	C 5	4
Fingal St. G20	F14	20	Forbes Dr. G40	L18	36	Freelands Ct., Old K.	C 5	4
Fingask St. G32	M23	55	Forbes Pl., Pais.	M 6	46	Freelands Pl., Old K.	D 5	4
Finglas Av., Pais.	N 7	47	Forbes St. G40	L18	36	Freelands Rd., Old K.	C 5	4
Fingleton Av., Barr.	R 8	59	Ford Rd. G12	H14	20	French St. G40	M18	52
Finhaven St. G32	M21	54	Fordneuk St. G40	L19	37	French St., Dalm.	D 6	4
Finlarig St. G34	K26	40	Fordoun St. G34	K26	40	French St., Renf.	J 7	31
Finlas St. G22	H17	22	Fordyce St. G11	J13	34	Freuchie St. G34	K25	40
Finlay Dr. G31	K19	37	Fore St. G14	H11	19	Friar Av., Bish.	D19	11
Finlay Dr., Linw.	L 1	28	Forehouse Rd., Kilb.	MO6	42	Friars Court Rd., Chr.	E25	14
Finnart Sq. G40	M18	52	Forest Dr., Udd.	Q28	69	Friars Pl. G13	F11	19
Finnart St. G40	M18	52	Forest Gdns., Lenz.	D22	12	Friarscourt Av. G13	E11	7
Finnieston Pl. G3	K15	35	Forest Pl., Lenz.	D22	12	Friarscourt La. G13	F11	19
Finnieston St.			Forest Pl., Pais.	N 6	46	*Arrowsmith Av.*		
Finnieston St. G3	K15	35	*Brodie Park Av.*			Friarton Rd. G43	P15	63
Finsbay St. G51	L12	33	Forest Rd., Cumb.	C 4	71	Friendship Way, Renf.	J 8	31
Fintry Av., Pais.	O 6	46	Forest Vw., Cumb.	B 4	71	Fruin Pl. G22	H17	22
Fintry Cres., Barr.	R 8	59	Forfar Av. G52	M10	48	Fruin Rd. G15	E 9	6
Fintry Cres., Bish.	E20	11	Forfar Cres., Bish.	F20	23	Fruin St. G22	H17	22
Fintry Dr. G44	O17	52	Forgan Gdns., Bish.	F20	23	Fulbar Av., Renf.	H 8	17
Fir Pl. G72	P23	67	Forge St. G21	J19	37	Fulbar Ct., Renf.	H 8	17
Caledonian Circuit			Forglen St. G34	J25	40	*Fulbar Av.*		
Fir Pl., Bail.	M25	56	Formby Dr. G23	E14	8	Fulbar La., Renf.	H 8	17
Fir Pl., John.	N 1	44	Forres Av. G46	Q14	62	Fulbar Rd. G51	K11	33
Firbank Ter., Barr.	R 9	60	Forres Gate, Giff.	R14	62	Fulbar Rd., Pais.	M 3	45
Firdon Cres. G15	E10	6	*Forres Av.*			Fulbar St., Renf.	H 8	17
Firhill Rd. G20	H16	21	Forres St. G23	E15	9	Fullarton Av. G32	N22	54
Firhill St. G20	H16	21	*Tolsta St.*			Fullarton Rd. G32	O21	54
Firpark Pl. G31	K18	36	Forrest St. G40	L19	37	Fullerton St., Pais	K 5	30
Firpark St.			Forrestfield St. G21	J19	37	Fullerton Ter., Pais.	K 6	30
Firpark Rd., Bish.	F19	23	Fortevoit Av., Bail.	L26	40	Fulmar Ct., Bish.	F18	22
Firpark St. G31	K18	36	Fortevoit Pl., Bail.	L26	40	Fulmar Pl., John.	O08	43
Firpark Ter. G31	K18	36	Forth Av., Pais.	N 3	45	Fulton Cres., Kilb.	M07	42
Ark La.			Forth Av., Renf.	J 8	31	Fulton St. G13	F11	19
First Av. G33	H22	24	*Third Av.*			Fulwood Av. G13	F 9	18
First Av. G44	R15	63	Forth Pl., John.	O08	43	Fulwood Av., Linw.	L 1	28
First Av., Bear.	D13	8	Forth Rd. G61	C11	7	Fulwood Pl. G13	F 9	18
First Av., Lenz.	E23	13	Forth Rd., Bear.	E11	7	Fynloch Pl., Clyde	B 6	4
First Av., Renf.	J 8	31	Forth St. G41	M15	51	Fyvie Av. G43	P13	62
First Av., Udd.	O27	57	Fortingall Av. G12	G14	20			
First Gdns. G41	M13	50	*Grantully Dr.*			Gadie Av., Renf.	J 9	32
First St., Udd.	O27	57	Fortingall Pl. G12	G14	20	Gadie St. G33	K20	37
First Ter., Clyde.	D 7	5	Fortrose St. G11	J13	34	Gadloch Av., Lenz.	E23	13
Firwood Dr. G44	P17	64	Foswell Pl. G15	C 9	6	Gadloch Gdns., Lenz.	D23	13
Fisher Cres., Clyde.	C 7	5	Fotheringay La. G41	N15	51	Gadloch St. G22	G17	22
Fisher Ct. G31	K18	36	*Beaton Rd.*			Gadloch Vw. G66	E23	13
Fishers Rd., Renf.	G 8	17	Fotheringay Rd. G41	N14	50	Gadsburn Ct. G21	G20	23
Fishescoates Av. G73	Q20	65	Foulis La. G13	G12	19	*Wallacewell Quadrant*		
Fishescoates Gdns.	P20	65	Foulis St. G13	G12	19	Gadshill St. G21	J18	36
G73			Foundry La., Barr.	R 7	59	Gailes Pk., Both.	R27	69
Fishescoates Rd.			*Main St.*			Gailes St. G40	M19	53
Fishescoates Rd. G73	P20	65	Foundry Open G31	L19	37	Gairbraid Av. G20	G14	20
Fitzalan Dr., Pais.	L 7	31	Fountain St. G31	L18	36	Gairbraid Ct. G20	G14	20
Fitzalan Rd., Renf.	J 7	31	Fountainwell Av. G.21	J17	36	Gairbraid Pl. G20	G14	20
Fitzroy La. G3	K15	35	Fountainwell Dr. G21	J17	36	Gairbraid Ter., Bail.	L28	41
Claremont St.			Fountainwell Pl. G21	J17	36	Gairn St. G11	J13	34
Fitzroy Pl. G3	K15	35	Fountainwell Rd. G21	J17	36	*Castlebank St.*		
Claremont St.			Fountainwell Sq. G21	J18	36	Gala Av., Renf.	J 9	32
Fitzroy Pl. G3	K15	35	Fountainwell Ter. G21	J18	36	Gala St. G33	J21	38
Sauchiehall St.			Fourth Av., G33	G22	24	Galbraith Av. G51	K12	33
Flax Rd., Udd.	P28	69	Fourth Av., Lenz.	E23	13	*Burghead Dr.*		
Fleet Av., Renf.	J 9	32	Fourth Av., Renf.	J 8	31	Galbraith Dr. G51	K11	33
Fleet St. G32	M22	54	*Third Av.*			Galbraith St. G51	K11	33
Fleming Av., Chr.	F26	26	Fourth Gdns. G41	M13	50	*Moss Rd.*		
Fleming Av., Clyde.	F 8	17	Fourth St., Udd.	N27	57	Galdenoch St. G33	J22	38
Fleming Rd., Cumb.	C 2	70	Fox La. G1	L17	36	Gallacher Av., Pais.	N 4	45
Fleming St. G31	L19	37	Fox St. G1	L16	35	Gallan Av. G23	E15	9
Fleming St., Pais.	K 6	30	Foxbar Cres., Pais.	O 3	45	Galloway Dr. G73	Q19	65
Flemington Rd. G72	R24	67	Foxbar Dr. G.13.	G10	18	Galloway St. G21	G18	22
Flemington St. G21	H18	22	Foxbar Dr. G78	O 3	45	Gallowflat St. G73	O19	53
Fleurs Av. G41	M13	50	Foxbar Rd., Pais.	O 3	45	Gallowgate G1	L17	36
Fleurs Rd. G41	M13	50	Foxes Gro. G66	C24	13	Gallowhill Av., Lenz.	C23	13
Floors St., John.	N09	43	Foxhills Pl. G23	E15	9	Gallowhill Gro., Lenz.	C23	13
Floorsburn Cres., John.	N09	43	Foxley St. G.32.	N23	55	Gallowhill Rd., Lenz.	C23	13
Flora Gdns., Bish.	E20	11	Foyers Ct. G13	G10	18	Gallowhill Rd., Pais.	L 6	30
Florence Dr., Giff.	R14	62	*Kirkton Av.*			Galston St. G53	P 9	60
Florence Gdns. G73	Q20	65	Foyers Ter. G21	H19	23	Gamrie Dr. G53	O10	48
Florence St. G5	L17	36	Francis St. G5	M16	51	Gamrie Gdns. G53	O10	48
Florence St. G73	M17	52	Frankfield Rd. G33	G24	25	Gamrie Rd. G53	O10	48

Name	Grid	Pg	Name	Grid	Pg	Name	Grid	Pg
Gannochy Dr., Bish.	E20	11	Garvald Ct. G40	M19	53	Glasgow Rd., Bail.	M24	55
Gantock Cres. G33	K22	38	Baltic St.			Glasgow Rd., Barr.	Q 8	59
Gardenside Av. G32	O22	54	Garvald St. G40	M19	53	Glasgow Rd., Blan.	R26	68
Gardenside Av., Udd.	P27	69	Garve Av. G44	Q16	63	Glasgow Rd., Clyde.	C 7	5
Gardenside Cres. G32	O22	54	Garvel Cres. G33	L24	39	Glasgow Rd., Clyde.	F 7	17
Gardenside Pl. G32	O22	54	Garvel Rd. G33	L24	39	Glasgow Rd., Cumb.	B 3	71
Gardenside St., Udd.	P27	69	Garvock Dr. G43	P13	62	Glasgow Rd., Cumb.	D 1	70
Gardner La., Bail.	M26	56	Gas St., John.	M 1	44	Glasgow Rd., Pais.	L 7	31
Church St.			Gask Pl. G13	F 9	18	Glasgow Rd., Renf.	H 9	18
Gardner St. G11	J13	34	Gatehouse St. G32	L22	38	Glasgow Rd., Udd.	O26	56
Gardyne St. G34	J25	40	Gateside Av. G72	P23	67	Glasgow St. G12	H15	21
Garfield St. G31	L19	37	Gateside Cres., Barr.	R 7	59	Glassel Rd. G34	J26	40
Garforth Rd., Bail.	M24	55	Gateside Pl., Kilb.	M07	42	Glasserton Pl. G43	P15	63
Gargrave Av., Bail.	M24	55	Gateside St., Barr.	R 7	59	Glasserton Rd. G43	P15	63
Garion Dr. G13	G10	18	Gateside St. G31	L19	37	Glassford St. G1	K17	36
Garion Dr. G13	G10	18	Gauldry Av. G52	M11	49	Glebe Av. G71	R28	69
Talbot Dr.			Gauze St., Pais.	L 6	30	Green St.		
Garlieston Rd. G33	L24	39	Gavins Rd., Clyde.	C 7	5	Glebe Ct. G4	K17	36
Garmouth Ct. G51	K12	33	Gavinton St. G44	Q15	63	Glebe Hollow G71	R28	69
Garmouth St.			Gear Ter. G40	N19	53	Glebe Wynd		
Garmouth Gdns. G51	K12	33	Geary St. G23	E14	8	Glebe Pl. G72	P22	66
Garmouth St. G51	K12	33	Torrin Rd,			Glebe Pl. G73	O18	52
Garnet La. G3	J16	35	Geddes Rd. G21	F20	23	Glebe St. G4	J17	36
Garnet St.			Gelston St. G32	M22	54	Glebe St., Renf.	H 8	17
Garnet St. G3	J16	35	General Terminus Quay	L15	35	Glebe Wynd G71	R28	69
Garnethill St. G3	J16	35	G51			Glebe, The, Both.	R28	69
Garngaber Av., Lenz.	C23	13	Generals Gate, Udd.	P27	69	Gleddoch Rd. G52	L 9	32
Garngaber Ct. G66	C24	13	Cobbleriggs Way			Glen Affric Av. G53	Q11	61
Woodleigh Rd.			Gentle Row, Clyde.	C 6	4	Glen Affric Dr. G53	Q11	61
Garnie Av., Renf.	F 5	16	George Av., Clyde.	D 8	5	Glen Affric Pl. G53	Q11	61
Garnie Cres., Renf.	E 5	4	Robert Burns Av.			Glen Alby Pl. G53	Q11	61
Garnie La., Renf.	E 5	4	George Cres., Clyde.	D 8	5	Glen Av. G32	L22	38
Garnie Oval, Renf.	E 5	4	George Gray St. G73	O20	53	Glen Av., Chr.	E27	15
Garnie Pl., Renf.	E 5	4	George Mann Ter. G73	P19	65	Glen Clunie Av. G53	Q11	61
Garnieland Rd., Renf.	E 5	4	George Pl., Pais.	M 6	46	Glen Clunie Dr. G53	Q11	61
Garnkirk La. G33	G24	25	George Reith Av. G12	G12	19	Glen Clunie Pl. G53	Q11	61
Garnkirk St. G21	J18	36	George Sq. G2	K17	36	Glen Cona Dr. G53	P11	61
Garnock St. G21	J18	36	George St. G1	K17	36	Glen Cres. G13	F 9	18
Garrell Way, Cumb.	C 2	70	George St., Bail.	M25	56	Glen Esk Dr. G53	Q11	61
Garrioch Cres. G20	G14	20	George St., Barr.	Q 7	59	Glen Gdns., John.	M 2	44
Garrioch Dr. G20	G14	20	George St., John.	M09	43	Glen La., Pais.	L 6	30
Garrioch Gate G20	G14	20	George St., Pais.	M 5	46	Glen Livet Pl. G53	Q11	61
Garrioch Quad. G20	G14	20	Gertrude Pl., Barr.	R 7	59	Glen Loy Pl. G53	Q11	61
Garrioch Rd. G20	G14	20	Gibb St. G21	J18	36	Glen Mallie Dr. G53	Q11	61
Garriochmill Rd. G20	H15	21	Royston Rd.			Glen Markie Dr. G53	Q11	61
Raeberry St.			Gibson Cres., John.	N09	43	Glen Moriston Rd.,	Q11	61
Garriochmill Way G20	H15	21	Gibson Rd., Renf.	J 7	31	Thorn. G53		
Woodside Rd.			Gibson St. G12	J15	35	Glen Nevis Pl. G73	R20	65
Garrowhill Dr., Bail.	M24	55	Gibson St. G40	L18	36	Glen Ogle St. G32	M23	55
Garry Av., Bear.	E13	8	Giffnock Park Av., Giff.	Q14	62	Glen Orchy Dr. G53	Q11	61
Garry Dr., Pais.	N 4	45	Gifford Dr. G52	L10	32	Glen Orchy Pl. G53	Q11	61
Garry St. G44	O16	51	Gilbert St. G3	K14	34	Glen Park Av., Thorn.	R12	61
Garscadden G13	F10	18	Gilbertfield Pl. G33	J22	38	Glen Rd. G32	K22	38
Garscadden Rd. G15	E10	6	Gilbertfield Rd. G72	Q23	67	Glen Sax Dr., Renf.	J 9	32
Garscadden Vw., Clyde.	D 8	5	Gilbertfield St. G33	J22	38	Glen Sq. G33	H22	24
Kirkoswald Dr.			Gilfillan Way, Pais.	O 3	45	Glen St. G72	Q23	67
Garscube Rd. G20	H16	21	Ashton Way			Glen St., Barr.	O 8	59
Gartcarron Hill, Cumb.	B 1	70	Gilhill St. G20	F14	20	Glen St., Pais.	L 6	30
Dunbrach Rd.			Gilia St. G72	P21	66	Glen Vw., Cumb.	B 4	71
Gartconnel Dr., Bear.	C12	7	Gillies La., Bail.	M26	56	Glenacre Cres., Udd.	O27	57
Gartconnel Gdns., Bear.	C12	7	Bredisholm Rd.			Glenacre Dr. G45	Q17	64
Gartconnel Rd., Bear.	C12	7	Gills Ct. G31	L19	37	Glenacre Quad. G45	Q17	64
Gartcosh Rd., Bail. & Gart.	K28	41	Gilmarton Rd., Linw.	L 1	28	Glenacre Rd., Cumb.	D 2	70
Gartcraig Rd. G33	K21	38	Gilmerton St. G32	M22	54	Glenacre St. G45	Q17	64
Gartferry Av., Chr.	E27	15	Gilmour Av., Clyde.	C 7	5	Glenacre Ter. G45	Q17	64
Gartferry Rd., Chr.	E27	15	Gilmour Cres. G73	O18	52	Glenallan Way, Pais.	O 3	45
Gartferry St. G21	H19	23	Gilmour Pl. G5	M17	52	Glenalmond Rd. G73	Q20	65
Garth St. G1	K17	36	Gilmour St., Clyde.	D 8	5	Glenalmond St. G32	M22	54
Garthamlock Rd. G33	J24	39	Gilmour St., Pais.	L 6	30	Glenapp Av., Pais.	N 7	47
Garthland Dr. G31	K19	37	Girthon St. G32	M23	55	Glenapp Rd., Pais.	N 7	47
Garthland La., Pais.	L 6	30	Girvan St. G33	J20	37	Glenapp St. G41	M15	51
Gartliston Ter., Bail.	L28	41	Gladney Av. G13	F 9	18	Glenarklet Dr., Pais.	N 7	47
Gartloch Cotts., Chr.	G25	26	Gladsmuir Rd. G52	L10	32	Glenartney Row, Chr.	E26	14
Gartloch Cotts., Gart.	H27	27	Gladstone Av., Barr.	R 7	59	Glenashdale Way, Pais.	N 7	47
Gartloch Rd. G33	J21	38	Gladstone St. G4	J16	35	Glenbrittle Dr.		
Gartly St. G44	Q15	63	Gladstone St., Dalm.	E 6	4	Glenavon Av. G73	Q20	65
Clarkston Rd.			Glaive Rd. G13	E11	7	Glenavon Rd. G20	F14	20
Gartmore Gdns., Udd.	O27	57	Glamis Av., John.	N 1	44	Thornton St.		
Gartmore La., Chr.	E28	15	Glamis Gdns., Bish.	D19	11	Glenavon Ter. G11	J13	34
Gartmore Rd., Pais.	M 8	47	Glamis Pl. G31	M20	53	Crow Rd.		
Gartmore Ter. G72	Q21	66	Glamis Rd.			Glenbank Av., Lenz.	D23	13
Gartness St. G31	K19	37	Glamis Rd. G31	M20	53	Glenbank Dr., Thorn.	R12	61
Gartocher Rd. G32	L23	39	Glanderston Av., Barr.	R 9	60	Glenbank Rd., Lenz.	D23	13
Gartochmill Rd. G20	H15	21	Glanderston Dr. G13	F10	18	Glenbarr St. G21	J18	36
Gartons Rd. G21	H20	23	Glaselune St. G34	K26	40	Glenbervie Pl. G23	E14	8
Gartshore Rd.,	C27	15	Lochdochart Rd.			Glenbrittle Dr., Pais.	N 7	47
Drumbreck			Glasgow Bridge	B21	12	Glenbrittle Way, Pais.	N 6	46
Garturk St. G42	N16	51	Glasgow Rd. G72	P21	66	Glenbuck Av. G33	G21	24
			Glasgow Rd. G72 & E.K.	R21	66	Glenbuck Dr. G33	G21	24
			Glasgow Rd. G73	N18	52	Glenburn Av. G73	P20	65

Street	Grid	Page
Glenburn Av., Bail.	L26	40
Glenburn Av., Chr.	E27	15
Glenburn Cres., Pais.	O 5	46
Glenburn Gdns., Bish.	E18	10
Glenburn Rd., Bear.	C11	7
Glenburn Rd., Giff.	R13	62
Glenburn Rd., Pais.	O 4	45
Glenburn St. G20	F15	21
Glenburnie Pl. G34	K25	40
Glencairn Dr. G41	N14	50
Glencairn Dr. G73	O18	52
Glencairn Dr., Chr.	E27	15
Glencairn Gdns. G41	N15	51
Glencairn Dr.		
Glencairn Rd., Cumb.	C 4	71
Glencairn Rd., Pais.	K 7	31
Glencally Av., Pais.	N 7	47
Glencart Gro., John.	N08	43
Milliken Park Rd.		
Glenclora Dr., Pais.	N 7	47
Glencloy St. G20	F14	20
Glencoe Pl. G13	F12	19
Glencoe Rd. G73	Q20	65
Glencoe St. G13	F12	19
Glencorse Rd., Pais.	N 5	46
Glencorse St. G32	K21	38
Glencroft Av., Udd.	O27	57
Glencroft Rd. G44	P17	64
Glencryan Rd., Cumb.	D 3	71
Glendale Cres., Bish.	F20	23
Glendale Dr., Bish.	F20	23
Glendale Pl. G31	L19	37
Glendale St.		
Glendale Pl. G64	F20	23
Glendale St. G31	L19	37
Glendaruel Av., Bear.	D13	8
Glendaruel Rd. G73	R21	66
Glendee Gdns., Renf.	J 8	31
Glendee Rd., Renf.	J 8	31
Glendenning Rd. G13	E12	7
Glendevon Pl., Dalm.	D 6	4
Glendevon Sq. G33	J22	38
Glendore St. G14	J12	33
Glendower Way	O 3	45
Spencer Dr.		
Glenduffhill Rd., Bail.	L24	39
Gleneagles Av., Cumb.	A 3	71
Muirfield Rd.		
Gleneagles Cotts. G14	H11	19
Dumbarton Rd.		
Gleneagles Dr., Bish.	D19	11
Gleneagles Gdns., Bish.	D19	11
Gleneagles La. N. G14	H11	19
Dunglass Av.		
Gleneagles Pk., Both.	R27	69
Gleneagles Ter. G14	H11	19
Dumbarton Rd.		
Glenelg Quad. G34	J26	40
Glenetive Pl. G73	R21	66
Glenfarg Cres., Bear.	D13	8
Glenfarg Rd. G73	Q19	65
Glenfarg St. G20	J16	35
Glenfield Cres., Pais.	P 5	58
Glenfield Rd., Pais.	P 5	58
Glenfinnan Dr. G20	G14	20
Glenfinnan Dr., Bear.	D14	8
Glenfinnan Pl. G20	G14	20
Glenfinnan Rd. G20	G14	20
Glenfruin Dr., Pais.	N 7	47
Glengarry Dr. G52	L10	33
Wedderlea Dr.		
Glengavel Cres. G33	G21	24
Glengyre St. G34	J26	40
Glenhead Cres. G22	G17	22
Glenhead Rd., Dalm.	C 7	5
Glenhead Rd., Lenz.	D23	13
Glenhead St. G22	G17	22
Glenholme, Pais.	N 4	45
Glenhove Rd., Cumb.	C 3	71
Gleniffer Av. G13	G10	18
Gleniffer Cres., John.	N 2	44
Gleniffer Dr., Barr.	P 7	59
Gleniffer Rd., Pais.	O 4	45
Gleniffer Rd., Renf.	J 7	31
Gleniffer Ter., Clyde.	D 8	5
Kirkoswald Dr.		
Glenisa Av., Chr.	D28	15
Glenisla St. G31	M20	53
Glenkirk Dr. G15	E10	6
Glenlee Cres. G52	M 9	48
Glenlora Dr. G53	O10	48
Glenlora Ter. G53	O10	48
Glenluce Dr. G32	M23	55
Glenlui Av. G73	P19	65
Glenlyon Pl. G73	Q20	65
Glenmalloch Pl., John.	M 2	44
Glenmanor Av., Chr.	E27	15
Glenmore Av. G42	O18	52
Glenmuir Dr. G53	P10	60
Glenpark Rd. G31	L19	37
Glenpark St. G31	L19	37
Glenpark Ter. G72	O21	54
Glenpatrick Bldgs., John.	N 2	44
Glenpatrick Rd., John.	N 2	44
Glenraith Rd. G33	H22	24
Glenraith Sq. G33	H22	24
Glenraith Wk. G33	H23	25
Glenshee St. G31	M20	53
Glenshiel Av., Pais.	N 7	47
Glenside Av. G53	N10	48
Glenside Dr. G73	P20	65
Glenspean Pl. G43	P14	62
Glenspean St.		
Glenspean St. G43	P14	62
Glentanar Pl. G22	F16	21
Glentarbert Rd. G73	Q20	65
Glenturret St. G32	M22	54
Glentyan Av., Kilb.	M07	42
Glentyan Dr. G53	P10	60
Glentyan Ter. G53	O10	48
Glenview Cres., Chr.	D28	15
Glenview Pl., Blan.	R26	68
Glenville Av., Giff.	Q13	62
Glenwood Ct., Kirk.	C22	12
Glenwood Dr., Thorn.	R12	61
Glenwood Gdns., Kirk.	C22	12
Glenwood Pl., Kirk.	C22	12
Glenwood Rd., Kirk.	C22	12
Gloucester Av. G73	P20	65
Gloucester St. G5	L16	35
Gockston Rd., Pais.	K 5	30
Gogar Pl. G33	K21	38
Gogar St. G33	K21	38
Goldberry Av. G14	G10	18
Goldie Rd., Udd.	Q28	69
Golf Ct. G44	R15	63
Golf Dr. G15	E 9	6
Golf Dr., Pais.	M 8	47
Golf Rd. G73	Q19	65
Golf Vw., Bear.	C10	6
Golf Vw., Dalm.	D 6	4
Golfhill Dr. G31	K19	37
Golfhill La. G31	K19	37
Whitehill St.		
Golfhill Ter. G31	K18	36
Firpark St.		
Golspie St. G51	K13	34
Goosedubbs G1	L17	36
Stockwell St.		
Gopher Av., Udd.	O28	57
Myrtle Rd.		
Gorbals Cross G5	L17	36
Gorbals La. G5	L16	35
Oxford St.		
Gorbals St. G5	L16	35
Gordon Av. G44	R15	63
Gordon Av., Bail.	L24	39
Gordon Dr. G44	Q15	63
Gordon La. G1	K16	35
Gordon St.		
Gordon Rd. G44	R15	63
Gordon St. G1	K16	35
Gordon St., Pais.	M 6	46
Gordon Ter., Blan.	R26	68
Gorebridge St. G32	K21	38
Gorget Av. G13	E11	7
Gorget Pl. G13	E11	7
Gorget Quad. G15	E10	6
Gorget Av.		
Gorse Dr., Barr.	Q 7	59
Gorse Pl., Udd.	O28	57
Myrtle Rd.		
Gorsewood, Bish.	E18	10
Gorstan Pl. G20	G14	20
Wyndford Rd.		
Gorstan St. G23	F14	20
Gosford La. G14	G 9	18
Dumbarton Rd.		
Goudie St., Pais.	K 5	30
Gough St. G33	K20	37
Gourlay Path G21	H17	22
Endrick St.		
Gourlay St. G21	H17	22
Gourlay St. G21	H18	22
Millarbank St.		
Gourock St. G5	M16	51
Govan Cross G51	K13	34
Govan Rd. G51	K12	33
Govanhill St. G42	N16	51
Gowanbank Gdns., John.	N09	43
Floors St.		
Gowanbrae, Lenz.	C23	13
Gallowhill Rd.		
Gowanlea Av. G15	E10	6
Gowanlea Dr., Giff.	Q14	62
Gowanlea Ter., Udd.	O28	57
Gower La. G51	L14	34
Gower St.		
Gower St. G43	M14	50
Gower Ter. G41	L14	34
Goyle Av. G15	D11	7
Grace Av., Bail.	L27	41
Grace St. G3	K15	35
Graffham Av., Giff.	Q14	62
Grafton Pl. G4	K17	36
Graham Av. G72	P23	67
Graham Av., Clyde.	D 7	5
Graham Sq. G31	L18	36
Graham St., Barr.	Q 7	59
Graham St., John.	N09	43
Graham Ter., Bish.	F19	23
Grahamston Cres., Pais.	O 8	47
Grahamston Ct., Pais.	O 8	47
Grahamston Pl., Pais.	O 8	47
Grahamston Rd.		
Grahamston Rd., Barr.	P 7	59
Craighead Av. G33	H20	23
Grainger Rd., Bish.	E20	11
Grampian Av., Pais.	O 5	46
Grampian Cres. G32	M22	54
Grampian Pl. G32	M22	54
Grampian St. G32	M22	54
Grampian Way, Barr.	R 8	59
Gran St., Clyde.	F 9	18
Granby La. G12	H14	20
Great George St.		
Granby Pl. G12	H14	20
Great George St.		
Grandtully Dr. G12	G14	20
Grange Gdns. G71	R28	69
Blairston Av.		
Grange Rd. G42	O16	51
Grange Rd., Bear.	C12	7
Grangeneuk Gdnd., Cumb.	C 1	70
Grant St. G3	J15	35
Grantlea Gro. G32	M23	55
Grantlea Ter. G32	M23	55
Grantley Gdns. G41	O14	50
Grantley St. G41	O14	50
Granton St. G5	N18	52
Granville St. G3	K15	35
Granville St., Clyde.	D 7	5
Gray Dr., Bear.	D12	7
Gray St. G3	J14	34
Great Dovehill G1	L17	36
Great George La. G12	H14	20
Great George St.		
Great George St. G12	H14	20
Great Hamilton St., Pais.	N 6	46
Great Kelvin La. G12	H15	21
Glasgow St.		
Great Western Rd. G12	H14	20
Great Western Ter. G12	H14	20
Great Western Terrace La. G12	H14	20
Westbourne Gdns. W.		
Green Av., Lenz.	B23	13
Green Farm Rd., Linw.	L 1	28
Green Lodge Ter. G40	M18	52
Greenhead St.		
Green Pk., Both.	R28	69
Green St.		
Green Rd. G73	O19	53
Green Rd., Pais.	M 4	45
Green St. G40	L18	36
Green St., Both.	R28	69
Green St., Clyde.	D 7	5

Street	Grid	Page
Green, The, G40	L18	36
Greenan Av. G42	O18	52
Greenbank Dr., Pais.	O 5	46
Greenbank Rd., Cumb.	C 1	70
Greenbank St. G43	P13	62
Harriet St.		
Greenbank St. G73	O19	53
Greendyke St. G1	L17	36
Greenend Av., John.	N08	43
Greenend Pl. G32	K23	39
Greenfaulds Cres.,	D 3	71
Cumb.		
Greenfaulds Rd., Cumb.	D 2	70
Greenfield Av. G32	K22	38
Greenfield Pl. G32	L22	38
Budhill Av.		
Greenfield Rd. G32	L23	39
Greenfield St. G51	K12	33
Greengairs Av. G51	K11	33
Greenhaugh St. G51	K13	34
Greenhead Rd., Bear.	D12	7
Greenhead Rd., Renf.	F 5	16
Greenhead St. G40	M18	52
Greenhill Av., Gart.	F27	27
Greenhill Av., Giff.	R13	62
Greenhill Cres., John.	N 2	44
Greenhill Cres., Linw.	L 2	28
Greenhill Ct. G73	O19	53
Greenhill Dr., Linw.	L 2	28
Greenhill Rd. G73	O19	53
Greenhill Rd., Pais.	L 5	30
Greenhill St. G73	O19	53
Greenhill, Bish.	E19	11
Greenholm Av., Udd.	O27	57
Greenholme St. G40	P16	63
Holmlea Rd.		
Greenknowe Rd. G43	P13	62
Greenlaw Av., Pais.	L 7	31
Greenlaw Dr., Pais.	L 7	31
Greenlaw Rd. G14	G 9	18
Greenlaw Ter., Pais.	L 7	31
Greenlaw Av.		
Greenlea Rd., Chr.	F25	26
Greenlea St. G13	G12	19
Greenlees Gdns. G72	Q21	66
Greenlees Pk. G72	Q22	66
Greenlees Rd. G72	P22	66
Greenloan Av. G51	K11	33
Greenmount G22	F16	21
Greenock Av. G44	P16	63
Greenock Rd., Pais.	K 5	30
Greenock Rd., Renf.	G 5	16
Greenrig St. G33	H20	23
Greenrig St., Udd.	P27	69
Greenrigg Rd., Cumb.	C 3	71
Greenshields Rd., Bail.	L25	40
Greenside Cres. G33	H21	24
Greenside St. G33	H21	24
Greentree Dr., Bail.	M24	55
Greenview St. G43	O14	50
Greenways Av., Pais.	N 4	45
Greenways Ct., John.	N 4	45
Greenwell Pl. G51	K13	34
Greenwell St. G51	K13	34
Govan Rd.		
Greenwood Av. G72	P24	67
Greenwood Av., Chr.	E27	15
Greenwood Dr., Bear.	D13	8
Greenwood Quad.,	E 8	5
Clyde.		
Greer Quad., Clyde.	D 7	5
Grenville Dr. G72	Q21	66
Greran Dr., Renf.	H 7	17
Gretna St. G40	M19	53
Greyfriars St. G32	K21	38
Greystone Av. G73	P20	65
Greywood St. G13	F12	19
Grier Path G31	L20	37
Grierson La. G33	K20	37
Lomak St.		
Grierson St. G33	K20	37
Grieve Rd., Cumb.	B 3	71
Griqua Ter. G71	R28	69
Grogary Rd. G15	D10	6
Springside Pl.		
Grosvenor Cres. G12	H14	20
Observatory Rd.		
Grosvenor Cres. La.	H14	20
G12		
Byers Rd.		
Grosvenor La. G12	H14	20
Byers Rd.		
Grosvenor Mansions	H14	20
G12		
Observatory Rd.		
Grosvenor Ter. G12	H14	20
Grove Pk., Lenz.	D23	13
Grove, The, Giff.	S13	62
Grove, The, Kilb.	M07	42
Groveburn Av., Thorn.	Q13	62
Grovepark Pl. G20	H16	21
Grovepark St. G20	H16	21
Groves, The, Bish.	F20	23
Woodhill Rd.		
Grudie St. G34	K25	40
Gryffe Av., Renf.	H 7	17
Gryffe Cres., Pais.	N 3	45
Gryffe St. G44	P16	63
Guildford St. G33	J23	39
Gullane Cres., Cumb.	A 2	70
Gullane St. G11	J13	34
Purdon St.		
Guthrie St. G20	G14	20
Hagg Cres., John.	M09	43
Hagg Pl., John.	M09	43
Hagg Rd., John.	N09	43
Haggs Rd. G41	N14	50
Haghill Rd. G31	K20	37
Haig Dr., Bail.	M24	55
Haig St. G21	H19	23
Hailes Av. G32	L23	39
Haining Rd., Renf.	H 8	17
Hairmyres St. G42	N16	51
Govanhill St.		
Hairst St., Renf.	H 8	17
Halbeath Av. G15	D 9	6
Halbert St. G41	N15	51
Haldane La. G14	H11	19
Haldane St.		
Haldane St. G14	H11	19
Halgreen Av. G15	D 9	6
Halifax Way, Renf.	J 8	31
Britannia Way		
Hall St., Clyde.	E 7	5
Hallbrae St. G33	J21	38
Halley Dr. G13	F 9	18
Halley Pl. G13	G 9	18
Halley Sq. G13	F 9	18
Halley St. G13	F 9	18
Hallhill Cres. G33	L24	39
Hallhill Rd. G32	L22	38
Hallhill Rd., John.	O08	43
Hallidale Cres., Renf.	J 9	32
Hallrule Dr. G52	L11	33
Hallside Av. G72	P24	67
Hallside Cres. G72	P24	67
Hallside Dr. G72	P24	67
Hallside Rd. G72	Q24	67
Hallside St. G5	M17	52
Hallydown Dr. G13	G11	19
Halton Gdns., Bail.	M24	55
Hamilton Av. G41	M13	50
Hamilton Cres. G72	Q23	67
Hamilton Cres., Bear.	B12	7
Hamilton Cres., Renf.	G 8	17
Hamilton Dr. G12	H15	21
Hamilton Dr. G72	P22	66
Hamilton Dr., Both.	R28	69
Hamilton Dr., Giff.	R14	62
Hamilton Park Av.	H15	21
G12		
Hamilton Rd. G32	N24	55
Hamilton Rd. G72 &	P22	66
Blan.		
Hamilton Rd. G73	O19	53
Hamilton Rd., Both.	R28	69
Hamilton Rd. G42	N17	52
Hamilton St., Clyde.	F 8	17
Hamilton St., Pais.	L 6	30
Hamilton Ter., Clyde.	F 8	17
Hamilton Vw., Udd.	O28	57
Hamiltonhill Rd. G22	H16	21
Hampden Dr. G42	O16	51
Cathcart Rd.		
Hampden La. G42	O16	51
Cathcart Rd.		
Hampden Ter. G42	O16	51
Cathcart Rd.		
Hampden Way, Renf.	J 8	31
Lewis Av.		
Hangingshaw Pl. G42	O17	52
Haning, The, Renf.	J 8	31
Hanover St. G1	K17	36
Hanson St. G31	K18	36
Hapland Av. G53	N11	49
Hapland Rd. G53	N11	49
Harbour La., Pais.	L 6	30
Harbour Rd., Pais.	K 6	30
Harburn Pl. G23	E15	9
Harbury Pl. G14	G 9	18
Harcourt Dr. G31	K19	37
Hardgate Dr. G51	K11	33
Hardgate Gdns. G51	K11	33
Hardgate Pl. G51	K11	33
Hardgate Rd. G51	K11	33
Hardie Av. G73	O20	53
Hardridge Av. G52	N11	49
Hardridge Rd.		
Hardridge Pl. G52	N12	49
Hardridge Rd. G52	N11	49
Harefield Dr. G14	G10	18
Harelaw Av. G44	Q15	63
Harelaw Av., Barr.	R 8	59
Harelaw Cres., Pais.	O 5	46
Harhill St. G51	K12	33
Harland Cotts. G14	J11	33
South St.		
Harland St. G14	H11	19
Harlaw Gdns. G64	E20	11
Harley St. G51	L14	34
Harmetray St. G22	G17	22
Harmony Pl. G51	K13	34
Harmony Row G51	K13	34
Harmony Sq. G51	K13	34
Harmsworth St. G11	J12	33
Harport St. G46	Q12	61
Harriet St. G73	O19	53
Harrington St. G20	G15	21
Maryhill Rd.		
Harris Rd. G23	E15	9
Harrison Dr. G51	L13	34
Harrow Ct. G51	D 9	6
Linkwood Dr.		
Harrow Pl. G15	D 9	6
Hart St. G31	L21	38
Hart St., Linw.	L 1	28
Hartfield Ter., Pais.	N 7	47
Hartlaw Cres. G52	L10	32
Hartree Av. G13	F 9	18
Hartstone Pl. G53	O10	48
Hartstone Rd. G53	O10	48
Hartstone Ter. G53	O10	48
Harvey St. G4	J17	36
Harvie St. G51	L14	34
Harwood St. G32	K21	38
Hastie St. G3	J14	34
Old Dumbarton Rd.		
Hatfield Dr. G12	G12	19
Hathaway Dr., Giff.	R13	62
Hathaway La. G20	G15	21
Avenuepark St.		
Hathaway St. G20	G15	21
Hathersage Av., Bail.	L25	40
Hathersage Dr., Bail.	L25	40
Hathersage Gdns., Bail.	L25	40
Hatters Row G40	M18	52
Dalmarnock Rd.		
Hatton Dr. G52	M10	48
Hatton Gdns. G52	M10	48
Haugh Rd. G3	K14	34
Haughburn Pl. G53	O10	48
Haughburn Rd. G53	O10	48
Haughburn Ter. G53	O11	49
Havelock La. G11	J14	34
Dowanhill St.		
Havelock St. G11	J14	34
Hawick Av. G78	N 4	45
Hawick St. G13	F 9	18
Hawkhead Av., Pais.	N 7	47
Hawkhead Rd., Pais.	M 7	47
Hawthorn Av., Bish.	F19	23
Hawthorn Av., Lenz.	C23	13
Hawthorn Av., Renf.	F 6	16
Hawthorn Cres., Renf.	E 5	4
Hawthorn Cres., Renf.	F 5	16
Hawthorn Dr., Barr.	S 8	59
Hawthorn Quad. G22	G17	22
Hawthorn Rd., Renf.	F 6	16

Name	Grid		
Hawthorn St. G22	G17	22	
Hawthorn St., Clyde.	D 7	5	
Hawthorn Wk. G72	P20	65	
Hawthorn Wk., Bish.	F20	23	
Letham Dr.			
Hawthornden Gdns.	E15	9	
G23			
Hawthorne Av., Bear.	B13	8	
Hawthorne Av., John.	N 1	44	
Hawthorne Ter., Udd.	O28	57	
Douglas St.			
Hay Dr., John.	M 1	44	
Hayburn Cres. G11	H13	20	
Hayburn Ct. G11	J13	34	
Hayburn La. G12	H13	20	
Queensborough Gdns.			
Hayburn St. G11	J13	34	
Hayfield St. G5	M17	52	
Hayhill Cotts., Gart.	G28	27	
Hayle Gdns., Chr.	D27	15	
Haylynn St. G14	J12	33	
Haymarket St. G32	K21	38	
Haystack Pl., Lenz.	D23	13	
Hayston Cres. G22	G16	21	
Hayston St. G22	G16	21	
Haywood St. G22	G16	21	
Hazel Av. G44	Q15	63	
Clarkston Rd.			
Hazel Av., John.	N 1	44	
Hazel Av., Lenz.	C23	13	
Hazel Dene, Bish.	E19	11	
Hazel Gro., Lenz.	C23	13	
Hazel Rd., Cumb.	B 4	71	
Hazel Ter., Udd.	O28	57	
Douglas St.			
Hazelden Gdns. G44	Q15	63	
Hazellea Dr., Giff.	Q14	62	
Hazelwood Av. G78	O 3	45	
Hazelwood Dr., Blan.	S26	68	
Hazelwood Gdns. G73	Q20	65	
Hazelwood Rd. G41	M14	50	
Hazlitt St. G20	G16	21	
Heath Av., Bish.	F19	23	
Heath Av., Lenz.	D23	13	
Heathcliffe Av., Blan.	R26	68	
Heathcot Av. G15	E 9	6	
Heathcot Pl. G15	E 9	6	
Heathcot Av.			
Heather Av., Barr.	P 7	59	
Heather Dr., Lenz.	D22	12	
Heather Gdns., Lenz.	D22	12	
Heather Pl., John.	N 1	44	
Heather Pl., Lenz.	C22	12	
Heather St. G41	L15	35	
Scotland St.			
Heatherbrae, Bish.	E18	10	
Heatheryknowe Rd.,	K27	41	
Bail.			
Heathfield Av., Chr.	E27	15	
Heathfield St. G33	K23	39	
Heathfield Ter. G21	G18	22	
Broomfield Rd.			
Heathside Rd., Giff.	Q14	62	
Heathwood Dr., Thorn.	Q13	62	
Hecla Av. G15	D 9	6	
Hecla Pl. G15	D 9	6	
Hector Rd. G41	O14	50	
Heggie Ter. G14	H11	19	
Dumbarton Rd.			
Helen St. G52	L12	33	
Helenburgh Dr. G13	G11	19	
Helenslea G72	Q23	67	
Helenvale Ct. G31	L20	37	
Helenvale St.			
Helenvale St. G31	M20	53	
Helmsdale Av., Blan.	Q26	68	
Helmsdale Ct. G72	P23	67	
Hemlock St. G13	F12	19	
Henderland Rd., Bear.	E12	7	
Henderson Av. G72	P23	67	
Henderson St. G20	H15	21	
Henderson St., Clyde.	F 9	18	
Henderson St., Pais.	L 5	30	
Henrietta St. G14	H11	19	
Henry St., Barr.	Q 7	59	
Hepburn Rd. G52	K10	32	
Herald Av. G13	E11	7	
Herald Way, Renf.	J 8	31	
Viscount Av.			
Herbert St. G20	H15	21	
Herbertson St. G5	L16	35	
Eglinton St.			
Hercules Way, Renf.	J 8	31	
Friendship Way			
Herichell St. G13	G12	19	
Foulis La.			
Heriot Av., Pais.	O 3	45	
Heriot Cres., Bish.	D19	11	
Heriot Rd., Lenz.	D23	13	
Herma St. G23	F15	21	
Hermiston Av. G32	L23	39	
Hermiston Pl. G32	L23	39	
Hermiston Rd. G32	K22	38	
Hermitage Av. G13	G11	19	
Heron Ct., Clyde.	C 7	5	
Heron Pl., John.	O08	43	
Heron St. G40	M18	52	
Heron Way, Renf.	J 8	31	
Britannia Way			
Herries Rd. G41	N14	50	
Herriet St. G41	M15	51	
Herschell St. G13	G12	19	
Foulis La.			
Hertford Av. G12	G13	20	
Hexham Gdns. G41	N14	50	
Heys St., Barr.	R 8	59	
Hickman St. G42	N16	51	
Hickory St. G42	G18	22	
High Barholm, Kilb.	M07	42	
High Calside, Pais.	M 5	46	
High Craighall Rd. G4	J16	35	
High Parksail, Renf.	F 5	16	
High Rd., Pais.	M 5	46	
High St. G1	L17	36	
High St. G73	O19	53	
High St., John.	M09	43	
High St., Pais.	M 5	46	
High St., Renf.	H 8	17	
Highburgh Dr. G73	P19	65	
Highburgh Rd. G12	J14	34	
Highburgh Ter. G12	J14	34	
Highburgh Rd.			
Highcraig Av., John.	N08	43	
Highcroft Av. G44	P17	64	
Highfield Av., Pais.	O 5	46	
Highfield Cres., Pais.	O 5	46	
Highfield Dr. G12	G13	20	
Highfield Dr. G73	Q20	65	
Highfield Pl. G12	G13	20	
Highkirk Vw., John.	N09	43	
Highland La. G51	K14	34	
Hilary Av. G73	P20	65	
Hilary Dr., Bail.	L24	39	
Hilda Cres. G33	H21	24	
Hill Path G52	L10	32	
Hill Pl. G52	L10	32	
Hill St. G3	J16	35	
Hillcrest Av. G32	O22	54	
Hillcrest Av. G44	Q15	63	
Hillcrest Av., Clyde.	B 7	5	
Hillcrest Av., Cumb.	C 2	70	
Hillcrest Av., Pais.	P 5	58	
Hillcrest Ct., Cumb.	C 2	70	
Hillcrest Rd. G32	O23	55	
Hillcrest Rd., Bear.	D12	7	
Hillcrest Rd., Udd.	O28	57	
Hillcrest Ter., Both.	Q28	69	
Churchill Cres.			
Hillcrest, Chr.	F26	26	
Hillcroft Ter., Bish.	F18	22	
Hillend Cres., Clyde.	B 6	4	
Hillend Rd. G22	F16	21	
Hillend Rd. G73	P19	65	
Hillfoot Av. G73	O19	53	
Hillfoot Av., Bear.	C12	7	
Hillfoot Dr., Bear.	C12	7	
Hillfoot Gdns., Udd.	O27	57	
Hillfoot St. G31	K19	37	
Hillfoot Ter., Bear.	C13	8	
Milngavie Rd.			
Hillhead Av. G73	Q19	65	
Hillhead Av., Chr.	E27	15	
Hillhead Gdns. G12	J14	34	
Hillhead St.			
Hillhead Pl. G12	J15	35	
Bank St.			
Hillhead St. G12	J14	34	
Hillhouse St. G21	H19	23	
Hillington Gdns. G52	M11	49	
Hillington Ind. Est. G52	K 9	32	
Hillington Pk. Cres. G52	L11	33	
Hillington Quad. G52	L10	32	
Hillington Rd. G52	J 9	32	
Hillington Rd. S., Renf.	L10	32	
Hillington Ter. G52	L10	32	
Hillkirk Pl. G21	H18	22	
Hillkirk St. G21	H18	22	
Hillkirk Street La. G21	H18	22	
Hillkirk St.			
Hillneuk Av., Bear.	C12	7	
Hillneuk Dr., Bear.	C13	8	
Hillpark Av., Pais.	N 5	46	
Hillpark Dr. G43	P14	62	
Hillsborough Rd., Bail.	L24	39	
Hillsborough Sq. G12	J14	34	
Hillhead St.			
Hillsborough Ter. G12	H15	21	
Bower St.			
Hillside Av., Bear.	C12	7	
Hillside Ct., Thorn.	Q12	61	
Hillside Dr., Barr.	Q 7	59	
Hillside Dr., Bear.	C13	8	
Hillside Dr., Bish.	E19	11	
Hillside Gardens La. G11	H13	20	
North Gardner St.			
Hillside Gdns. G11	H13	20	
Turnberry Rd.			
Hillside Gro., Barr.	Q 7	59	
Hillside Quad. G43	P13	62	
Hillside Rd. G43	P13	62	
Hillside Rd., Barr.	Q 7	59	
Hillside Rd., Pais.	N 7	47	
Hillswick Cres. G22	F16	21	
Hilltop Rd., Chr.	E27	15	
Eastwood Rd.			
Hillview Cres., Udd.	O27	57	
Hillview Dr., Blan.	R26	68	
Hillview Rd., John.	N 2	44	
Hillview St. G32	L21	38	
Hilton Gardens La. G13	F12	19	
Fulton St.			
Hilton Gdns. G13	F12	19	
Hilton Pk., Bish.	D18	10	
Hilton Rd., Bish.	D18	10	
Hilton Ter. G13	F12	19	
Hilton Ter. G72	Q21	66	
Hilton Ter., Bish.	D18	10	
Hinshaw St. G20	H16	21	
Hinshelwood Dr. G51	L13	34	
Hinshelwood Pl. G51	L13	34	
Edmiston Dr.			
Hirsel Pl., Bush.	R28	69	
Lomond Dr.			
Hobart Cres., Dalm.	C 5	4	
Hobart St. G22	H16	21	
Hobden St. G21	H19	23	
Hoddam Av. G45	Q19	65	
Hoddam Av. G45	Q19	65	
Ardencraig Rd.			
Hoddam Ter. G45	Q19	65	
Hoey St. G51	K14	34	
Hogan Ct., Clyde.	C 6	4	
Dalgleish Av.			
Hogarth Av. G32	K20	37	
Hogarth Cres. G32	K20	37	
Hogarth Dr. G32	K20	37	
Hogarth Gdns. G32	K20	37	
Hogg Av., John.	N09	43	
Hogganfield St. G33	J20	37	
Holburn Av., Pais.	L 4	29	
Hole Brae, Cumb.	B 3	71	
Holeburn Rd. G43	P14	62	
Holehouse Dr. G13	G10	18	
Holland St. G2	K16	35	
Hollinwell Rd. G23	F15	21	
Hollowglen Rd. G32	L22	38	
Hollows Av., Pais.	O 3	45	
Hollows Cres., Pais.	O 3	45	
Holly Pl., John.	O 1	44	
Holly St., Clyde.	D 7	5	
Hollybank Pl. G72	Q22	66	
Hollybank St. G21	J19	37	
Hollybrook St. G42	N16	51	
Hollybush Av., Pais.	O 4	45	
Hollybush Rd. G52	L 9	32	
Hollymount, Bear.	E12	7	
Holm Av., Pais.	N 6	46	
Holm Av., Udd.	O27	57	
Holm Pl., Linw.	K 1	28	
Holm St. G2	K16	35	

Name	Grid	Page
Holmbank Av. G41	O14	50
Holmbrae Av., Udd.	O27	57
Holmbrae Rd., Udd.	O27	57
Holmbyre Rd. G45	R17	64
Holmbyre Ter. G45	R17	64
Holmes Av., Renf.	J 8	31
Holmfauldhead Dr. G51	K12	33
Holmhead Cres. G44	P16	63
Holmhead Pl. G44	P16	63
Holmhead Rd. G44	P16	63
Holmhill Av. G72	Q22	66
Holmhills Dr. G72	Q21	66
Holmhills Gdns. G72	Q21	66
Holmhills Gro. G72	Q21	66
Holmhills Pl. G72	Q21	66
Holmhills Rd. G72	Q21	66
Holmhills Ter. G72	Q21	66
Holmlea Rd. G44	O16	51
Holms Pl., Gart.	F27	27
Holmswood Av., Blan.	R26	68
Holmwood Av., Udd.	O27	57
Holmwood Gdns., Udd.	P27	69
Holyrood Cres. G20	J15	35
Holyrood Quad. G20	J15	35
Holywell St. G31	L19	37
Homeston Av., Udd.	Q28	69
Honeybog Rd. G52	L 9	32
Hood St., Clyde.	E 8	5
Hope St. G2	K16	35
Hopefield Av. G12	G14	20
Hopehill Pl. G20	H16	21
Hopehill Rd		
Hopehill Rd. G20	H16	21
Hopeman Av. G46	Q12	61
Hopeman Dr. G46	Q12	61
Hopeman Rd. G46	Q12	61
Hopeman St. G46	Q12	61
Hopetoun Pl. G23	E15	9
Hornal Rd., Udd.	Q28	69
Hornbeam Dr., Dalm.	D 7	5
Hornbeam Rd., Udd.	O28	57
Myrtle Rd.		
Horndean Cres. G33	J23	39
Horndean Ct., Bish.	D19	11
Horne St. G22	G18	22
Hawthorn St.		
Hornshill Dr. G33	F24	25
Hornshill St. G21	H19	23
Horsburgh St. G33	J23	39
Horse Shoe La., Bear.	D12	7
Horse Shoe Rd., Bear.	C12	7
Horslethill Rd. G12	H14	20
Hospital St. G5	M16	51
Hotspur St. G20	H15	21
Houldsworth La. G3	K15	35
Finnieston St.		
Houldsworth St. G3	K15	35
Househillmuir Cres. G53	O11	49
Househillmuir La. G53	O11	49
Househillmuir Pl. G53	O11	49
Househillmuir Rd. G53	P10	60
Househillwood Cres. G53	O10	48
Househillwood Rd. G53	P10	60
Housel Av. G13	F10	18
Houston Pl. G5	L15	35
Houston Pl., John.	N 2	44
Houston Rd., Loanhead	H 1	28
Houston Sq., John.	M09	43
Houston St. G5	L15	35
Houston St., Renf.	H 8	17
Howard St. G1	L16	35
Howard St., Pais.	M 7	47
Howat St. G51	K13	34
Howden Dr., Linw.	L 1	28
Howe St., Pais.	M 3	45
Howford Rd. G52	M10	48
Howgate Av. G15	D 9	6
Howieshill Av. G72	P22	66
Howieshill Rd. G72	Q22	66
Howth Dr. G13	F12	19
Howth Ter. G13	F12	19
Howwood St. G41	L15	35
Hoylake Pk., Both.	R27	69
Hoylake Pl. G23	E15	9
Hozier Cres., Udd.	O27	57
Hozier St. G40	M18	52
Hubbard Dr. G11	J12	33
Hugh Murray Gro. G72	P23	67
Hughenden Dr. G12	H13	20
Hughenden Gdns. G12	H13	20
Hughenden La. G12	H13	20
Hughenden Rd. G12	H13	20
Hughenden Ter. G12	H13	20
Hughenden Rd.		
Hugo St. G20	G15	21
Hume Dr., Both.	Q28	69
Hume Dr., Udd.	O27	57
Hume Rd., Cumb.	B 3	71
Hume St., Clyde.	E 7	5
Hunter Pl. G78	N07	42
Hunter Rd. G73	N20	53
Hunter St. G4	L18	36
Hunter St., Pais.	L 6	30
Hunterfield Dr. G72	P21	66
Hunterhill Av., Pais.	M 6	46
Hunterhill Rd.		
Hunterhill Rd., Pais.	M 6	46
Huntersfield Rd., John.	N08	43
Huntershill St. G21	G18	22
Huntershill Rd., Bish.	F18	22
Huntershill Way, Bish.	F18	22
Crowhill Rd.		
Huntingdon Sq. G21	J18	36
Huntingdon Rd.		
Huntingdon Rd. G21	J18	36
Huntingtower Rd., Bail.	M25	56
Huntley Dr., Bear.	B12	7
Tweedsmuir Dr.		
Huntley Rd. G52	K 9	32
Huntly Av., Giff.	R14	62
Huntly Dr. G72	Q22	66
Huntly Gdns. G12	H14	20
Huntly Path, Chr.	E28	15
Burnbrae Av.		
Huntly Rd. G12	H14	20
Huntly Ter., Pais.	N 7	47
Hurlet Rd., Pais.& G53	N 8	47
Hurley Hawkin, Bish.	F20	23
Hurlford Av. G13	F 9	18
Hutcheson Rd., Thorn.	R13	62
Hutcheson St. G1	K17	36
Hutchinson Ct. G2	K16	35
Hope St.		
Hutchinson Pl. G72	Q24	67
Berryhill Rd.		
Hutchison Dr., Bear.	E13	8
Hutton Dr. G51	K12	33
Huxley St. G20	G15	21
Hydepark Pl. G21	G18	22
Springburn Rd.		
Hydepark St. G3	K15	35
Hyndal Av. G53	N11	49
Hyndford St. G51	K13	34
Hyndland Av. G11	J13	34
Hyndland Rd. G12	H13	20
Hyndland St. G11	J14	34
Hyndlee Dr. G52	L11	33
Hyslop Pl., Clyde.	D 7	5
Albert Rd.		
Iain Dr., Bear.	C11	7
Iain Rd., Bear.	C11	7
Ibrox St. G51	L14	34
Ibrox Ter. G51	L13	34
Ibrox Terrace La. G51	L13	34
Ibroxholm La. G51	L14	34
Paisley Rd. W.		
Ibroxholm Oval G51	L13	34
Ibroxholm Pl. G51	L14	34
Ilay Av., Bear.	F12	19
Ilay Ct., Bear.	F13	20
Ilay Rd., Bear.	F13	20
Inchbrae Rd. G52	M11	49
Inchfad Dr. G15	D 9	6
Inchholm St. G11	J12	33
Inchinnan Rd., Pais.	K 6	30
Inchinnan Rd., Renf.	H 7	17
Inchkeith Pl. G32	K22	38
Inchlee St. G14	J12	33
Inchmurrin Dr. G73	R20	65
Inchmurrin Gdns. G73	R20	65
Inchmurrin Pl. G73	R20	65
Inchoch St. G33	J24	39
Inchrory Pl. G15	D 9	6
Incle St., Pais.	L 6	30
India Dr., Renf.	G 5	16
India St. G2	K16	35
India St. G73	O19	53
Inga St. G20	F15	21
Ingerbreck Av. G73	Q20	65
Ingleby Dr. G31	K19	37
Inglefield St. G42	N16	51
Ingleneuk Av. G33	G22	24
Inglestone Av., Thorn.	R13	62
Inglis St. G31	L19	37
Ingram St. G1	K17	36
Inishail Rd. G33	J23	39
Inkerman Rd. G52	L 9	32
Innerwick Dr. G52	L10	32
Inver Rd. G33	K24	39
Inverary Dr., Bish.	D19	11
Invercanny Dr. G15	D 9	6
Invercanny Pl. G15	D10	6
Inverclyde Gdns. G11	H12	19
Broomhill Dr.		
Inverclyde Gdns. G73	Q21	66
Inveresk Cres. G32	L22	38
Inveresk St. G32	L22	38
Inverewe Av. G46	Q11	61
Inverewe Dr. G46	R11	61
Inverewe Gdns. G46	R11	61
Inverewe Pl. G46	Q11	61
Invergarry Av. G46	R11	61
Invergarry Ct. G46	R11	61
Invergarry Dr. G46	R11	61
Invergarry Gdns. G46	R11	61
Invergarry Gro. G46	R11	61
Invergarry Pl. G46	R11	61
Invergarry Quad. G46	R12	61
Invergarry Vw. G46	R12	61
Inverglas Av., Renf.	J 9	32
Morriston Cres.		
Invergordon Av. G43	O15	51
Invergyle Dr. G52	L10	32
Inverkar Dr., Pais.	N 4	45
Inverkip St. G5	L17	36
Inverlair Av. G43	P15	63
Inverleith St. G32	L20	37
Inverlochy St. G33	J23	39
Inverness St. G51	L11	33
Inveroran Dr., Bear.	D13	8
Invershiel Rd. G23	E14	8
Invershin Dr. G20	G14	20
Wyndford Rd.		
Inverurie St. G21	H17	22
Inzievar Ter. G32	N22	54
Iona Ct. G51	K13	34
Iona Dr., Pais.	O 5	46
Iona La., Chr.	E28	15
Heathfield Av.		
Iona Rd. G73	Q21	66
Iona Rd., Renf.	J 8	31
Iona St. G51	K13	34
Irongray St. G31	K20	37
Irvine Dr., Linw.	L 1	28
Irvine St. G40	M19	53
Irving Av., Clyde.	C 7	5
Stewart Dr.		
Irving Quad., Clyde.	C 7	5
Stewart Dr.		
Iser La. G41	O15	51
Island Rd., Cumb.	D 1	70
Islay Av. G73	Q21	66
Islay Cres., Pais.	O 5	46
Ivanhoe Rd. G13	F11	19
Ivanhoe Rd., Cumb.	D 2	70
Ivanhoe Rd., Pais.	N 3	45
Ivanhoe Way, Pais.	N 3	45
Ivanhoe Rd.		
Ivybank Ave. G72	Q23	67
Jacks Rd., Udd.	P28	69
Jagger Gdns., Bail.	M24	55
Jamaica St. G1	L16	35
James Dunlop Gdns., Bish.	F19	23
Graham Ter.		
James Gray St. G41	O15	51
James Morrison St. G1	L17	36
St. Andrews Sq.		
James Nisbet St. G21	K18	36
James St. G40	M18	52
James Watt La. G2	K16	35
James Watt St.		
James Watt St. G2	K16	35
Jamieson Ct. G42	N16	51
Jamieson Ct., Clyde.	B 7	5

Name	Map Ref	Page
Jamieson Path G42	N16	51
Jamieson St.		
Jamieson St. G42	N16	51
Janebank Av. G72	Q23	67
Janefield Av., John.	N 9	43
Janefield St. G31	L19	37
Janes Brae, Cumb.	D 2	70
Janetta St., Clyde.	D 7	5
Jardine St. G20	H15	21
Jardine Ter., Gart.	G27	27
Jasgray St. G42	N15	51
Jean Armour Dr., Clyde.	D 8	5
Jedburgh Av. G73	O19	53
Jedburgh Dr., Pais.	N 4	45
Jedburgh Gdns. G20	H15	21
Jedworth Av. G15	D10	6
Jellicoe St. Dalm.	D 6	4
Jennys Well Rd., Pais.	N 7	47
Jerviston Rd. G33	J23	39
Jessie St. G42	N17	52
Jessiman Sq., Renf.	J 7	31
John Brown Pl., Chr.	F26	26
John Knox La. G4	K18	36
Drygate		
John Knox St. G4	K18	36
John Knox St., Clyde.	F 8	17
John Lang St., John.	M 1	44
John St. G1	K17	36
John St., Barr.	Q 7	59
John St., Pais.	M 5	46
Johnshaven St. G43	O14	50
Bengal St.		
Johnston Rd., Gart.	G28	27
Johnston St., Pais.	M 6	46
Gordon St.		
Johnstone Av. G52	L10	32
Johnstone Av., Clyde.	F 8	17
Johnstone Cotts., Kirk.	B21	12
Johnstone Dr. G72	P22	66
Johnstone Dr. G73	O19	53
Joppa St. G33	K21	38
Jordan St. G14	J11	33
Jordanhill Cres. G13	G11	19
Jordanhill Dr. G13	G11	19
Jordanhill La. G13	G12	19
Austen Rd.		
Jordanvale Av. G14	J11	33
Jowitt Av., Clyde.	E 8	5
Joycelyn Sq. G1	L17	36
Jubilee Bank, Lenz.	D23	13
Heriot Rd.		
Jubilee Path, Bear.	D12	7
Jubilee Ter., John.	N08	43
Julian Av. G12	H14	20
Julian La. G12	H14	20
Julian Av.		
Juniper Ct., Lenz.	C22	12
Juniper Pl. G32	M24	55
Juniper Pl., John.	O 1	44
Juniper Ter. G32	M24	55
Jura Av., Renf.	J 8	31
Jura Ct. G52	L12	33
Jura Dr., Blan.	Q26	68
Jura Rd., Pais.	O 5	46
Jura St. G52	L12	33
Kaim Dr. G53	P11	61
Kames St. G5	M16	51
Karol Path G4	J16	35
St. Peters St.		
Katewell Av. G15	D 9	6
Katrine Av., Bish.	E19	11
Katrine Dr., Pais.	N 3	45
Kay St. G21	H18	22
Kaystone Rd. G15	E10	6
Keal Av. G15	F10	18
Keal Cres. G15	F10	18
Keal Dr. G15	F10	18
Keal Pl. G15	F10	18
Kearn Av. G15	E10	6
Kearn Pl. G15	E10	6
Keats Pk., Udd.	Q28	69
Keir Dr., Bish.	E18	10
Keir St. G41	M15	51
Keirhill Rd, Cumb.	C 1	70
Woodburn Rd.		
Keirs Wk. G72	P22	66
Keith Av., Giff.	Q14	62
Keith Ct. G11	J14	34
Keith St.		
Keith St. G11	J14	34
Kelbourne St. G20	H15	21
Kelburn St., Barr.	R 7	59
Kelburne Dr., Pais.	L 7	31
Kelburne Gdns., Bail.	M25	56
Kelburne Gdns., Pais.	L 7	31
Kelburne Oval, Pais.	L 7	31
Kelhead Av. G52	L 9	32
Kelhead Dr. G52	L 9	32
Kelhead Path G52	L10	32
Kelhead Pl. G52	L 9	32
Kellas St. G51	L13	34
Kells Pl. G15	D 9	6
Kelso Av. G73	O19	53
Kelso Av., Pais.	N 4	45
Kelso St. G13	G 9	18
Kelton St. G32	M22	54
Kelty Pl. G5	L16	35
Bedford St.		
Kelty St. G5	M16	51
Eglinton St.		
Kelvin Av. G52	J 9	32
Kelvin Cres., Bear.	E12	7
Kelvin Ct. G12	G12	19
Kelvin Dr. G20	H14	20
Kelvin Dr., Barr.	R 8	59
Kelvin Dr., Bish.	E19	11
Kelvin Dr., Chr.	E27	15
Kelvin Rd., Cumb.	D 3	71
Kelvin Rd., Udd.	O27	57
Kelvin Way G3	J14	34
Kelvin Way, Udd.	Q28	69
Bracken Ter.		
Kelvindale Bldgs. G12	G14	20
Kelvindale Rd.		
Kelvindale Cotts. G12	G14	20
Kelvindale Rd.		
Kelvindale Glen G12	G14	20
Kelvindale Rd.		
Kelvindale Pl. G20	G14	20
Kelvindale Rd. G12	G14	20
Kelvingrove St. G3	K15	35
Kelvingrove Ter. G3	K15	35
Kelvingrove St.		
Kelvinhaugh Pl. G3	K14	34
Kelvinhaugh St.		
Kelvinhaugh St. G3	K14	34
Kelvinside Av. G20	H15	21
Queen Margaret Dr.		
Kelvinside Gdns. E. G20	H15	21
Kelvinside Gdns. G20	H15	21
Kelvinside Ter. S. G20	H15	21
Kelvinside Ter. W. G20	H15	21
Kemp Av., Renf.	J 7	31
Kemp St. G21	H18	22
Kempock St. G31	M20	53
Kempsthorn Cres. G53	N10	48
Kempsthorn Path G53	N10	48
Kempsthorn Rd. G53	N10	48
Kendal Av., Giff.	Q14	62
Kendal Dr. G12	G13	20
Kendal Ter. G12	G13	20
Kendoon Av. G15	D 9	6
Kenilworth Av. G41	O14	50
Kenilworth Cres., Bear.	C11	7
Kenilworth Way, Pais.	O 3	45
Kenmar Gdns., Udd.	O26	56
Kenmore Gdns., Bear.	D13	8
Kenmore Rd., Cumb.	C 3	71
Kenmore St. G32	L22	38
Kenmuir Av. G32	M24	55
Kenmuir Rd. G32	O23	55
Kenmuirhill Rd. G32	N23	55
Kenmure Av., Bish.	E18	10
Kenmure Cres., Bish.	E18	10
Kenmure Dr., Bish.	E18	10
Kenmure Gdns., Bish.	E18	10
Kenmure Row G22	E16	9
Kenmure St. G41	M15	51
Kenmure Way G73	Q19	65
Kennedar Dr. G51	K12	33
Kennedy Ct., Giff.	Q14	62
Braidholm Cres.		
Kennedy St. G4	K17	36
Kennet St. G21	J19	37
Kennishead Av. G46	P12	61
Kennishead Pl. G46	P12	61
Kennishead Rd. G46	P12	61
Kennishead Rd. G53	Q11	61
Kennisholm Av. G46	P12	61
Kennisholm Pl. G46	P12	61
Kennoway Dr. G11	J12	33
Kennoway La. G11	J12	33
Thornwood Dr.		
Kennyhill Sq. G31	K19	37
Kensington Dr., Giff.	R14	62
Kensington Gate G12	H14	20
Kensington Rd.		
Kensington Rd. G12	H14	20
Kent Dr. G73	P20	65
Kent Rd. G3	K15	35
Kent St. G40	L18	36
Kentallen Rd. G33	L24	39
Kentigern Ter., Bish.	F19	23
Keppel Dr. G44	O18	52
Keppoch St. G21	H17	22
Keppochhill Rd. G22	H17	22
Kerfield Pl. G15	D 9	6
Kerr St. G40	L18	36
Kerr St., Barr.	R 7	59
Kerr St., Blan.	S27	69
Kerr St., Pais.	L 5	30
Kerrera Pl. G33	L23	39
Kerrera Rd. G33	L23	39
Kerry Pl. G15	D 9	6
Kerrycroy Av. G42	O17	52
Kerrycroy Pl. G42	O17	52
Kerrycroy Av.		
Kerrycroy St. G42	O17	52
Kerrydale St. G40	M19	53
Kerrylamont Av. G42	O18	52
Kersland La. G12	H14	20
Kersland St.		
Kersland St. G12	H14	20
Kessington Dr., Bear.	D13	8
Kessington Rd., Bear.	D13	8
Kestral Ct., Clyde.	C 7	5
Kestrel Pl., John.	O08	43
Kestrel Rd. G13	G11	19
Kew Gdns. G12	H14	20
Ruthven St.		
Kew Gdns., Udd.	O28	57
Kew La. G12	H14	20
Saltoun St.		
Kew Ter. G12	H14	20
Keyden St. G41	L15	35
Kibbleston Rd., Kilb.	M07	42
Kidston St. G5	M17	52
Kierhill Rd., Cumb.	C 1	70
Kilbarchan Rd., John.	N08	43
Kilbarchan St. G5	L16	35
Bedford St.		
Kilbeg Ter. G46	Q11	61
Kilberry St. G21	J19	37
Kilbirnie St. G5	M16	51
Kilbowie Ct., Clyde.	D 7	5
Crown Av.		
Kilbowie Rd., Clyde.	C 7	5
Kilbowie Rd., Cumb.	C 3	71
Kilbrennan Rd., Linw.	L 1	28
Kilbride St. G5	N17	52
Kilbride Vw., Udd.	O28	57
Hamilton Vw.		
Kilburn Gro., Blan.	R26	68
Kilburn Pl. G13	G10	18
Kilchattan Dr. G44	O17	52
Kilchoan Rd. G33	J23	39
Kilcloy Av. G15	D10	6
Kildale St. G73	O18	52
Kildale Way G73	O18	52
Kildary Av. G44	P16	63
Kildary Rd. G44	P16	63
Kildermorie Rd. G34	K25	40
Kildonan Dr. G11	J13	34
Kildonan Ter. G51	L13	34
Copland Rd.		
Kildrostan St. G41	N15	51
Terregles Av.		
Kildrum Rd., Cumb.	B 3	71
Kilearn Rd., Pais.	K 7	31
Kilfinan St. G22	F16	21
Kilkerran Dr. G33	G21	24
Killarn Way, Pais.	K 7	31
Killearn Dr., Pais.	M 9	48
Killearn St. G22	H16	21
Killermont Av., Bear.	E13	8
Killermont Ct., Bear.	D13	8
Killermont Meadows, Both.	R27	69

Name	Grid	Page
Killermont Rd., Bear.	D13	8
Killermont St. G1	K17	36
Killermont Vw. G20	E13	8
Killiegrew Rd. G41	N14	50
Killin Dr., Linw.	L 1	28
Killin St. G32	M22	54
Killoch Av., Pais.	L 4	29
Killoch Dr. G13	F10	18
Killoch Dr., Barr.	R 8	59
Killoch Rd., Pais.	L 4	29
Kilmailing Rd. G44	P16	63
Kilmair Pl. G20	G14	20
Wyndford Rd.		
Kilmaluag Ter. G46	Q11	61
Kilmany Dr. G32	L21	38
Kilmardinny Av., Bear.	C12	7
Kilmardinny Cres.,	C12	7
Bear.		
Kilmardinny Dr., Bear.	C12	7
Kilmardinny Gate, Bear.	C12	7
Kilmardinny Av.		
Kilmardinny Gro., Bear.	C12	7
Kilmarnock Rd. G43	P14	62
Kilmartin Pl., Thorn.	Q12	61
Kilmaurs Dr., Giff.	Q15	63
Kilmaurs St. G51	L12	33
Kilmorie Dr. G73	O18	52
Kilmory Av., Udd.	O28	57
Spindlehow Rd.		
Kilmuir Cres. G46	Q11	61
Kilmuir Dr. G46	Q12	61
Kilmuir Rd. G46	Q12	61
Kilmuir Rd., Udd.	N27	57
Kilmun La. G20	F14	20
Kilmun St.		
Kilmun Pl. G20	F14	20
Kilmun St.		
Kilmun St. G20	F14	20
Kilnside Rd., Pais.	L 6	30
Kiloran St. G46	Q12	61
Kilpatrick Av., Pais.	N 4	45
Kilpatrick Cres., Pais.	N 5	46
Kiltearn Rd. G33	K24	39
Kilvaxter Dr. G46	Q12	61
Kilwynet Way, Pais.	K 7	31
Kimberley St., Dalm.	C 5	4
Kinalty Rd. G44	P16	63
Kinarvie Cres. G53	O 9	48
Kinarvie Gdns. G53	O 9	48
Kinarvie Rd.		
Kinarvie Pl. G53	O 9	48
Kinarvie Rd. G53	O 9	48
Kinarvie Ter. G53	O 9	48
Kinbuck St. G22	H17	22
Kincardine Cres., Bish.	F19	23
Graham Ter.		
Kincardine Pl., Bish.	F19	23
Kincardine Pl., Bish.	F20	23
Kincardine Sq. G33	J23	39
Kincath Av. G73	Q20	65
Kinclaven Av. G15	D10	6
Kincraig St. G51	L11	33
Kinellan Rd., Bear.	E12	7
Kinellar Dr. G14	G10	18
Kinfauns Dr. G15	D 9	6
Kinfauns Ter. G51	L13	34
Copland Rd.		
King Edward Rd. G13	G12	19
King George V Bridge	L16	35
G5		
King St. G1	L17	36
King St. G73	O19	53
King St., Clyde.	F 8	17
King St., Pais.	L 5	30
Kingarth St. G42	N16	51
Kinghorn Dr. G44	O17	52
Kinglas Rd., Bear.	E11	7
Kings Cres. G72	P22	66
Kings Cres., John.	M 2	44
Kings Cross G31	K18	36
Kings Dr. G40	M18	52
Kings Dr., Cumb.	A 2	70
Kings Inch Rd., Renf.	G 8	17
Kings La. W., Renf.	H 8	17
Bell St.		
Kings Park Av. G44	P17	64
Kings Park Rd. G44	O16	51
Kings Pl. G22	F16	21
Kings Rd., John.	N 1	44
Kingsacre Rd. G44	O17	52
Kingsbarns Dr. G44	O16	51
Kingsborough Gate G12	H13	20
Prince Albert Rd.		
Kingsborough Gdns.	H13	20
G12		
Kingsborough Ter. G12	H13	20
Hyndland Rd.		
Kingsbrae Dr. G44	O17	52
Kingsbridge Cres. G44	P17	64
Kingsbridge Dr. G44	P17	64
Kingsburgh Dr., Pais.	L 7	31
Kingsburn Dr. G73	P19	65
Kingsburn Gro. G73	P19	65
Kingscliffe Av. G44	P17	64
Kingscourt Av. G44	P17	64
Kingsdale Av. G44	O17	52
Kingsdyke Av. G44	O17	52
Kingsford Av. G44	Q15	63
Kingshall Cotts., Gart.	H28	27
Kingsheath Av. G73	P18	64
Kingshill Dr. G44	P17	64
Kingshouse Av. G44	P17	64
Kingshurst Av. G44	O17	52
Kingsknowe Dr. G73	P18	64
Kingsland Cres. G52	L10	32
Kingsland Dr. G52	L10	32
Kingsley Av. G42	N16	51
Kingsley Ct., Udd.	O28	57
Kingslynn Dr. G44	P17	64
Kingslynn La. G44	P17	64
Kingslynn Dr.		
Kingsmuir Dr. G73	P18	64
Kingston Bri. G3	L15	34
Kingston Pl., Dalm.	D 5	4
Kingston St. G5	L16	35
Kingsway Ct. G14	G10	18
Kingsway G14	G10	18
Kingswood Dr. G44	P17	64
Kingussie Dr. G44	P17	64
Kiniver Dr. G15	E10	6
Kinloch Av. G72	Q22	66
Kinloch Av., Linw.	L 1	28
Pentland Dr.		
Kinloch Rd., Renf.	J 7	31
Kinloch St. G40	M20	53
Kinmount Av. G44	O16	51
Kinmount La. G44	O16	51
Kinmount Av.		
Kinnaird Cres., Bear.	D13	8
Kinnaird Dr., Linw.	L 1	28
Kinnaird Pl. G64	F19	23
Kinnear Rd. G40	M19	53
Kinnell Av. G52	M11	49
Kinnell Cres. G52	M11	49
Kinnell Pl. G52	N12	49
Mosspark Dr.		
Kinnell Sq. G52	M11	49
Kinning St. G5	L15	35
Kinnoul Pl. G12	H13	20
Crown Rd.		
Kinpurnie Rd., Pais.	L 8	31
Kinross Av. G52	M10	48
Kinsail Dr. G52	L 9	32
Kinstone Av. G14	G10	18
Kintessack Pl., Bish.	E20	11
Kintillo Dr. G13	G10	18
Kintore Rd. G43	P15	63
Kintra St. G51	L13	34
Kintyre Av., Linw.	L 1	28
Kintyre St. G21	J19	37
Kippen St. G22	G17	22
Kippford St. G32	M23	55
Kirk La. G43	O14	50
Riverbank St.		
Kirk Pl., Udd.	P27	69
Kirk Rd., Bear.	C12	7
Kirkaig Av., Renf.	J 9	32
Kirkbean Av. G73	Q19	65
Kirkburn Av. G72	Q22	66
Kirkcaldy Rd. G41	N14	58
Kirkconnel Av. G13	G 9	18
Kirkconnel Dr. G73	P18	64
Kirkdale Dr. G52	M12	49
Kirkfield Rd., Udd.	Q28	69
Kirkford Rd., Chr.	E27	15
Bridgeburn Dr.		
Kirkhill Av. G72	Q22	66
Kirkhill Dr. G20	G14	20
Kirkhill Gdns. G72	Q22	66
Kirkhill Gro. G72	Q22	66
Kirkhill Pl. G20	G14	20
Kirkhill Rd., Gart.	G27	27
Kirkhill Rd., Udd.	O27	57
Kirkhill Ter. G72	Q22	66
Kirkhope Dr. G15	E10	6
Kirkinner Rd. G32	M23	55
Kirkintilloch Rd., Bish.	F18	22
Kirkintilloch Rd., Lenz.	C23	13
Kirkland St. G20	H15	21
Kirklandneuk Rd., Renf.	H 7	17
Kirklands Cres., Udd.	Q28	69
Kirklea Av., Pais.	L 4	29
Kirklee Circus G12	H14	20
Kirklee Gardens La. G12	G14	20
Bellshaugh Rd.		
Kirklee Gdns. G12	G14	20
Bellshaugh Rd.		
Kirklee Pl. G12	H14	20
Kirklee Quad. G12	H14	20
Kirklee Quad. La. G12	H14	20
Kirklee Quad.		
Kirklee Rd. G12	H14	20
Kirklee Ter. G12	H14	20
Kirklee Terrace La. G12	H14	20
Kirklee Ter.		
Kirkliston St. G32	L21	38
Kirkmuir Av., Renf.	J 7	31
Kirkmuir Dr. G73	Q19	65
Kirknewton St. G32	L22	38
Kirkoswald Dr., Clyde.	D 8	5
Kirkoswald Rd. G43	P14	62
Kirkpatrick St. G40	L19	37
Kirkriggs Av. G73	P19	65
Kirkriggs Gdns. G73	P19	65
Kirkriggs Way, Ruth.	P19	65
Kirkstall Gdns., Bish.	D19	11
Kirkstonside, Barr.	R 7	59
Kirkton Av. G13	G10	18
Kirkton Cres. G13	G10	18
Kirkton Rd. G72	P22	66
Kirkview Gdns., Udd.	O27	57
Glencroft Av.		
Kirkville Pl. G15	E10	6
Kirkwall Av., Blan.	Q26	68
Kirkwall, Cumb.	A 3	71
Kirkwell Rd. G44	P16	63
Kirkwood Av., Clyde.	E 8	5
Kirkwood Quad., Clyde.	E 8	5
Kirkwood Av.		
Kirkwood Rd., Udd.	N27	57
Newlands Rd.		
Kirkwood St. G51	L14	34
Kirkwood St. G73	O19	53
Kirn St. G20	F14	20
Kilmun St.		
Kirriemuir Av. G52	M11	49
Kirriemuir Gdns., Bish.	E20	11
Kirriemuir Rd., Bish.	E20	11
Kirtle Dr., Renf.	J 9	32
Kirton Av., Barr.	R 7	59
Kishorn Pl. G32	J23	39
Knapdale St. G22	F16	21
Knightsbridge Rd. G13	G11	19
Knightscliffe Av. G13	F11	19
Knightswood Cross G13	F11	19
Knightswood Rd. G13	E11	7
Knightswood Ter., Blan.	R27	69
Knock Way, Pais.	K 7	31
Knockburnie Rd., Udd.	Q28	69
Knockhall St. G33	J23	39
Knockhill Dr. G44	O16	51
Knockhill La. G44	O16	51
Mount Annan Dr.		
Knockhill Rd., Renf.	J 7	31
Knockside Av., Pais.	O 5	46
Knowe Rd., Chr.	F26	26
Knowe Rd., Pais.	K 7	31
Knowe Ter. G22	F16	21
Hillend Rd.		
Knowehead Dr., Udd.	P27	69
Knowehead Gdns. G41	M15	51
Knowehead Ter.		
Knowehead Gdns., Udd.	P27	69
Knowehead Ter. G41	M15	51
Knowetap St. G20	F15	21
Knox St., Pais.	M 4	45
Kyle Dr., Giff.	Q14	62
Kyle Rd., Cumb.	B 3	71
Kyle Sq. G73	P19	65
Kyle St. G4	J17	36

Kyleakin Gdns., Blan.	R25 68	
Kyleakin Rd. G46	Q11 61	
Kyleakin Ter. G46	Q11 61	
Kylepark Av., Udd.	P26 68	
Kylepark Cres., Udd.	O26 56	
Kylepark Dr., Udd.	O26 56	
Kylerhea Rd. G46	Q11 61	
La Belle Pl. G3	J15 35	
Laburnum Gdns., Lenz.	C22 12	
Laburnum Gro.		
Laburnum Gro., Lenz.	C22 12	
Laburnum Pl., John.	O 1 44	
Laburnum Rd. G41	M14 50	
Laburnum Rd., Cumb.	C 4 71	
Lacrosse Ter. G12	H15 21	
Lacy St., Pais.	L 7 31	
Lade Ter. G52	M10 48	
Ladeside Dr., John.	N08 43	
Ladhope Pl. G13	F 9 18	
Lady Anne St. G14	G 9 18	
Lady Isle Cres., Udd.	P27 69	
Lady Jane Gate, Both.	Q27 69	
Lady La., Pais.	M 5 46	
Ladybank Dr. G52	M12 49	
Ladyburn St., Pais.	M 7 47	
Ladyhill Dr., Bail.	M25 56	
Ladykirk Cres. G52	L10 32	
Ladykirk Cres., Pais.	M 6 46	
Ladykirk Dr. G52	L10 32	
Ladyloan Av. G15	D 9 6	
Ladyloan Pl. G15	D 9 6	
Ladymuir Cres. G53	N11 49	
Ladysmith Av., Kilb.	N08 43	
Ladywell St. G4	K18 36	
Wishart St.		
Laggan Rd. G43	P15 63	
Laggan Rd., Bish.	E19 11	
Laggan Ter., Renf.	H 7 17	
Laidlaw Gdns., Udd.	N27 57	
Laidlaw St. G5	L16 35	
Laigh Kirk La., Pais.	M 6 46	
Causeyside St.		
Laigh Possil Rd. G23	F16 21	
Balmore Rd.		
Laighcartside St., John.	M 1 44	
Laighlands Rd. G71	R28 69	
Laighmuir St., Udd.	P27 69	
Laighpark Harbour, Pais.	K 6 30	
Lainshaw Dr. G45	R16 63	
Laird St. G40	M18 52	
Lairds Hill, Cumb.	C 2 70	
Lairg Dr., Blan.	R26 68	
Lamb St. G22	G16 21	
Lambhill St. G41	L14 34	
Lamerton Dr. G52	L10 32	
Lamerton Rd., Cumb.	C 4 71	
Lamington Rd. G52	M10 48	
Lamlash Cres. G33	K22 38	
Lammermoor Av. G52	M11 49	
Lammermoor Dr., Cumb.	D 2 70	
Lammermuir Dr., Pais.	O 6 46	
Lamont Rd. G21	G19 23	
Lanark St. G1	L17 36	
Lancaster Cres. G12	H14 20	
Lancaster Cres. La. G12	G13 20	
Clevedon Rd.		
Lancaster Rd., Bish.	D19 11	
Lancaster Ter. G12	H14 20	
Westbourne Gdns. W.		
Lancaster Ter. La. G12	H14 20	
Westbourne Gdns. W.		
Lancefield Quay G3	K15 35	
Lancefield St. G3	K15 35	
Landemer Dr. G73	P18 64	
Landressy St. G40	M18 52	
Lanfine Rd., Pais.	M 7 47	
Lang Av., Renf.	J 8 31	
Lang St., Pais.	M 7 47	
Langa St. G20	F15 21	
Langbank St. G5	M16 51	
Eglinton St.		
Langbar Cres. G33	K24 39	
Langbar Path G33	K23 39	
Langcraigs Dr., Pais.	P 5 58	
Langcraigs Ter., Pais.	P 5 58	
Langcroft Dr. G72	Q23 67	
Langcroft Pl. G51	K11 33	
Langcroft Rd. G51	K11 33	
Langcroft Ter. G51	K11 33	

Langdale Av. G33	H21 24	
Langdale Av., Cumb.	C 1 70	
Langdale St. G33	H21 24	
Langfaulds Cres., Clyde.	C 8 5	
Langford Av. G53	Q10 60	
Langford Dr. G53	Q10 60	
Langford Pl. G53	Q10 60	
Langford Dr.		
Langhill Dr., Cumb.	B 1 70	
Langholm Ct., Chr.	E28 15	
Heathfield Av.		
Langholm Dr., Linw.	L 2 28	
Langholm St. G14	G 9 18	
Langlands Av. G51	K11 33	
Langlands Dr. G51	K11 33	
Langlands Path G51	K12 33	
Langlands Rd. G51	K11 33	
Langlands Rd. G51	K13 34	
Langlea Av. G72	Q20 65	
Langlea Gro. G72	Q21 66	
Langlea Rd. G72	Q21 66	
Langley Av. G13	F10 18	
Langmuir Rd., Bail.	L28 41	
Langmuirhead Rd., Lenz.	F22 24	
Langness Rd. G33	K22 38	
Langrig Rd. G21	H19 23	
Langshot St. G51	L14 34	
Langside Av. G41	N15 51	
Langside Av., Udd.	P29 69	
Langside Dr. G43	P15 63	
Langside Dr. G78	N07 42	
Langside Gdns. G42	O16 51	
Langside La. G42	N16 51	
Langside Pk. G78	N07 42	
Langside Pl. G41	O15 51	
Langside Rd. G42	O16 51	
Langside Rd., Both.	R28 69	
Langside St., Clyde.	C 9 6	
Langstile Pl. G52	L 9 32	
Langstile Rd. G52	L 9 32	
Langton Cres. G53	N11 49	
Langton Cres., Barr.	R 8 59	
Langton Gdns., Bail.	M24 55	
Langton Rd. G53	N11 49	
Langtree Av., Giff.	R13 62	
Lanrig Pl., Chr.	F26 26	
Lanrig Rd., Chr.	F26 26	
Lansbury Gdns., Pais.	K 5 30	
Cowdie St.		
Lansdowne Cres. G20	J15 35	
Lansdowne Cres. La. G12	H15 21	
Great Western Rd.		
Lanton Dr. G52	L10 32	
Lanton Rd. G43	P15 63	
Lappin St., Clyde.	F 8 17	
Larch Av., Bish.	F19 23	
Larch Av., Lenz.	C23 13	
Larch Cres., Lenz.	C23 13	
Larch Ct., Cumb.	B 4 71	
Larch Gro. G67	B 5 71	
Larch Pl., John.	O 1 44	
Larch Rd. G41	M13 50	
Larch Rd., Cumb.	B 4 71	
Larches, The, Chr.	D28 15	
Larchfield Av. G14	H10 18	
Larchfield Dr. G73	Q19 65	
Larchfield Pl. G14	H10 18	
Larchfield Rd. G69	E27 15	
Larchfield Rd., Bear.	E12 7	
Larchgrove Av. G32	L23 39	
Larchgrove Pl. G32	K23 39	
Larchgrove Rd.		
Larchgrove Rd. G32	K23 39	
Larchwood Ter., Barr.	R 9 60	
Largie Rd. G43	P15 63	
Largo Pl. G51	K12 33	
Largs St. G31	K19 37	
Larkfield Rd., Lenz.	C24 13	
Larkfield St. G42	N16 51	
Cathcart Rd.		
Larkin Gdns., Pais.	K 5 30	
Lasswade St. G14	G 9 18	
Latherton Dr. G20	G14 20	
Latherton Pl. G20	G14 20	
Latherton Dr.		
Latimer Gdns. G52	M10 48	
Lauder Dr. G73	O20 53	
Lauder Dr., Linw.	L 1 28	
Lauder Gdns., Blan.	R26 68	

Lauder St. G5	M16 51	
Eglinton St.		
Lauderdale Gdns. G12	H13 20	
Laundry La. G33	G23 25	
Laurel Av., Dalm.	D 5 4	
Laurel Av., Lenz.	C23 13	
Laurel Bank Rd., Chr.	F25 26	
Laurel Pl. G11	J13 34	
Laurel St. G11	J13 34	
Laurel Way, Barr.	Q 7 59	
Graham St.		
Laurel Wk. G73	Q20 65	
Laurence Dr., Bear.	C11 7	
Laurie Ct., Udd.	O28 57	
Hillcrest Rd.		
Laurieston La. G51	L14 34	
Paisley Rd.		
Laurieston Way G73	Q19 65	
Laverock Ter., Chr.	E27 15	
Laverockhall St. G21	H18 22	
Law St. G40	L19 37	
Lawers Rd. G43	P13 62	
Lawers Rd., Bear.	C11 7	
Lawers Rd., Renf.	J 8 31	
Lawhill Av. G44	Q17 64	
Lawmoor Av. G5	M17 52	
Lawmoor La. G5	L17 36	
Ballater St.		
Lawmoor Rd. G5	M17 52	
Lawmoor St. G5	M17 52	
Lawn St., Pais.	L 6 30	
Lawrence Av., Giff.	R14 62	
Lawrence St. G11	J14 34	
Lawrie St. G11	J13 34	
Lawside Dr. G53	O11 49	
Laxford Av. G44	Q16 63	
Laxton Dr., Lenz.	D24 13	
Leabank Av., Pais.	O 6 46	
Leadburn Rd. G21	H20 23	
Rye Rd.		
Leadburn St. G32	K21 38	
Leader St. G33	J20 37	
Leander Cres., Renf.	J 9 32	
Leckethill St. G21	H18 22	
Springburn Rd.		
Leckie St. G43	O14 50	
Ledaig Pl. G31	K20 37	
Ledaig St. G31	K20 37	
Ledard Rd. G42	O15 51	
Ledcameroch Cres.,	D11 7	
Bear.		
Ledcameroch Pk., Bear.	D11 7	
Ledcameroch Rd.		
Ledcameroch Rd.,	D11 7	
Bear.		
Ledgowan Pl. G20	F14 20	
Ledi Dr., Bear.	B10 6	
Ledi Rd. G43	P14 62	
Ledmore Dr. G15	D 9 6	
Lednock Rd. G33	G23 25	
Lednock Rd. G52	L10 32	
Lee Av. G33	J21 38	
Lee Cres., Bish.	F18 22	
Leebank Dr. G44	R15 63	
Leefield Av. G44	R15 63	
Leehill Rd. G21	F18 22	
Leeside Rd. G21	F18 22	
Leewood Dr. G44	R15 63	
Leicester Av. G12	G13 20	
Leighton St. G20	G15 21	
Leitchland Rd. G78	O 2 44	
Leitchs Ct. G1	L17 36	
Trongate		
Leith St. G33	K20 37	
Leithland Av. G53	O10 48	
Leithland Rd. G53	N10 48	
Lendale La., Bish.	D19 11	
Lendel Pl. G51	L15 35	
Paisley Rd. W.		
Lenhall Dr. G45	R18 64	
Lenhall Ter. G45	R18 64	
Lennox Av. G14	H11 19	
Lennox Cres., Bish.	F18 22	
Lennox Ct., Bear.	B12 7	
Lennox Dr., Bear.	C12 7	
Lennox Dr., Clyde.	B 8 5	
Lennox La. W. G14	H11 19	
Lennox Av.		
Lennox Pl. G14	H11 19	
Scotstoun St.		

Lennox Pl., Dalm.	D 6 4
Swindon St.	
Lennox Rd., Cumb.	C 2 70
Lennox Ter., Pais.	K 7 31
Lennox Vw., Clyde.	D 7 5
Granville St.	
Lentran St. G34	K26 40
Leny St. G20	H16 21
Lenzie Dr. G21	G18 22
Lenzie Rd. G33	G23 25
Lenzie St. G21	G18 22
Lenziemill Rd., Cumb.	D 3 71
Lerwick St. G4	J16 35
Dobbies Loan	
Leslie Rd. G41	N15 51
Leslie St. G41	M15 51
Lesmuir Dr. G14	G10 18
Lesmuir Pl. G14	G 9 18
Letham Ct. G43	P15 63
Letham Dr. G43	P15 63
Letham Dr. G64	F20 23
Lethamhill Cres. G33	J21 38
Lethamhill Pl. G33	J21 38
Lethamhill Rd. G33	J21 38
Letherby Dr. G44	O16 51
Lethington Av. G41	O15 51
Letterickhills Cres. G72	Q24 67
Lettoch St. G51	L13 34
Leven Av., Bish.	E19 11
Leven Ct., Barr.	P 7 59
Leven Dr., Bear.	D12 7
Leven Sq., Renf.	H 7 17
Leven St. G41	M15 51
Leven Vw., Clyde.	D 7 5
Radnor St.	
Leven Way, Pais.	N 3 45
Levern Cres., Barr.	R 7 59
Levern Gdns., Barr.	Q 7 59
Chappel St.	
Levernside Av., Barr.	R 7 59
Levernside Cres. G53	N10 48
Levernside Rd. G53	N10 48
Lewis Av., Renf.	J 8 31
Lewis Ct., Kilb.	N07 42
Lewis Gdns., Bear.	C10 6
Lewiston Dr. G23	E14 8
Lewiston Rd.	
Lewiston Pl. G23	E14 8
Lewiston Rd.	
Lewiston Rd. G23	E14 8
Lexwell Av., John.	M 2 44
Lexwell Rd., Pais.	N 3 45
Leyden Ct. G20	G15 21
Leyden St.	
Leyden Gdns. G20	G15 21
Leyden St.	
Leyden St. G20	G15 21
Leys, The, Bish.	E19 11
Liberton St. G33	K20 37
Liberty Av., Bail.	L28 41
Libo Av. G53	N11 49
Liddale Way G73	O18 52
Liddel Rd., Cumb.	C 2 70
Liddell St. G32	N23 55
Liddesdale Av.	O 2 44
Liddesdale Pl. G22	F17 22
Liddesdale Sq.	
Liddesdale Rd. G22	F17 22
Liddesdale Sq. G22	F17 22
Liddesdale Ter. G22	F18 22
Liff Gdns., Bish.	F20 23
Liff Pl. G34	J26 40
Lightburn Pl. G32	K22 38
Lightburn Rd. G72	Q23 67
Lilac Av., Dalm.	D 6 4
Lilac Pl., John.	N 1 44
Lily St. G40	M19 53
Lilybank Av. G72	Q23 67
Lilybank Av., Chr.	F26 26
Lilybank Gardens La. G12	H14 20
Great George St.	
Lilybank Gdns. G12	J14 34
Lilybank Ter. G12	H14 20
Great George St.	
Lilybank Terrace La. G12	H14 20
Great George St.	
Lilyburn Pl. G15	C 9 6
Lime Gro., Blan.	R26 68
Lime Gro., Lenz.	C23 13
Lime St. G14	H11 19
Limecraigs Cres., Pais.	O 5 46
Limecraigs Rd., Pais.	O 5 46
Limekiln St., Clyde.	B 8 5
Limeside Av. G73	O19 53
Limeside Gdns. G73	O20 53
Calderwood Rd.	
Limetree Av., Udd.	O28 57
Limetree Dr., Dalm.	D 7 5
Linacre Dr. G32	L23 39
Linacre Gdns. G32	L23 39
Linbank Av. G53	O11 49
Linburn Pl. G52	L10 32
Linburn Rd. G52	K 9 32
Linclive Link Rd., Linw.	L 3 29
Linclive Ter., Linw.	L 2 28
Lincoln Av. G13	G10 18
Lincoln Av., Udd.	N27 57
Lincuan Av., Giff.	S14 62
Lindams, Udd.	P27 69
Linden St. G13	F12 19
Lindores Av. G73	O19 53
Lindores St. G42	O16 51
Somerville Dr.	
Lindrick Dr. G23	E15 9
Lindsay Dr. G12	G13 20
Lindsay Pl. G12	G13 20
Lindsay Pl., Lenz.	D23 13
Lindsaybeg Rd., Lenz.& Chr.	D24 13
Linfern Rd. G12	H14 20
Links Rd. G32	M23 55
Links Rd. G44	Q17 64
Linkwood Av. G15	D 9 6
Kinfauns Dr.	
Linkwood Cres. G15	D 9 6
Linkwood Dr. G15	D 9 6
Linkwood Pl. G15	D 9 6
Kinfauns Dr.	
Linlithgow Gdns. G32	L23 39
Linn Cres., Pais.	O 5 46
Linn Dr. G44	Q15 63
Linnet Av., John.	O08 43
Linnhe Av. G44	Q16 63
Linnhe Av., Bish.	E19 11
Linnhe Dr., Barr.	P 7 59
Linnhe Pl., Blan.	R26 68
Linnhead Dr. G53	P10 60
Linnhead Pl. G14	H10 18
Linnpark Av. G44	R15 63
Linnpark Ct. G44	R15 63
Linnpark Gdns., John.	N 1 44
Lunn Brae	
Linside Av., Pais.	M 7 47
Lintfield Loan, Udd.	P28 69
Myers Cres.	
Linthaugh Rd. G53	N10 48
Linthouse Bldgs. G51	K12 33
Lintlaw Dr. G52	L11 33
Lintlaw, Blan.	R26 68
Linton St. G33	K21 38
Linwell Cres., Pais.	O 5 46
Linwood Ct. G44	P16 63
Bowling Green Rd.	
Linwood Moss Rd., Linw.	L 2 28
Linwood Rd., John.	L 2 28
Linwood Ter. G12	H15 21
Glasgow St.	
Lismore Av., Renf.	J 8 31
Lismore Dr., Pais.	O 5 46
Lismore Gdns., John.	N08 43
Lismore Pl., Chr.	D28 15
Altnacreag Gdns.	
Lismore Rd. G12	H13 20
Lister Rd. G52	K10 32
Lister St. G4	J17 36
Lithgow Cres., Pais.	N 7 47
Little Dovehill G1	L17 36
Little Holm, Dalm.	D 6 4
Little St. G3	K15 35
Littlehill St. G21	H18 22
Edgefauld Rd.	
Littleton Dr. G23	E14 8
Rothes Dr.	
Littleton St. G23	E14 8
Rothes Dr.	
Livingstone Av. G52	K10 32
Livingstone Cres., Blan.	R26 68
Livingstone St. G21	H17 22
Keppochhill Rd.	
Livingstone St., Clyde.	E 8 5
Lloyd Av. G32	N22 54
Lloyd St. G31	K19 37
Loanbank Quad. G51	K13 34
Loancroft Av., Bail.	M26 56
Loancroft Gdns., Udd.	B27 69
Loancroft Pl., Bail.	M25 56
Loanend Cotts. G72	R24 67
Loanfoot Av. G13	F10 18
Loanhead Av., Renf.	H 8 17
Loanhead St. G32	K21 38
Loaning, The, Lenz.	B23 13
Lobnitz Av., Renf.	H 8 17
Loch Achray St. G32	M23 55
Loch Katrine St. G32	M23 55
Loch Laidon St. G32	M23 55
Loch Rd., Lenz.	B23 13
Loch Voil St. G32	M23 55
Lochaber Dr. G73	Q20 65
Lochaber Rd., Bear.	E13 8
Lochaline Av. G78	N 4 45
Lochaline Dr. G44	Q16 63
Lochalsh Dr., Pais.	N 4 45
Lochalsh Pl., Blan.	R25 68
Lochar Cres. G53	N11 49
Lochard Dr., Pais.	N 4 45
Lochay St. G32	M23 55
Lochbrae Dr. G73	Q20 65
Lochbridge Rd. G33	K25 40
Lochbroom Dr., Pais.	N 4 45
Lochburn Cres. G20	F15 21
Lochburn Gro. G20	F15 21
Cadder Rd.	
Lochburn Pass. G20	F15 21
Lochburn Rd. G20	G14 20
Lochdochart Path G34	K26 40
Lochdochart Rd.	
Lochdochart Rd. G34	K26 40
Lochearn Cres., Pais.	N 4 45
Lochearnhead Rd. G33	G23 25
Lochend Av., Gart.	F27 27
Lochend Cres., Bear.	D11 7
Lochend Dr., Bear.	D11 7
Lochend Rd. G34	J25 40
Lochend Rd., Bear.	D12 7
Lochend Rd., Gart.	F27 27
Locher Rd., Kilb.	M06 42
Locherbie Av. G43	P15 63
Lochfauld Rd. G23	E16 9
Lochfield Cres., Pais.	N 6 46
Lochfield Dr., Pais.	N 7 47
Lochfield Rd., Pais.	N 6 46
Lochgilp St. G20	F14 20
Lochgoin Av. G15	D 9 6
Lochgreen St. G33	H21 24
Lochhead Av., Linw.	L 1 28
Lochiel La. G73	Q20 65
Lochiel Rd., Thorn.	Q12 61
Lochinver Cres., Pais.	N 4 45
Lochinver Dr. G44	Q16 63
Lochinver Gro. G72	P23 67
Andrew Sillars Av.	
Lochlea Av., Clyde.	D 8 5
Lochlea Rd. G43	P14 62
Lochlea Rd. G73	P18 64
Lochlea Rd., Cumb.	B 4 71
Lochleven La. G42	O16 51
Battlefield Rd.	
Lochleven Rd. G42	O16 51
Lochlibo Av. G13	G 9 18
Lochlibo Cres., Barr.	R 7 59
Lochlibo Rd., Barr.	R 7 59
Lochmaben Rd. G52	M 9 48
Lochmaddy Av. G44	Q16 63
Lochside G41	N15 51
Minard Rd.	
Lochside, Bear.	D12 7
Drymen Rd.	
Lochside, Gart.	G27 27
Lochview Cotts., Gart.	H27 27
Lochview Cres. G33	H21 24
Lochview Dr. G33	H21 24
Lochview Gdns. G33	H21 24
Lochview Pl. G33	H21 24
Lochview Rd., Bear.	D12 7
Lochview Ter., Gart.	G27 27
Lochwood St. G33	J21 38
Lochy Av., Renf.	J 9 32

Name	Ref
Lochy Gdns., Bish.	E19 11
Lockhart Av. G72	P23 67
Lockhart Dr. G72	P23 67
Lockhart St. G21	J19 37
Locksley Av. G13	F11 19
Locksley Rd., Pais.	N 3 45
Logan Dr., Cumb.	B 1 70
Logan Dr., Pais.	L 5 30
Logan St. G5	N17 52
Logan Tower G72	Q24 67
Claude Av.	
Loganswell Dr. G46	R11 61
Loganswell Gdns. G46	R12 61
Loganswell Pl. G46	R12 61
Loganswell Rd. G46	R12 61
Logie St. G51	K13 34
Lomax St. G33	K20 37
Lomond Av., Renf.	J 7 31
Lomond Cres., Pais.	O 5 46
Lomond Ct., Barr.	R 8 59
Lomond Dr., Barr.	Q 7 59
Lomond Dr., Udd.	Q28 69
Lomond Gdns., John.	N 2 44
Lomond Pl. G33	H23 25
Lomond Rd., Bear.	E12 7
Lomond Rd., Bish.	D18 10
Lomond Rd., Lenz.	C23 13
Lomond Rd., Udd.	N27 57
Lomond St. G22	G16 21
Lomond Vw., Clyde.	D 7 5
Granville St.	
London Arcade G1	L17 36
London Rd.	
London La. G1	L17 36
London Rd.	
London Rd. G1	L17 36
London St., Renf.	G 8 17
Long Row, Bail.	L26 40
Longay Pl. G22	F17 22
Longay St. G22	F17 22
Longcroft Dr., Renf.	H 8 17
Longdale Rd., Chr.	E27 15
Longden St., Clyde.	F 8 17
Longford St. G33	K20 37
Longlee, Bail.	M25 56
Longmeadow, John.	N08 43
Longstone Rd. G33	K22 38
Longwill Ter., Cumb.	B 3 71
Lonmay Rd. G33	K23 39
Lonsdale Av., Giff.	Q14 62
Loom St. G40	L18 36
Stevenson St.	
Loom Wk., Kilb.	M07 42
Shuttle St.	
Lora Dr. G52	M12 49
Loretto Pl. G33	K21 38
Loretto St. G33	K21 38
Lorne Av., Chr.	F26 26
Lorne Cres., Bish.	E20 11
Lorne Dr., Linw.	L 1 28
Lorne Pl. G42	O16 51
Cathcart Rd.	
Lorne Rd. G52	K 9 32
Lorne St. G51	L14 34
Lorne Ter. G72	Q21 66
Lorraine Gdns. G12	H14 20
Kensington Rd.	
Lorraine Rd. G12	H14 20
Loskin Dr. G22	F16 21
Lossie Cres., Renf.	J 9 32
Lossie St. G33	J20 37
Lothian Cres., Pais.	N 5 46
Lothian Dr., Clark.	R14 62
Lothian Gdns. G20	H15 21
Lothian St. G52	K 9 32
Loudon Gdns.	M 1 44
Loudon Rd. G33	G22 24
Loudon Ter. G12	H14 20
Observatory Rd.	
Lounsdale Cres., Pais.	N 4 45
Lounsdale Dr., Pais.	N 4 45
Lounsdale Pl. G14	H10 18
Lounsdale Rd., Pais.	N 4 45
Lourdes Av. G52	M11 49
Lovat Pl. G73	Q20 65
Lovat St. G4	J17 36
Love St., Pais.	L 6 30
Low Barholm, Kilb.	N07 42
Low Cres., Clyde.	F 9 18
Low Parksail, Renf.	F 5 16
Low Rd., Pais.	M 5 46
Lower Bourtree Dr. G73	Q20 65
Lower English Bldgs. G42	M16 51
Lower Millgate, Udd.	O27 57
New Sneddon St.	
Lowndes La., Pais.	L 6 30
Lowndes St., Barr.	R 8 59
Lowther Ter. G12	H14 20
Loyne Dr., Renf.	J 9 32
Morriston Cres.	
Luath St. G51	K13 34
Lubas Av. G42	O17 52
Lubas Pl. G42	O17 52
Lubnaig Rd. G43	P15 63
Luckingsford Av., Renf.	F 5 16
Luckingsford Dr., Renf.	F 5 16
Luckingsford Rd., Renf.	F 5 16
Lucy Brae, Udd.	O27 57
Ludovic Sq., John.	M09 43
Luffness Gdns. G32	N22 54
Lugar Dr. G52	M12 49
Lugar Pl. G44	P18 64
Luggiebank Pl., Bail.	M28 57
Luing Rd. G52	L12 33
Lumloch St. G21	H19 23
Lumsden La. G3	K14 34
Lumsden St.	
Lumsden St. G3	K14 34
Lunan Dr., Bish.	F20 23
Lunan Pl. G51	K12 33
Luncarty Pl. G32	M22 54
Luncarty St. G32	M22 54
Lunderston Dr. G53	O10 48
Lundie Gdns., Bish.	F20 23
Lundie St. G32	M21 54
Lunn Brae, John.	N09 43
Luss Rd. G51	K12 33
Lusset Vw., Clyde.	D 7 5
Radnor St.	
Lusshill Ter., Udd.	N25 56
Lyall Pl. G21	H17 22
Keppochhill Rd.	
Lyall St. G21	H17 22
Lybster Cres. G73	Q20 65
Lye Brae, Cumb.	C 3 71
Lye Ter., Pais.	N 6 46
Lymburn St. G3	K14 34
Lyndale Pl. G20	F14 20
Lyndale Rd. G20	F14 20
Lyndhurst Gdns. G20	H15 21
Lyne Croft, Bish.	D19 11
Lyne Dr. G23	E15 9
Lynedoch Cres. G3	J15 35
Lynedoch Pl. G3	J15 35
Lynedoch St. G3	J15 35
Lynedoch Ter. G3	J15 35
Lynn Gdns. G12	H14 20
Great George St.	
Lynn Wk., Udd.	P28 69
Flax Rd.	
Lynnhurst, Udd.	O27 57
Lynton Av., Giff.	R13 62
Lyon Cross Av., Barr.	R 8 59
Lyon Rd., Pais.	N 3 45
Lyoncross Cres., Barr.	Q 8 59
Lyoncross Rd. G53	N10 48
Lytham Dr. G23	E15 9
Lytham Meadows, Both.	R27 69
Macbeth Pl. G31	M20 53
Macbeth St.	
Macbeth St. G31	M20 53
Macdougal St. G43	O14 50
Macdowall St., John.	M09 43
Macdowall St., Pais.	L 5 30
Macduff Pl. G31	M20 53
Macduff St. G31	M20 53
Mace Rd. G13	E11 7
Macfarlane Rd., Bear.	E12 7
Machrie Dr. G45	Q18 64
Machrie Rd. G45	Q18 64
Machrie St. G45	Q18 64
Mackean St., Pais.	L 5 30
Mackeith St. G40	M18 52
Mackenchnie St. G31	K13 34
Mackenzie Dr. John.	O07 42
Mackie St. G4	H17 22
Borron St.	
Mackiesmill Rd., John.	O 2 44
Mackinlay St. G5	M16 51
Maclay Av., Kilb.	N07 42
Maclean St. G41	L15 35
Maclean St. G51	L14 34
Maclean St., Clyde.	F 9 18
Wood Quadrant	
Maclehose Rd., Cumb.	B 4 71
Maclellan St. G41	L14 34
Madison Av. G44	P16 63
Madison La. G44	P16 63
Carmunnock Rd.	
Madras Pl. G40	M18 52
Madras St.	
Madras St. G40	M18 52
Mafeking St. G51	L13 34
Magdalen Way, Pais.	O 2 44
Magnus Cres. G44	Q16 63
Mahon Ct., Chr.	E27 15
Maida St. G43	O13 50
Maidland Rd. G53	O11 49
Mailerbeg Gdns., Chr.	D27 15
Mailing Av., Bish.	E19 11
Main Rd., John.	M 2 44
Main Rd., Pais.	M 5 46
Main St. G40	M18 52
Main St. G72	P22 66
Main St. G73	O19 53
Main St., Bail.	M25 56
Main St., Barr.	R 7 59
Main St., Both.	R28 69
Main St., Chr.	E26 14
Main St., Cumb.	A 3 71
Main St., Thorn.	Q12 61
Main St., Udd.	P27 69
Mainhead Ter., Cumb.	A 3 71
Roadside	
Mainhill Av., Bail.	L26 40
Mainhill Pl., Bail.	L26 40
Mainhill Rd., Bail.	L27 41
Mains Av., Giff.	R13 62
Mains Dr., Renf.	E 5 4
Mains Hill, Renf.	E 5 4
Mains Holm, Renf.	E 5 4
Mains River, Renf.	E 5 4
Mains Wood, Renf.	E 5 4
Mainscroft, Renf.	E 5 4
Mair St. G51	L15 35
Maitland Pl., Renf.	J 7 31
Maitland St. G4	J16 35
Malcolm St. G31	L20 37
Malin Pl. G33	K21 38
Mallaig Path G51	K11 33
Mallaig Pl. G51	K11 33
Mallaig Rd. G51	K11 33
Mallard Rd., Clyde.	C 7 5
Malloch Cres., John.	N 1 44
Malloch St. G20	G15 21
Malta St., Clyde.	F 8 17
Maltbarns St. G20	H16 21
Malvern Ct. G31	L19 37
Malvern Way, Pais.	K 5 30
Mambeg Dr. G51	K12 33
Mamore Pl. G43	P14 62
Mamore St. G43	P14 62
Manchester Dr. G12	G13 20
Manitoba Pl. G31	L19 37
Janefield St.	
Mannering Ct. G41	O14 50
Pollokshaws Rd.	
Mannering Rd. G41	O14 50
Mannering Rd., Pais.	O 3 45
Mannofield, Bear.	D11 7
Chesters Rd.	
Manor Rd. G14	H12 19
Manor Rd. G15	E 9 6
Manor Rd., Gart.	G27 27
Manor Rd., Pais.	N 3 45
Manor Way G73	Q19 65
Manse Av., Bear.	C12 7
Manse Brae G44	P16 63
Manse Ct., Barr.	Q 8 59
Manse Rd. G32	M23 55
Manse Rd., Bail.	L27 41
Manse Rd., Bear.	C12 7
Manse St., Renf.	H 8 17
Mansefield Av. G72	Q22 66
Mansefield Dr., Udd.	P28 69
Mansefield Gdns. G11	J14 34
Mansel St. G21	G18 22
Mansewood Rd. G43	P13 62

Street	Grid	Pg
Mansfield Rd. G52	K 9	32
Mansion Ct. G72	P22	66
Mansion St. G22	G17	22
Mansion St. G72	P22	66
Mansionhouse Av. G32	O23	55
Mansionhouse Dr. G32	L23	39
Mansionhouse Gdns. G41	O15	51
Mansionhouse Rd.		
Mansionhouse Rd. G32	M24	55
Mansionhouse Rd. G42	O15	51
Mansionhouse Rd., Pais.	L 7	31
Maple Ct., Barr.	S 8	59
Oakbank Dr.		
Maple Dr., Dalm.	C 6	4
Maple Dr., John.	O 1	44
Maple Dr., Lenz.	C22	12
Maple Rd. G41	M13	50
Mar Gdns. G73	Q20	65
March La. G41	N15	51
Nithsdale Dr.		
March St. G41	N15	51
Marchfield Av., Pais.	K 5	30
Marchfield, Bish.	D18	10
Marchfield, Bish.	D18	10
Westlands		
Marchglen Pl. G51	K11	33
Mallaig Rd.		
Marchmont Gdns., Bish.	D18	10
Marchmont Ter. G12	H14	20
Observatory Rd.		
Maree Dr. G52	M12	49
Maree Gdns., Bish.	E19	11
Maree Rd., Pais.	N 4	45
Marfield St. G32	L21	38
Margaret St. G41	K17	36
Martha St.		
Margarette Bldgs. G44	P16	63
Clarkston Rd.		
Marguerite Av., Lenz.	C23	13
Marguerite Dr., Lenz.	C23	13
Marguerite Gdns., Lenz.	C23	13
Marguerite Gdns., Udd.	Q28	69
Marguerite Gro., Lenz.	C23	13
Mariscat Rd. G41	N15	51
Marjory Dr., Pais.	K 7	31
Marjory Rd., Renf.	J 7	31
Market Rd., Lenz.	B25	14
Market St. G40	L18	36
Markinch St. G5	L16	35
West St.		
Marlborough Av. G11	H12	19
Marlinford Rd., Renf.	H10	18
Marlow St. G41	M15	51
Marlow Ter. G41	L15	35
Seaward St.		
Marmion Pl., Cumb.	D 2	70
Marmion Rd., Cumb.	D 2	70
Marmion Rd., Pais.	O 3	45
Marmion St. G20	H15	21
Marne St. G31	K19	37
Marnock Ter., Pais.	N 7	47
Marnock Way, Chr.	E27	15
Braeside Av.		
Marr St. G51	K13	34
Marshalls La., Pais.	M 6	46
Mart St. G1	L17	36
Martha St. G1	K17	36
Martin Cres., Bail.	L26	40
Martin St. G40	M18	52
Martlet Dr., John.	O08	43
Martyr St. G4	K18	36
Martyrs Pl. G64	F19	23
Marwick St. G31	K19	37
Marwood Av., Chr. & Waterside	C25	14
Mary St. G4	J16	35
Mary St., John.	M 1	44
Mary St., Pais.	N 6	46
Maryhill Rd., Bear.& G20	E13	8
Maryland Dr. G52	L12	33
Maryland Gdns. G52	L12	33
Marys La., Renf.	H 8	17
Maryston Pl. G33	J20	37
Maryston St. G33	J20	37
Maryview Gdns., Udd.	N26	56
Edinburgh Rd.		
Maryville Av., Giff.	R14	62
Maryville Vw., Udd.	N26	56
Marywood Sq. G41	N15	51
Masonfield Av., Cumb.	C 1	70
Masterton St. G21	H17	22
Mathieson La. G5	M17	52
Mathieson St.		
Mathieson Rd. G73	N20	53
Mathieson St. G5	M17	52
Mathieson St., Pais.	L 7	31
Matilda Rd. G41	M15	51
Mauchline St. G5	M16	51
Maukinfauld Ct. G31	M21	54
Maukinfauld Rd. G32	M21	54
Mauldslie St. G40	M19	53
Maule Dr. G11	J13	34
Mause Av., Both.	R28	69
Mavis Bank, Bish.	F18	22
Mavisbank Rd. G51	K13	34
Govan Rd.		
Mavisbank Ter., Pais.	M 6	46
Maxton Av., Barr.	Q 7	59
Maxton Gro., Barr.	Q 7	59
Maxton Ter. G72	Q21	66
Maxwell Av. G41	M15	51
Maxwell Av., Bail.	M25	56
Maxwell Av., Bear.	E12	7
Maxwell Dr. G41	M14	50
Maxwell Dr., Bail.	L25	40
Maxwell Gdns. G41	M14	50
Maxwell Gro. G41	M14	50
Maxwell Oval G41	M15	51
Maxwell Pl. G41	M16	51
Maxwell Rd. G41	M15	51
Maxwell Sq. G41	M15	51
Maxwell St. G18	L17	36
Maxwell St., Bail.	M25	56
Maxwell St., Dalm.	D 6	4
Maxwell St., Pais.	L 6	30
Maxwellton Rd. G78	M 4	45
Maxwellton St., Pais.	M 5	46
Maxwelton Rd. G33	J20	37
May Rd., Pais.	O 6	46
May Ter. G42	O16	51
Prospecthill Rd.		
May Ter., Giff.	Q14	62
Maybank La. G42	N16	51
Victoria Rd.		
Maybank St. G42	N16	51
Mayberry Cres. G32	L23	39
Mayberry Gdns. G32	L23	39
Maybole St. G53	P 9	60
Mayfield St. G20	G15	21
McAlpine St. G2	L16	35
McArthur St. G43	O14	50
Pleasance St.		
McArthur St., Clyde.	G 8	17
McAslin Ct. G4	K17	36
McAslin St. G4	K18	36
McCallum Av. G73	O19	53
McClue Av., Renf.	H 7	17
McClue Rd., Renf.	H 7	17
McCracken Av., Renf.	J 7	31
McCreery St., Clyde.	F 8	17
McCulloch St. G41	M15	51
McDonald Av., John.	N09	43
McDonald Cres., Clyde.	F 8	17
McEwan St. G31	L20	37
McFarlane St. G4	L18	36
McFarlane St., Pais.	K 5	30
McGhee St., Clyde.	D 7	5
McGown St., Pais.	L 5	30
McGregor Av., Renf.	J 7	31
Porterfield Rd.		
McGregor Rd., Cumb.	C 2	70
McGregor St. G51	L12	33
McGregor St., Clyde.	F 8	17
McIntoch Ct. G31	K18	36
McIntoch St.		
McIntoch St. G31	K18	36
McIntyre Pl., Pais.	N 5	46
McIntyre St. G72	K15	35
McIntyre Ter. G72	P22	66
McIver St. G72	P23	67
McKay Cres., John.	N 1	44
McKenzie Av., Clyde.	D 7	5
McKenzie St., Pais.	L 5	30
McKerrel St., Pais.	L 7	31
McLaren Av., Renf.	J 8	31
Newmains Rd.		
McLaurin Cres., John.	N08	43
McLean Pl., Pais.	K 5	30
McLean Sq. G51	L14	34
McLean St., Clyde.	F 9	18
Wood Quad.		
McLennan St. G42	O16	51
McNair St. G32	L22	38
McNeil St. G5	M17	52
McNeill Av., Clyde.	E 9	6
McPhail St. G40	M18	52
McPhater St. G4	J16	35
Dunblane St.		
McPherson Dr., Udd.	Q28	69
Wordsworth Way		
McPherson St. G1	L17	36
High St.		
McTaggart Rd., Cumb.	D 2	70
Meadow La., Renf.	G 8	17
Meadow Rd. G11	J13	34
Meadow Vw., Cumb.	B 4	71
Meadowbank La., Udd.	P27	69
Meadowburn Av. G66	C24	13
Meadowburn, Bish.	D19	11
Meadowhead Av., Chr.	E27	15
Meadowpark St. G31	K19	37
Meadowside Av., John.	N 2	44
Meadowside St. G11	J13	34
Meadowside St., Renf.	G 8	17
Meadowwell St. G32	L22	38
Meadside Av. G78	M07	42
Meadside Rd., Kilb.	M07	42
Mears Way, Bish.	E20	11
Medlar Rd., Cumb.	C 4	71
Medwin St. G72	P24	67
Mill Rd.		
Medwyn St. G14	H11	19
Meek Pl. G72	P22	66
Meetinghouse La., Pais.	L 6	30
Moss St.		
Megan Gate G40	M18	52
Megan St.		
Megan St. G40	M18	52
Meikle Av., Renf.	J 8	31
Meikle Rd. G53	O11	49
Meiklerig Cres. G53	N11	49
Meikleriggs Dr., Pais.	N 4	45
Meiklewood Rd. G51	L11	33
Melbourne Av., Dalm.	C 5	4
Melbourne Ct., Giff.	Q14	62
Melbourne St. G31	L18	36
Meldon Pl. G51	K12	33
Meldrum Gdns. G41	N14	50
Meldrum St., Clyde.	F 9	18
Melford Av., Giff.	R14	62
Melford Way, Pais.	K 7	31
Knock Way		
Melfort Av., Clyde.	D 7	5
Melfort Av., G41	M13	50
Melfort Gdns., John.	N08	43
Milliken Park Rd.		
Mellerstain Dr. G14	G 9	18
Melness Pl. G51	K11	33
Mallaig Rd.		
Melrose Av. G73	O19	53
Melrose Av., Bail.	L27	41
Melrose Av., Linw.	L 1	28
Melrose Av., Pais.	N 4	45
Melrose Gdns. G20	H15	21
Melrose Gdns., Udd.	N27	57
Lincoln Av.		
Melrose Pl., Blan.	R26	68
Melrose St. G4	J16	35
Queens Cres.		
Melvaig Pl. G20	G14	20
Melvick Pl. G51	K11	33
Mallaig Rd.		
Melville Ct. G1	K17	36
Brunswick St.		
Melville Gdns., Bish.	E19	11
Melville St. G41	M15	51
Memel St. G21	G18	22
Memus Av. G52	M11	49
Mennock Dr., Bish.	D19	11
Menock Rd. G44	P16	63
Menteith Av., Bish.	E19	11
Menteith Dr. G73	R20	65
Menteith Pl. G73	R20	65
Menzies Dr. G21	G19	23
Menzies Pl. G21	G19	23
Menzies Rd. G21	G19	23
Merchant La. G1	L17	36
Clyde St.		

Merchants Clo., Pais. M07 42
Church St.
Merchiston Av., Linw. L 1 28
Merchiston St. G32 K21 38
Merkland Ct. G11 J13 34
Vine St.
Merkland St. G11 J13 34
Merksworth Way, Pais. K 5 30
Mosslands Rd.
Merlewood Av. G71 Q28 69
Merlin Way, Pais. K 7 31
Merrick Gdns. G51 L13 34
Merrick Ter., Udd. O28 57
Merrick Way G73 Q19 65
Merryburn Av., Giff. P14 62
Merrycrest Av., Giff. Q14 62
Merrycroft Av., Giff. Q14 62
Merryland Pl. G51 K14 34
Merryland St. G51 K13 34
Merrylee Cres., Giff. P14 62
Merrylee Park Av., Giff. Q14 62
Merrylee Park La., Giff. Q14 62
Merrylee Park Ms., Q14 62
Giff.
Merrylee Rd. G43 P14 62
Merryton Av. G15 D10 6
Merryton Av., Giff. Q14 62
Merryton Pl. G15 D10 6
Merryvale Av., Giff. Q14 62
Merryvale Pl., Giff. P14 62
Merton Dr. G52 L10 32
Meryon Gdns. G32 N23 55
Meryon Rd. G32 N23 55
Methil St. G14 H11 19
Methuen Rd., Renf. J 7 31
Methven Av., Bear. C13 8
Methven St. G31 M20 53
Methven St., Dalm. D 6 4
Metropole La. G1 L16 35
Howard St.
Michillen Rd., C14 8
Bear.& G23
Mid Cotts., Gart. H26 26
Midcroft Av. G44 P17 64
Midcroft, Bish. D18 10
Middle Hard St., Clyde. B 8 5
Middlemuir Av., Lenz. C23 13
Middlemuir Rd., Lenz. C23 13
Middlerigg Rd., Cumb. C 1 70
Middlesex St. G41 L15 35
Middleton Cres., Pais. L 5 30
Middleton Rd., Linw. K 2 28
Middleton St. G51 L14 34
Midland St. G1 L16 35
Midlem Dr. G52 L11 33
Midlem Oval G52 L11 33
Midlock St. G51 L14 34
Midlothian Dr. G41 N14 50
Midton Cotts., Chr. E28 15
Midton St. G21 H18 22
Midwharf St. G4 J17 36
Migvie Pl. G20 G14 20
Wyndford Rd.
Milan St. G41 M16 51
Milford St. G33 K22 38
Mill Cres. G40 M18 52
Mill Ct. G73 O19 53
Mill Pl., Linw. L 1 28
Mill Rd. G72 Q23 67
Mill Rd., Barr. Q 7 59
Mill Rd., Both. R28 69
Mill Rd., Clyde. F 8 17
Mill River, Lenz. D23 13
Mill Road Gdns. G40 L18 36
Mill St. G40 M18 52
Mill St. G73 O19 53
Mill St., Pais. M 6 46
Mill Vennel, Renf. H 9 18
High St.
Mill Way, Lenz. C25 14
Millands Av., Blan. R26 68
Millar St., Pais. L 6 30
Millar Ter. G73 N19 53
Millarbank St. G21 H18 22
Millarston Av., Pais. M 4 45
Millarston Dr., Pais. M 4 45
Millbeg Cres. G33 L24 39
Millbeg Pl. G33 L24 39
Millbrae Cres. G13 F 8 17
Millbrae Cres. G42 O15 51

Millbrae Ct. G42 O15 51
Millbrae Rd.
Millbrae Rd. G42 O15 51
Millbrix Av. G14 G10 18
Millburn Av. G73 P19 65
Millburn Av., Clyde. F 9 18
Millburn Av., Renf. H 9 18
Millburn Dr., Renf. H 8 17
Millburn Rd., Renf. H 8 17
Millburn St. G21 J19 37
Millburn Way, Renf. H 9 18
Millcroft Rd. G73 N18 52
Millcroft Rd., Cumb. C 3 71
Miller St. G1 K17 36
Miller St., Bail. M25 56
Miller St., Clyde. E 7 5
Miller St., John. M 1 44
Millerfield Pl. G40 M19 53
Millerfield Rd. G40 M19 53
Millers Pl., Lenz. D23 13
Millersneuk Av., Lenz. D23 13
Millersneuk Cres. G33 G22 24
Millersneuk Dr., Lenz. D23 13
Millerston St. G31 L19 37
Millford Dr., Linw. L 1 28
Millgate Av., Udd. O27 57
Millgate, Udd. O27 57
Millholm Rd. G44 Q16 63
Millhouse Cres. G20 F14 20
Millhouse Dr. G20 F14 20
Milliken Dr., Kilb. N08 43
Milliken Park Rd., Kilb. N08 42
Millpond Dr. G40 L18 36
Millport Av. G44 O17 52
Millroad Dr. G40 L18 36
Millroad St. G40 L18 36
Millwood St. G41 O15 51
Milncroft Rd. G33 J22 38
Milner Rd. G13 G12 19
Milngavie Rd., Bear. D12 7
Milnpark Gdns. G41 L15 35
Milnpark St. G41 L15 35
Milovaig St. G23 E14 8
Milrig Rd. G73 O18 52
Milton Av. G72 P21 66
Milton Douglas Rd., C 7 5
Clyde.
Milton Dr., Bish. F18 22
Milton Gdns., Udd. O27 57
Milton Mains Rd., Dalm. C 7 5
Milton St. G4 J17 35
Milverton Av., Bear. C11 7
Milverton Rd., Giff. R13 62
Minard Rd. G41 N15 51
Minard Way, Udd. O28 57
Newton Dr.
Minerva St. G3 K15 35
Minerva Way G3 K15 35
Mingarry La. G20 H14 20
Clouston St.
Mingary St. G20 H15 21
Mingulay Cres. G22 F17 22
Mingulay Pl. G22 F18 22
Mingulay St. G22 F17 22
Minmoir Rd. G53 O 9 48
Minstrel Rd. G13 E11 7
Minto Av. G73 Q20 65
Minto Cres. G52 L12 33
Minto St. G52 L12 33
Mireton St. G22 G16 21
Mirrlees Dr. G12 H14 20
Mirrlees La. G12 H14 20
Redlands Rd.
Mitchell Av. G72 P24 67
Mitchell Av., Renf. J 7 31
Mitchell Dr. G73 P19 65
Mitchell La. G1 K16 35
Buchanan St.
Mitchell Rd., Cumb. C 3 71
Mitchell St. G1 K16 35
Mitchell St., Coat. M28 57
Mitchellhill Rd. G42 R18 64
Mitchison Rd., Cumb. B 3 71
Mitre Ct. G14 H11 19
Mitre Rd.
Mitre La. G14 H12 19
Mitre La. W. G14 H12 19
Mitre La.
Mitre Rd. G14 H12 19

Moat Av. G13 F11 19
Mochrum Rd. G43 P15 63
Moffat Pl., Blan. R26 68
Moffat St. G5 M17 52
Mogarth Av., Pais. O 4 45
Amochrie Rd.
Moidart Av., Renf. H 7 17
Moidart Cres. G52 L12 33
Moidart Rd.
Moidart Ct., Barr. P 8 59
Moidart Pl. G52 L12 33
Moidart Rd.
Moidart Rd. G52 L12 33
Moir La. G1 L17 36
Moir St.
Moir St. G1 L17 36
Molendinar St. G1 L17 36
Mollinsburn St. G21 H18 22
Monach Rd. G33 K23 39
Monachie Gdns. E20 11
Muirhead Way
Moncrieff Av., Lenz. C23 13
Moncrieff Gdns., Lenz. C23 13
Moncrieff Pl. G4 J16 35
North Woodside Rd.
Moncrieff St. G4 J16 35
Balnain St.
Moncur St. G40 L18 36
Moness Dr. G52 M12 49
Monifieth Av. G52 M11 49
Monikie Gdns., Bish. E20 11
Muirhead Way
Monkcastle Dr. G73 P22 66
Monkland Av., Lenz. C23 13
Monkland View Cres., L28 41
Bail.
Monkland Vw, Udd. N28 57
Lincoln Av.
Monksbridge Av. G13 E11 7
Monkscroft Av. G11 H13 20
Monkscroft Ct. G11 J13 34
Monkscroft Gdns. G11 H13 20
Monkscroft Av.
Monkton Dr. G15 E10 6
Monmouth Av. G12 G13 20
Monreith Av., Bear. E11 7
Monreith Rd. E. G44 P16 63
Monreith Rd. G43 P14 62
Monroe Dr., Udd. N27 57
Monroe Pl., Udd. N27 57
Montague La. G12 H13 20
Montague St. G4 J15 35
Montague Ter. G12 H13 20
Hyndland Rd.
Montclair Pl., Linw. L 1 28
Monteith Dr., Clark. S15 63
Monteith Gdns., Clark. S15 63
Monteith Pl. G40 L18 36
Monteith Pl., Blan. R27 69
Monteith Row G40 L18 36
Monteith Row La. G40 L18 36
Monteith Pl.
Montford Av. G44 O17 52
Montgomerie Gdns. G14 H11 19
Lennox Av.
Montgomery Av., Pais. K 7 31
Montgomery Dr., Giff. R15 62
Montgomery Dr., Kilb. M07 42
Meadside Av.
Montgomery La. G42 O16 51
Somerville Dr.
Montgomery Rd., Pais. K 7 31
Montgomery St. G42 M18 52
London Rd.
Montgomery St. G72 P24 67
Mill Rd.
Montrave St. G52 M11 49
Montrave St. G73 N19 53
Montreal Ho., Dalm. C 5 4
Perth Cres.
Montron Dr. G15 E10 6
Moraine Av.
Montrose Av. G32 N22 54
Montrose Av. G52 K 9 32
Montrose Dr., Bear. B12 7
Montrose Gdns., Blan. R26 68
Montrose Pl., Linw. L 1 28
Montrose Rd., Pais. O 3 45
Montrose St. G4 K17 36
Montrose St., Clyde. E 7 5

Montrose Ter., Bish.	F20	23
Monymusk Gdns., Bish.	E20	11
Monymusk Pl. G15	C 9	6
Moodies Ct. G2	K16	35
Argyle St.		
Moodiesburn St. G33	J20	37
Moorburn Av., Giff.	Q13	62
Moore Dr., Bear.	D12	7
Moore St. G31	L19	37
Gallowgate		
Moorehouse Av. G13	G 9	18
Moorehouse Av., Pais.	N 4	45
Moorfoot Av. G46	Q13	62
Moorfoot Av., Pais.	N 5	46
Moorfoot St. G32	L21	38
Moorfoot, Bish.	E20	11
Moorhouse Av. G13	G 9	18
Moorhouse St., Barr.	R 8	59
Moorpark Av. G52	L 9	32
Moorpark Av., Chr.	F26	26
Moorpark Dr. G52	L10	32
Moorpark Pl. G52	L 9	32
Moorpark Sq., Renf.	J 7	31
Morag Av., Blan.	R26	68
Moraine Av. G15	E10	6
Moraine Circus G15	E10	6
Moraine Dr. G15	E10	6
Moraine Pl. G15	E10	6
Moraine Dr.		
Morar Cres., Bish.	E18	10
Morar Ct., Cumb.	DO	70
Morar Dr. G73	Q19	65
Morar Dr., Bear.	D13	8
Morar Dr., Cumb.	DO	70
Morar Dr., Linw.	L 1	28
Morar Dr., Pais.	N 4	45
Morar Pl., Renf.	H 7	17
Morar Rd. G52	L12	33
Morar Ter., Udd.	O28	57
Moravia Av., Both.	Q28	69
Moray Gate, Both.	Q27	69
Moray Gdns., Udd.	O27	57
Moray Pl. G41	N15	51
Moray Pl., Bish.	E20	11
Moray Pl., Linw.	L 1	28
Mordaunt St. G40	M19	53
Moredun Cres. G32	K23	39
Moredun Dr., Pais.	N 4	45
Moredun Rd., Pais.	N 4	45
Moredun St. G32	K23	39
Morefield Rd. G51	K11	33
Morgan Ms. G42	M16	51
Morion Rd. G13	F11	19
Morley St. G42	O16	51
Morna Pl. G14	J12	33
Victoria Park Dr. S.		
Morningside St. G33	K20	37
Morrin Path G21	H18	22
Crichton St.		
Morrin Sq. G4	K18	36
Collins St.		
Morrin St. G21	H18	22
Morris Pl. G40	L18	36
Morrison Quad., Clyde.	E 9	6
Morrison St. G5	L16	35
Morrison St., Clyde.	C 6	4
Morrisons Ct. G2	K16	35
Argyle St.		
Morriston Cres., Renf.	J 9	32
Morriston St. G72	P22	66
Mortimer St. G20	H15	21
Hotspur St.		
Morton Gdns. G41	N14	50
Morven Av., Bish.	E20	11
Morven Av., Blan.	R26	68
Morven Av., Pais.	O 5	46
Morven Dr., Linw.	L 1	28
Morven Gdns., Udd.	O27	57
Morven Rd. G72	Q21	66
Morven Rd., Bear.	C12	7
Morven St. G52	L12	33
Mosesfield St. G21	G18	22
Mosesfield Ter. G21	G18	22
Balgray Hill Rd.		
Moss Av., Linw.	L 1	28
Moss Dr., Barr.	P 7	59
Moss Heights Av. G52	L11	33
Moss Knowe, Cumb.	C 4	71
Moss Rd. G51	K11	33
Moss Rd., Chr.	F26	26
Moss Rd., Cumb.	B 4	71
Moss Rd., Lenz.	C23	13
Moss Sq. G33	J22	38
Moss St., Pais.	L 6	30
Moss-side Rd. G41	N15	51
Mossbank Dr. G33	H21	24
Mosscastle Rd. G33	J23	39
Mossend La. G33	K23	39
Mossend Rd., Pais.	K 5	30
Mosslands Rd.		
Mossend St. G33	K23	39
Mossgiel Av. G73	P19	65
Mossgiel Dr., Clyde.	D 8	5
Mossgiel Gdns., Udd.	O27	57
Mossgiel Pl. G73	P19	65
Mossgiel Rd. G43	P14	62
Mossgiel Rd., Cumb.	C 3	71
Mossgiel Ter., Blan.	R26	68
Mosshead Rd., Bear.	B13	8
Mossland Rd. G52	K 9	32
Mosslands Rd. G52	J 9	32
Mosslands Rd., Pais.	K 5	30
Mossneuk Dr., Pais.	O 5	46
Mosspark Av. G52	M12	49
Mosspark Boulevard G52	M12	49
Mosspark Dr. G52	M11	49
Mosspark La. G52	N12	49
Mosspark Dr.		
Mosspark Oval G52	M12	49
Mosspark Sq. G52	M12	49
Mossvale Cres. G33	J23	39
Mossvale La., Pais.	L 5	30
Mossvale Path G33	H23	25
Mossvale Rd. G33	H22	24
Mossvale Sq. G33	J24	39
Mossvale Sq. G33	J23	39
Mossvale St., Pais.	K 5	30
Mossvale Ter., Chr.	D28	15
Mossvale Way G33	J23	39
Mossvale Wk. G33	J23	39
Mossview Cotts., Chr.	G26	26
Mossview Quad. G52	L11	33
Mossview Rd. G33	G24	25
Mote Hill Rd., Pais.	L 7	31
Moulin Circus G52	M10	48
Moulin Pl. G52	M10	48
Moulin Rd. G52	M10	48
Moulin Ter. G52	M10	48
Mount Annan Dr. G44	O16	51
Mount Harriet Av. G33	G24	25
Mount Harriet Dr. G33	G23	25
Mount St. G20	H15	21
Mount Stuart St. G41	O15	51
Mount Vernon Av. G32	M24	55
Mountainblue St. G31	L19	37
Mountblow Ho., Dalm.	C 5	4
Melbourne Av.		
Mountblow Rd., Dalm.	C 6	4
Mountgarrie Path G51	K11	33
Mountgarrie Rd.		
Mountgarrie Rd. G51	K11	33
Mowbray Av., Gart.	G27	27
Mowcraigs Ct., Clyde.	F 8	17
Yokerburn Ter.		
Moy St. G11	J14	34
Church St.		
Moyne Rd. G53	N10	48
Muckcroft Rd., Chr.	D25	14
Muir Park Ter. G64	F18	22
Muir St. G21	H18	22
Muir St., Bish.	E19	11
Muir St., Renf.	H 8	17
Muir Ter., Pais.	K 7	31
Muirbank Av. G73	O18	52
Muirbank Gdns. G73	O18	52
Muirbrae Rd. G73	Q19	65
Muirbrae Way G73	Q19	65
Muirburn Av. G44	Q15	63
Muirdrum Av. G52	M11	49
Muirdykes Av. G52	L10	32
Muirdykes Cres., Pais.	L 4	29
Muirdykes Rd. G52	L10	32
Muirdykes Rd., Pais.	L 4	29
Muiredge Ct., Udd.	P27	69
Watson St.		
Muiredge Ter., Bail.	M25	56
Muirend Av. G44	Q15	63
Muirend Rd. G44	Q15	63
Muirfield Cres. G23	E15	9
Muirfield Rd., Cumb.	A 3	71
Muirhead Ct., Bail.	M26	56
Muirhead Dr., Linw.	L 1	28
Muirhead Gdns., Bail.	M26	56
Muirhead Rd., Udd. & Bail.	M25	56
Muirhead St. G11	J13	34
Purdon St.		
Muirhead Way, Bish.	E20	11
Muirhill Av., G44	Q15	63
Muirhill Cres., G13	F10	18
Muirhouse St. G41	N15	51
Pollokshaws Rd.		
Muirkirk Dr. G13	F12	19
Muirpark Av., Renf.	J 8	31
Muirpark Dr., Bish.	F19	23
Muirpark St. G11	J13	34
Muirpark Ter., Bish.	F18	22
Crowhill Rd.		
Muirshiel Av. G53	P11	61
Muirshiel Cres. G53	P11	61
Muirside Av. G32	M24	55
Muirside Rd., Bail.	M25	56
Muirside St., Bail.	M25	56
Muirskeith Cres. G43	P15	63
Muirskeith Pl. G43	P15	63
Muirskeith Rd. G43	P15	63
Muirton Dr., Bish.	D18	10
Muirton Gdns., Bish.	D18	10
Muiryfauld Dr. G31	M21	54
Mulben Cres. G53	O 9	48
Mulben Pl. G53	O 9	48
Mulben Ter. G53	O 9	48
Mulberry Rd. G43	P14	62
Mull Av., Pais.	O 6	46
Mull Av., Renf.	J 8	31
Mull St. G21	J19	37
Mullardoch St. G23	E14	8
Rothes Dr.		
Mungo Pl., Udd.	N28	57
Lincoln Av.		
Munlochy Rd. G51	K11	33
Munro Ct., Clyde.	C 6	4
Gentle Row		
Munro La. G13	G12	19
Munro Pl. G13	G12	19
Munro Pl., Udd.	N28	57
Kirkwood Rd.		
Munro Rd. G13	G12	19
Munro Vw., Udd.	N28	57
Kirkwood Rd.		
Murano St. G20	H15	21
Murdoch St. G21	G18	22
Lenzie St.		
Muriel St., Barr.	Q 8	59
Murray Pl., Barr.	Q 8	59
Murray Rd., Both.	Q28	69
Murray St., Pais.	L 5	30
Murray St., Renf.	H 8	17
Murrayfield Dr., Bear.	E12	7
Murrayfield St. G32	K21	38
Murrayfield, Bish.	D19	11
Ashfield		
Murrin Av., Bish.	E20	11
Murroes Rd. G51	K11	33
Muslin St. G40	M18	52
Mybster Pl. G51	K11	33
Mybster Rd. G51	K11	33
Myers Cres., Udd.	P28	69
Myres Rd. G53	O11	49
Myreside Pl. G32	L20	37
Myreside St. G32	L20	37
Myrie Gdns., Bish.	E19	11
Myroch Pl. G34	J26	40
Myrtle Av., Lenz.	C23	13
Myrtle Hill La. G42	O17	52
Myrtle Hill Vw. G42	O17	52
Myrtle Pk. G42	N17	52
Myrtle Pl. G42	O17	52
Myrtle Rd., Dalm.	D 5	4
Myrtle Rd., Udd.	O28	57
Myrtle Sq., Bish.	F19	23
Myrtle St., Blan.	R26	68
Myrtle Wk. G72	P21	66
Naburn St. G5	M17	52
Nairn Av., Blan.	R26	68
Nairn Gdns., Bear.	D11	7
Nairn Pl., Dalm.	D 6	4
Dumbarton Rd.		

Name	Grid		Name	Grid		Name	Grid
Nairn St. G3	J14 34		Nevis Rd., Bear.	B10 6		Nithsdale St. G41	N15 51
Nairn St., Dalm.	D 6 4		Nevis Rd., Renf.	J 7 31		Nitshill Rd. G53	P 9 60
Nairnside Rd. G21	F20 23		New City Rd. G4	J16 35		Niven St. G20	G14 20
Naismith St. G32	O23 55		New Edinburgh Rd.,	O27 57		Noldrum Av. G32	O23 55
Nansen St. G20	H16 21		Udd.			Noldrum Gdns. G32	O23 55
Napier Ct., Old.K.	C 5 4		New Inchinnan Rd.,	K 6 30		Norbreck Dr., Giff.	Q14 62
Freelands Rd.			Pais.			Norby Rd. G11	H12 19
Napier Dr. G51	K13 34		New Kirk Pl., Bear.	C12 7		Norfield Dr. G44	O16 51
Napier Gdns., Linw.	L 2 28		*New Kirk Rd.*			Norfolk Cres., Bish.	D18 10
Napier Pl. G51	K13 34		New Kirk Rd., Bear.	C12 7		Norfolk Ct. G5	L16 35
Napier Pl., Old.K.	C 5 4		New Rd. G72	Q24 67		Norfolk La. G5	L16 35
Old Dalnottar Rd.			New Sneddon St., Pais.	L 6 30		*Norfolk St.*	
Napier Rd. G52	J 9 32		New St., Clyde.	C 7 5		Norfolk St. G5	L16 35
Napier Rd. G63	K13 34		New St., Kilb.	M07 42		Norham St. G41	N15 51
Napier St. G51	K14 34		New St., Pais.	M 6 46		Norman St. G40	M18 52
Napier St., Clyde.	F 8 17		New Wynd G1	L17 36		Norse La. N. G14	H11 19
Napier St., Linw.	L 2 28		Newark Dr. G41	M14 50		*Ormiston Av.*	
Napier Ter. G51	K13 34		Newark Dr., Pais.	O 5 46		Norse La. S. G14	H11 19
Napiershall La. G20	J15 35		Newbattle Ct. G32	N22 54		*Duncan Av.*	
Napiershall St.			Newbattle Gdns. G32	N22 54		Norse La. S. G14	H11 19
Napiershall Pl. G20	J15 35		Newbattle Pl. G32	N22 54		*Verona Av.*	
Napiershall St.			Newbattle Rd. G32	N22 54		Norse Rd. G14	H11 19
Napiershall St. G20	J15 35		Newbold Av. G21	F18 22		North Av. G72	P21 66
Naseby Av. G11	H12 19		Newburgh St. G43	O14 50		North Av., Clyde.	E 7 5
Nasmyth Rd. G52	K10 32		Newcastleton Dr.	E15 9		North Bank Pl., Clyde.	F 8 17
Nasmyth Rd. N. G52	K10 32		Newcroft Dr. G44	P17 64		*North Bank St.*	
Nasmyth Rd. S. G52	K10 32		Newfield Pl. G73	O18 52		North Bank St., Clyde.	F 8 17
National Bank La. G2	K16 35		Newfield Pl., Thorn.	R12 61		North Brae Pl., G13	F10 18
St. Vincent St.			*Rouken Glen Rd.*			North British Rd., Udd.	P27 69
Navar Pl., Pais.	N 7 47		Newfield Sq. G53	P10 60		North Canalbank St. G4	J17 36
Naver St. G33	J21 38		Newhall St. G40	M18 52		North Carbrain Rd.,	D 2 70
Neilsland Oval G53	O11 49		Newhaven Rd. G33	K22 38		Cumb.	
Neilsland Sq. G53	N11 49		Newhaven St. G32	K22 38		North Claremont St. G3	J15 35
Neilston Av. G53	P11 61		Newhills Rd. G33	K24 39		North Corsebar Av.,	N 5 46
Neilston Rd., Barr.	R 7 59		Newington St. G32	L21 38		Pais.	
Neilston Rd., Pais.	M 6 46		Newlands Gdns., John.	N 2 44		North Court La. G1	K17 36
Neilvaig Dr. G73	Q20 65		*Renshaw Rd.*			*Buchanan St.*	
Nelson Mandela Pl. G1	K17 36		Newlands Rd. G43	P15 63		North Croft St., Pais.	L 6 30
Buchanan St.			Newlands Rd., Udd.	O27 57		North Deanpark Av.,	Q28 69
Nelson Pl., Bail.	M25 56		Newlandsfield Rd. G43	O14 50		Udd.	
Nelson St. G5	L16 35		Newluce Dr. G32	M23 55		North Douglas St.,	F 8 17
Nelson St., Bail.	M25 56		Newmains Rd., Renf.	J 7 31		Clyde.	
Nelson Ter. G12	H15 21		Newmill Rd. G21	G20 23		North Dr. G1	L17 36
Glasgow St.			Newnham Rd., Pais.	M 9 48		North Dr., Linw.	L 1 28
Neptune St. G51	K13 34		Newshot Ct., Clyde.	F 8 17		North Elgin St., Clyde.	F 8 17
Nerston Av. G53	O11 49		*Clydeholm Ter.*			North Erskine Pk., Bear.	C11 7
Ness Av., John.	O08 43		Newshot Dr., Renf.	E 5 4		North Frederick St. G1	K17 36
Ness Dr., Blan.	R27 69		Newstead Gdns. G23	E15 9		North Gardner St. G11	H13 20
Ness Gdns., Bish.	E19 11		Newton Av. G72	P23 67		North Grange Rd., Bear.	C12 7
Ness Rd., Renf.	H 7 17		Newton Av., Barr.	R 8 59		North Greenhill Rd.,	K 5 30
Ness St. G33	J21 38		Newton Av., John.	M 3 45		Pais.	
Netham St. G51	K13 34		Newton Av., Pais.	K 7 31		North Hanover Pl. G4	J17 36
Nether Auldhouse Rd.	P13 62		Newton Brae G72	P24 67		North Hanover St. G1	K17 36
G43			Newton Dr., John.	M 3 45		North Iverton Park Rd.,	M 1 44
Netherburn Av. G44	R15 63		Newton Dr., Udd.	O28 57		John.	
Netherby Dr. G41	M14 50		Newton Farm Rd. G72	O24 55		North Lodge Rd., Renf.	H 8 17
Nethercairn Rd. G43	Q14 62		Newton Pl. G3	J15 35		North Moraine La. G15	E11 7
Nethercliffe Av. G44	R15 63		Newton Rd., Lenz.	D24 13		*Moraine Av.*	
Nethercommon Harbour,	K 6 30		Newton St., Pais.	M 5 46		North Park Av., Thorn.	Q12 61
Pais.			Newton Station Rd. G72	P24 67		North Park St. G20	H15 21
Nethercraig Cotts., Pais.	P 5 58		Newton Ter. G3	K15 35		North Pl. G3	K15 35
Glenfield Rd.			*Sauchiehall St.*			*North St.*	
Nethercraigs Dr., Pais.	O 5 46		Newton Terrace La. G3	J15 35		North Portland St. G1	K17 36
Nethercraigs Rd., Pais.	O 4 45		*Elderslie St.*			North Queen St. G2	K17 36
Netherdale Dr., Pais.	M 9 48		Newtongrange Av. G32	N22 54		*George Sq.*	
Netherfield St. G31	L20 37		Newtongrange Gdns.	N22 54		North Rd., John.	N09 43
Netherhill Av. G44	R15 63		G32			North Spiers Wf. G4	J16 35
Netherhill Cres., Pais.	L 7 31		Newtyle Pl., Bish.	E20 11		North St. G3	K15 35
Netherhill Rd., Chr.	E27 15		Newtyle Rd., Pais.	M 8 47		North St., Clyde.	E 7 5
Netherhill Rd., Pais.	L 6 30		Nicholas St. G1	K17 36		*Dumbarton Rd.*	
Netherhouse Av., Lenz.	D24 13		Nicholson La. G5	L16 35		North St., Pais	L 6 30
Netherhouse Pl., Bail.	K27 41		*Nicholson St.*			North Vw., Bear.	E11 7
Netherhouse Rd.			Nicholson St. G5	L16 35		North Wallace St. G4	J17 36
Netherhouse Rd., Bail.	K26 40		Niddrie Rd. G42	N15 51		North Way, Bail.	R26 68
Netherlee Rd., G44	Q15 63		Niddrie Sq. G42	N15 51		North Woodside Rd.	H15 21
Netherpark Av. G44	R15 63		Niddry St., Pais.	L 6 30		G20	
Netherplace Cres. G53	O10 48		Nigel Gdns. G41	N14 50		Northampton Dr. G12	G13 20
Netherplace Rd. G53	O10 48		Nigg Pl. G34	K25 40		Northampton La. G12	G13 20
Netherton Ct. G22	R18 64		Nightingale Pl., John.	O08 43		*Northampton Dr.*	
Netherton Dr., Barr.	R 9 60		Nimmo Dr. G51	K12 33		Northbank Av. G72	P23 67
Netherton Rd. G13	F12 19		Nisbet St. G31	L20 37		Northbank St. G72	P23 67
Netherton St. G13	F12 19		Nith Av., Pais.	N 3 45		Northcroft Rd. G21	H18 22
Crow Rd.			Nith Pl., John.	O08 43		Northcroft Rd., Chr.	E27 15
Nethervale Av. G44	R15 63		Nith St. G33	J20 37		Northgate Quad. G21	F20 23
Netherview Rd. G44	R16 63		Nithsdale Cres., Bear.	C11 7		Northgate Rd. G21	F20 23
Netherway G44	R15 63		Nithsdale Dr. G41	N15 51		Northinch St. G14	J11 33
Nethy Way, Renf.	J 9 32		Nithsdale Pl. G41	M15 51		Northland Dr. G14	G11 19
Teith Av.			*Shields Rd.*			Northland La. G14	H11 19
Neuk Way G32	O23 55		Nithsdale Rd. G41	M13 50		*Northland Dr.*	
Nevis Rd. G43	P13 62					Northmuir Rd. G15	D10 6

Name	Grid	Page
Northpark Ter. G12	H15	21
Hamilton Dr.		
Northumberland St. G20	H15	21
Norval St. G11	J13	34
Norwich Dr. G12	G13	20
Norwood Dr., Giff.	R13	62
Norwood Ter. G12	J15	35
Southpark Av.		
Norwood Ter., Udd.	O28	57
Norwood, Bear.	D12	7
Nottingham Av. G12	G13	20
Nottingham La. G12	G13	20
Northampton Dr.		
Novar Dr. G12	H13	20
Novar Gdns., Bish.	E18	10
Numrow Ct., Clyde.	C 6	4
Nuneaton St. G40	M19	53
Nurseries Rd., Bail.	L24	39
Nursery La. G41	N15	51
Nursery St. G41	N15	51
Pollokshaws Rd.		
Nursery Street La. G41	N15	51
Nithsdale Dr.		
Nutberry Ct. G42	N16	51
Oak Cres., Bail.	M25	56
Oak Dr. G72	Q23	67
Oak Dr., Lenz.	C22	12
Oak Pl., Bish.	E19	11
Oak Rd., Dalm.	C 6	4
Oak Rd., Pais.	N 7	47
Oakbank Dr., Barr.	S 8	59
Oakbank La. G20	H16	21
Oakbank Ter. G20	H16	21
Oakdene Av., Udd.	O28	57
Oakfield Av. G12	J15	35
Oakfield Ter. G12	J15	35
Oakhill Av.		
Oakhill Av., Bail.	M24	55
Oakley Dr. G44	Q15	63
Oakley Ter. G31	K18	36
Oaks, The, John.	N08	43
Oakshaw School Brae, Pais.	L 5	30
Oakshaw St., Pais.	L 5	30
Oakshawhead, Pais.	L 5	30
Oakwood Av., Pais.	N 4	45
Oatfield St. G21	H19	23
Oban Ct. G22	H15	21
Oban Dr. G20	H15	21
Observatory La. G12	H14	20
Observatory Rd.		
Observatory Rd. G12	H14	20
Ochil Dr., Barr.	R 8	59
Ochil Dr., Pais.	O 6	46
Ochil Pl. G32	M22	54
Ochil Rd., Bish.	E20	11
Ochil Rd., Renf.	J 7	31
Ochil St. G32	M22	54
Ogilvie Pl. G31	M21	54
Ogilvie St. G31	M20	53
Old Bothwell Rd., Both.	R28	69
Old Castle Rd. G44	P16	63
Old Dalmarnock Rd. G40	M18	52
Old Dalnottar Rd., Old K.	C 5	4
Old Dumbarton Rd. G3	J14	34
Old Edinburgh Rd., Udd.	N27	57
Old Gartcosh Rd., Gart.	G27	27
Old Glasgow Rd., Udd.	O26	56
Old Govan Rd., Renf.	H 9	18
Old Greenock Rd., Renf.	F 5	16
Old Manse Rd. G32	L23	39
Old Mill Rd. G72	P23	67
Old Mill Rd., Both.	R28	69
Old Mill Rd., Clyde.	C 7	5
Old Mill Rd., Udd.	P27	69
Old Rd., John.	M 2	44
Old Renfrew Rd., Renf.	J10	32
Old Roundknowe Rd., Udd.	N26	56
Old Rutherglen Rd. G5	M17	52
Old Shettleston Rd. G32	L21	38
Old Sneddon St., Pais.	L 6	30
Old St., Clyde.	C 6	4
Old Wood Rd., Bail.	M25	56
Old Wynd G1	L17	36
Oldhall Rd., Pais.	L 8	31
Olifard Av., Udd.	Q28	69
Oliphant Cres., Pais.	O 3	45
Olive St. G33	H20	23
Olrig Ter. G41	M15	51
Shields Rd.		
Olympia St. G40	L18	36
Onslow Dr. G31	K19	37
Onslow Rd., Clyde.	E 8	5
Onslow Sq. G31	K19	37
Onslow Dr.		
Oran Gate G20	H15	21
Oran Gdns. G20	G15	21
Oran Pl. G20	G15	21
Oran St. G20	G15	21
Oransay Cres., Bear.	D13	8
Orcades Dr. G44	Q16	63
Orchard Av. G17	R28	69
Orchard Ct. G32	O22	54
Orchard Ct., Thorn.	Q13	62
Orchard Dr. G73	O18	52
Orchard Dr., Giff.	Q13	62
Orchard Gro., Giff.	Q13	62
Orchard Park Av., Thorn. & Giff.	Q13	62
Orchard Pk., Giff.	Q14	62
Orchard Pl., Lenz.	B24	13
Orchard Sq., Pais.	M 6	46
Orchard St., Pais.	M 6	46
Orchard St., Renf.	H 8	17
Orchardfield, Lenz.	D23	13
Orchy Cres., Bear.	E11	7
Orchy Cres., Pais.	N 3	45
Orchy Ct., Clyde.	C 8	5
Orchy Dr., Clark.	R15	63
Orchy Gdns., Clark.	R15	63
Orchy St. G44	P16	63
Oregon Pl. G5	M17	52
Orkney Pl. G51	K13	34
Orkney St.		
Orkney St. G51	K13	34
Orleans Av. G14	H12	19
Orleans La. G14	H12	19
Ormiston Av. G14	H11	19
Ormiston La. G14	H11	19
Ormiston Av.		
Ormiston La. S. G14	H11	19
Ormiston Av.		
Ormonde Av. G44	Q15	63
Ormonde Cres. G44	Q15	63
Ormonde Ct. G44	Q15	63
Ormonde Dr. G44	Q15	63
Ornsay St. G22	F17	22
Orr Pl. G40	L18	36
Orr Sq., Pais.	L 6	30
Orr St. G40	L18	36
Orr St., Pais.	L 6	30
Orr St., Pais.	M 6	46
Orton St. G51	L13	34
Orwell St. G21	H18	22
Osborn Ter. G51	L13	34
Copland Rd.		
Osborne St. G1	L17	36
Osborne St., Clyde.	D 7	5
Osborne Vill. G44	P16	63
Holmhead Rd.		
Osprey Dr., Udd.	O28	57
Ossian Av., Pais.	L 9	32
Auchmannoch Av.		
Ossian Rd. G43	P15	63
Oswald La. G1	L16	35
Oswald St.		
Oswald St. G1	L16	35
Otago La. G12	J15	35
Otago St.		
Otago La. N. G12	J15	35
Otago St.		
Otago St. G12	J15	35
Ottawa Cres., Dalm.	D 5	4
Otter La. G11	J13	34
Castlebank St.		
Otterburn Dr., Giff.	R14	62
Otterswick Pl. G33	J23	39
Oval, The, Clark.	R15	63
Overbrae Pl. G15	C 9	6
Overdale Av. G42	O15	51
Overdale Gdns. G42	O15	51
Overdale St. G42	O15	51
Overdale Vills. G42	O15	51
Overdale St.		
Overlea Av. G73	P20	65
Overnewton Pl. G3	K14	34
Kelvinhaugh St.		
Overnewton Sq. G3	K14	34
Overnewton St. G3	J14	34
Overton Cres., John.	M 1	44
Overton Rd. G72	Q23	67
Overton Rd., John.	N 1	44
Overton St. G72	Q23	67
Overtoun Ct., Dalm.	D 6	4
Dunswin Av.		
Overtoun Dr. G73	O19	53
Overtoun Dr., Dalm.	D 6	4
Overtoun Rd., Dalm. & Clyde.	D 6	4
Overtown Av. G53	P10	60
Overtown St. G31	L19	37
Overwood Dr. G44	P17	64
Oxford Dr., Linw.	L 1	28
Oxford La. G5	L16	35
Oxford Rd., Renf.	H 8	17
Oxford St. G5	L16	35
Oxgang Pl., Lenz.	B24	13
Oxton Dr. G52	L10	32
Paisley Ct., Barr.	Q 7	59
Paisley Rd.		
Paisley Rd. G5	L15	35
Paisley Rd. W. G5	M10	48
Paisley Rd., Barr.	Q 7	59
Paisley Rd., Renf.	J 7	31
Palace St. G31	M20	53
Paladin Av. G13	F11	19
Palermo St. G21	H18	22
Palmer Av. G13	E11	7
Palmerston Pl. G3	K14	34
Kelvinhaugh St.		
Palmerston Pl., John.	O08	43
Pandora Way, Udd.	O28	57
Hillcrest Rd.		
Panmure St. G20	H16	21
Park Av. G3	J15	35
Park Av., Bar.	R 7	59
Park Av., Bish.	D19	11
Park Av., John.	N 2	44
Park Av., Pais.	N 5	46
Park Bank, Renf.	E 4	4
Park Brae, Renf.	F 5	16
Park Dr.		
Park Burn Av., Lenz.	B23	13
Park Circus C3	J15	35
Park Circus La. G3	J15	35
Lynedoch Pl.		
Park Circus Pl. G3	J15	35
Park Cres., Bear.	C10	6
Park Cres., Bish.	D19	11
Park Cres., Renf.	F 5	16
Park Ct., Bish.	D19	11
Park Ct., Dalm.	D 6	4
Little Holm		
Park Ct., Giff.	Q13	62
Belmont Dr.		
Park Ct., Giff.	R13	62
Park Dr. G3	J15	35
Park Dr. G73	O19	53
Park Dr., Renf.	F 5	16
Park Gardens La. G3	J15	35
Clifton St.		
Park Gate G3	J15	35
Park Gdns. G3	J15	35
Park Gdns., Kilb.	M07	42
Park Gro., Renf.	F 5	16
Park La. G40	L18	36
Park La., Blan.	S26	69
Park La., Pais.	L 6	30
Netherhill Rd.		
Park Pl. G20	F14	20
Fingal St.		
Park Quad. G3	J15	35
Park Rd. G4	J15	35
Park Rd., Bail.	L27	41
Park Rd., Bish.	E19	11
Park Rd., Chr.	F26	26
Park Rd., Dalm.	D 6	4
Park Rd., Giff.	R14	62
Park Rd., John.	N09	43
Park Rd., Pais.	N 5	46
Park Rd., Renf.	F 5	16
Park Ridge, Renf.	F 5	16
Park Dr.		

Park St. S. G3   J15 35
Park Ter. G3   J15 35
Park Ter. G42   N15 51
Queens Dr.
Park Ter., Giff.   R14 62
Park Top, Renf.   F 5 16
Park Way, Cumb.   B 3 71
Park Winding, Renf.   F 5 16
Park Wood, Renf.   E 4 4
Parkburn Av., Lenz.   C23 13
Parker St. G14   J12 33
Parkglade, Renf.   F 4 16
Parkgrove Av., Giff.   Q14 62
Parkgrove Ct., Giff.   Q14 62
Parkgrove Ter. G3   J15 35
Parkgrove Ter. La. G3   K15 35
Derby St.
Parkhall Rd., Dalm.   D 6 4
Parkhall Ter., Dalm.   C 6 4
Parkhead Cross G31   L20 37
Parkhill Dr. G73   O19 53
Parkhill Rd. G43   O14 50
Parkholm La. G5   L15 35
Paisley Rd.
Parkhouse La. G4   K18 36
Parkhouse Path G53   Q10 60
Parkhouse Rd. G53   Q 9 60
Parklands Rd. G44   Q15 63
Parklea, Bish.   D18 10
Midcroft
Parkmoor, Renf.   F 4 16
Parkneuk Rd. G43   Q14 62
Parksail Dr., Renf.   F 5 16
Parksail, Renf.   F 5 16
Parkview Av., Lenz.   C23 13
Parkview Ct., Lenz.   B23 13
Parkview Dr. G33   G24 25
Parkview G78   M07 42
Parkview, Pais.   N 5 46
Parliament Rd. G21   K18 36
Parnie St. G1   L17 36
Parson St. G4   K18 36
Partick Bridge St. G11   J14 34
Partickhill Av. G11   H13 20
Partickhill Ct. G11   H13 20
Partickhill Av.
Partickhill Rd. G11   H13 20
Paterson St. G5   L16 35
Pathead Gdns. G33   G21 24
Patna St. G40   M19 53
Paton St. G31   K19 37
Patrick St., Pais.   M 6 46
Patterton Dr., Barr.   R 8 59
Pattison St., Dalm.   D 6 4
Payne St. G4   J17 36
Peacock Dr., Pais.   M 3 45
Pearce St. G51   K13 34
Pearson Dr., Renf.   J 8 31
Pearson Pl., Linw.   L 1 28
Peat Pl. G53   P10 60
Peat Rd. G53   P10 60
Peathill Av., Chr.   F25 26
Peathill St. G21   H17 22
Peebles Dr. G73   P20 65
Peel Glen Rd.,
   Bear. & G15   C10 6
Peel La. G11   J13 34
Burgh Hall St.
Peel Pl., Both.   Q28 69
Peel St. G11   J13 34
Peel Vw., Clyde.   D 8 5
Kirkoswald Dr.
Peirshill St. G32   K21 38
Pembroke St. G3   K15 35
Pencaitland Dr. G32   M22 54
Falside Rd.
Pencaitland Gro. G32   M22 54
Falside Rd.
Pencaitland Pl. G23   E15 9
Pendeen Cres. G33   L24 39
Pendeen Pl. G33   L24 39
Pendeen Rd. G33   L24 39
Pendicle Cres., Bear.   D11 7
Pendicle Rd., Bear.   D11 7
Penicuik St. G32   L20 37
Penilee Rd., Pais.   L 9 32
Penilee Ter. G52   K 9 32
Peninver Dr. G51   K12 33
Penman Av. G73   O18 52
Pennan Pl. G14   G10 18

Penneld Rd. G52   L 9 32
Penrith Av., Giff.   R14 62
Penrith Dr. G12   G13 20
Penryn Gdns. G32   M23 55
Penston Rd. G33   K23 39
Pentland Cres., Pais.   O 5 46
Pentland Ct., Barr.   R 7 59
Pentland Dr., Barr.   R 8 59
Pentland Dr., Bish.   E20 11
Pentland Dr., Linw.   L 1 28
Pentland Dr., Renf.   K 7 31
Pentland Pl. G40   M18 52
Pentland Pl., Bear.   B10 6
Pentland Rd. G43   P14 62
Pentland Rd., Chr.   F26 26
Penzance Way, Chr.   D27 15
Peockland Gdns.   M 1 44
Peockland Pl., John.   M 1 44
Percy Dr., Giff.   R14 62
Percy Rd., Renf.   K 7 31
Percy St. G51   L14 34
Perran Gdns., Chr.   E27 15
Perth Cres., Dalm.   C 5 4
Peters Ct. G20   F14 20
Maryhill Rd.
Petershill Ct. G21   H19 23
Petershill Dr. G21   H19 23
Petershill Pl. G21   H19 23
Petershill Rd. G21   H18 22
Petition Pl., Udd.   P28 69
Pettigrew St. G32   L22 38
Peveril Av. G41   N14 50
Peveril Av. G73   P20 65
Pharonhill St. G31   L21 38
Quarrybrae St.
Phoenix Park Ter. G4   J16 35
Corn St.
Phoenix Pl., John.   M 2 44
Phoenix Rd. G4   J16 35
Great Western Rd.
Piccadilly St. G3   K15 35
Pikeman Av. G13   G11 19
Pikeman Rd. G13   G11 19
Pilmuir Av. G44   Q15 63
Pilrig St. G32   K21 38
Pilton Rd. G15   D10 6
Pine Cres., John.   N 1 44
Pine Gro., Udd.   O28 57
Douglas Cres.
Pine Pl. G5   M17 52
Pine Pl., Cumb.   B 5 71
Pine Rd., Cumb.   B 5 71
Pine Rd., Dalm.   D 5 4
Pine St., Pais.   N 7 47
Pinelands, Bish.   D19 11
Pinewood Av., Lenz.   C22 12
Pinewood Ct., Lenz.   C22 12
Pinewood Pl., Kirk.   C22 12
Pinewood Pl., Lenz.   C22 12
Pinkerton Av. G73   O18 52
Pinkston Dr. G21   J17 36
Pinkston Rd. G21   H17 22
Pinmore Path G53   P 9 60
Pinmore Pl. G53   P 9 60
Pinmore St. G53   P 9 60
Pinwherry Pl., Udd.   Q28 69
Hume Dr.
Pirn St. G40   M18 52
Pitcairn St. G31   M21 54
Pitcaple Dr. G43   P13 62
Pitlochry Dr. G52   M10 48
Pitmedden Rd., Bish.   E20 11
Pitmilly Rd. G15   D11 7
Pitreavie Pl. G33   J23 39
Pitt St. G2   K16 35
Pladda Rd., Renf.   J 8 31
Plane Tree Pl., John.   N 1 44
Planetree Rd., Dalm.   C 7 5
Planetrees Av., Pais.   N 6 46
Carriagehill Dr.
Plant St. G31   L20 37
Plantation Pl. G51   L15 35
Govan Rd.
Plantation Sq. G51   L15 35
Playfair St. G40   M19 53
Pleaknowe Cres., Chr.   E27 15
Pleamuir Pl., Cumb.   C 1 70
Plean St. G14   G10 18
Pleasance La. G43   O14 50
Pleasance St. G43   O14 50

Plover Pl., John.   O08 43
Pollock Dr., Bish.   E18 10
Pollock Rd., Bear.   D13 8
Pollokshaws Rd.   O13 50
Polmadie Av. G42   N17 52
Polmadie Rd. G5   N17 52
Polmadie St. G42   N17 52
Polnoon Av. G13   G10 18
Polson Dr., John.   N09 43
Polwarth Gdns. G12   H13 20
Novar Dr.
Polwarth La. G12   H13 20
Novar Dr.
Polwarth St. G12   H13 20
Poplar Av. G11   H12 19
Poplar Av., John.   N 1 44
Poplar Cotts. G14   G 9 18
Dumbarton Rd.
Poplar Dr., Dalm.   C 6 4
Poplar Dr., Lenz.   C22 12
Poplar Pl., Blan.   R26 68
Poplar Rd. G41   L13 34
Urrdale Rd.
Poplin St. G40   M18 52
Porchester St. G33   J23 39
Port Dundas Pl. G2   K17 36
Port Dundas Rd. G4   J17 36
Port St. G3   K15 35
Portal Rd. G13   F11 19
Porterfield Rd., Renf.   J 7 31
Portman Pl. G12   J15 35
Cowan St.
Portman St. G41   L15 35
Portmarnock Dr. G23   F14 20
Portreath Rd., Chr.   D27 15
Portsoy Av. G13   F 9 18
Portsoy Pl. G13   F 9 18
Portugal La. G5   L16 35
Bedford St.
Portugal St. G5   L16 35
Norfolk Ct.
Possil Cross G22   H16 21
Possil Rd. G4   H16 21
Post La., Renf.   H 8 17
Potassels Rd., Chr.   F26 26
Potter Pl. G32   M21 54
Potter St. G32   M21 54
Potterhill Av., Pais.   O 6 46
Potterhill Rd. G53   N10 48
Powburn Cres., Udd.   O26 56
Powfoot St. G31   L20 37
Powrie St. G33   H23 25
Preston Pl. G42   N16 51
Prestwick St. G53   P10 60
Priesthill Av. G53   P11 61
Priesthill Cres. G53   P11 61
Priesthill Rd. G53   P10 60
Primrose Ct. G14   H11 19
Primrose St. G14   H11 19
Prince Albert Rd. G12   H13 20
Prince Edward St. G42   N16 51
Prince of Wales Gdns.   F14 20
   G20
Prince of Wales Ter. G12   H14 20
Byres Rd.
Princes Gate G73   O19 53
Greenbank St.
Princes Gdns. G12   H13 20
Princes Pl. G12   H14 20
Princes Sq. G1   K17 36
Princes Sq., Barr.   Q 8 59
Princes St. G73   O19 53
Princes Ter. G12   H14 20
Princess Cres., Pais.   L 7 31
Priory Av., Pais.   K 7 31
Priory Cotts., Blan.   R26 68
Priory Dr., Udd.   O26 56
Priory Pl. G13   F11 19
Priory Rd. G13   F11 19
Prosen St. G32   M21 54
Prospect Av. G72   P21 66
Prospect Av., Udd.   O27 57
Prospect Rd. G43   O14 50
Prospecthill Circus G42   N17 52
Prospecthill Cres. G42   O18 52
Prospecthill Dr. G42   O17 52
Prospecthill Pl. G42   O18 52
Prospecthill Rd. G42   O16 51
Prospecthill Sq. G42   O17 52
Provan Rd. G33   J20 37

Street	Ref	Pg
Provand Hall Cres., Bail.	M25	56
Provanhill Pl. G21	J18	36
Provanmill Pl. G33	H20	23
Provanmill Rd.		
Provanmill Av. G33	H20	23
Purdon St. G11	J13	34
Pykestone Rd. G33	J23	39
Quadrant Rd. G43	P15	63
Quadrant, The, Clark.	S15	63
Quarrelton Rd., John.	N09	43
Quarry Av. G72	Q24	67
Quarry Pl. G72	P21	66
Quarry Rd., Barr.	Q 7	59
Quarry Rd., Pais.	N 6	46
Quarry St., John.	M09	43
Quarrybank, John.	N08	43
Quarrybrae St. G31	L21	38
Quarryknowe G73	O18	52
Quarryknowe St. G31	L21	38
Quarrywood Av. G21	H20	23
Quarrywood Rd. G21	H20	23
Quay Rd. G73	N19	53
Quay Rd. N. G73	N19	53
Quebec Ho., Dalm.	C 5	4
Perth Cres.		
Queen Arc. G2	K16	5
Renfrew St.		
Queen Elizabeth Av. G52	K 9	32
Queen Elizabeth Sq. G5	M17	52
Queen Margaret Cres. G12	H15	21
Hamilton Dr.		
Queen Margaret Ct. G20	H15	21
Queen Margaret Dr. G12	H14	20
Queen Margaret Dr. G20	H15	21
Queen Margaret Rd. G20	H15	21
Queen Mary Av. G42	N16	51
Queen Mary Av., Clyde.	E 8	5
Queen Mary St. G40	M18	52
Queen Sq. G41	N15	51
Queen St. G1	K17	36
Queen St. G73	O19	53
Queen St., Pais.	M 5	46
Queen St., Renf.	H 8	17
Queen Victoria Dr. G14	H11	19
Queen Victoria Gate G13	G11	19
Queenbank Av., Gart.	F27	27
Queens Av. G72	P22	66
Queens Cres. G4	J16	35
Queens Cres., Bail.	L27	41
Queens Cross G20	H15	21
Queens Dr. G42	N15	51
Queens Dr., Cumb.	A 2	70
Queens Drive La. G42	N16	51
Queens Gdns. G12	H14	20
Victoria Crescent Rd.		
Queens Park Av. G42	N16	51
Queens Pl. G12	H14	20
Queens Rd., John.	N 2	44
Queensborough Gdns. G12	H13	20
Queensferry St. G5	N18	52
Rosebery St.		
Queenshill St. G21	H18	22
Queensland Ct. G52	L11	33
Queensland Dr. G52	L11	33
Queensland Gdns. G52	L11	33
Queensland La. E. G52	L10	32
Kingsland Dr.		
Queensland La. W. G52	L11	33
Queensland Dr.		
Queenslie Ind. Est. G33	K23	39
Queenslie St. G33	J20	37
Quentin St. G41	N15	51
Quinton Gdns., Bail.	L25	40
Raasay Dr., Pais.	O 5	46
Raasay Pl. G22	F17	22
Raasay St. G22	F17	22
Rachan St. G34	J26	40
Radnor St. G3	K15	35
Argyle St.		
Radnor St., Clyde.	D 7	5
Raeberry St. G20	H15	21
Raeswood Dr. G53	O 9	48
Raeswood Gdns. G53	O 9	48
Raeswood Pl. G53	O 9	48
Raeswood Rd. G53	O 9	48
Raglan St. G4	J16	35
Raith Av. G44	Q17	64
Raithburn Av. G45	Q17	64
Raithburn Rd. G45	Q17	64
Ralston Av., Pais. & G52	M 9	48
Ralston Ct. G52	M 9	48
Ralston Dr. G52	M 9	48
Ralston Path G52	M 9	48
Ralston Dr.		
Ralston Pl. G52	M 9	48
Ralston Rd., Bear.	C12	7
Ralston St., Barr.	R 8	59
Ralston St., Pais.	M 7	47
Seedhill Rd.		
Ram St. G32	L21	38
Rampart Av. G13	F10	18
Ramsay Av., John.	N09	43
Ramsay Cres., John.	O07	42
Ramsay Pl., John.	N09	43
Ramsay St., Dalm.	D 6	4
Ranald Gdns. G73	Q20	65
Randolph Av., Clark.	R15	63
Randolph Dr., Clark.	R15	63
Randolph Gdns., Clark.	R15	63
Randolph Rd. G11	H12	19
Randolph Ter. G72	P22	66
Hamilton Rd.		
Ranfurley Rd. G52	L 9	32
Rankine Pl., John.	M09	43
Rankine St.		
Rankine St., John.	M09	43
Rankines La., Renf.	H 8	17
Manse St.		
Rannoch Av., Bish.	E19	11
Rannoch Dr., Bear.	E13	8
Rannoch Dr., Renf.	H 8	17
Rannoch Gdns., Bish.	E19	11
Rannoch Pl., Pais.	M 7	47
Rannoch Rd., John.	N09	43
Rannoch Rd., Udd.	N27	57
Rannoch St. G44	P16	63
Ranza Pl. G33	H20	23
Raploch Av. G14	H10	18
Ratford St. G51	K13	34
Rathlin St. G51	K13	34
Ratho Dr. G21	G18	22
Rattray St. G32	M21	54
Ravel Row G31	L20	37
Ravelston Rd., Bear.	E12	7
Ravelston St. G32	L20	37
Ravens Ct., Bish.	F18	22
Lennox Cres.		
Ravenscliffe Dr., Giff.	Q13	62
Ravenscraig Av., Pais.	N 5	46
Ravenscraig Dr. G53	P10	60
Ravenscraig Ter. G53	P11	61
Ravenshall Rd. G42	O14	50
Ravenstone Rd., Giff.	Q14	62
Ravenswood Av. G78	O 3	45
Ravenswood Dr. G41	N14	50
Ravenswood Rd., Bail.	L26	40
Rayne Pl. G15	D10	6
Red Rd. G21	H19	23
Red Road Ct. G21	H19	23
Redan St. G40	L18	36
Redcastle Sq. G33	J23	39
Redford St. G33	K20	37
Redgate Pl. G14	H10	18
Redhill Rd., Cumb.	B 1	70
Redlands La. G12	H14	20
Kirklee Rd.		
Redlands Rd. G12	H14	20
Redlands Ter. G12	H14	20
Redlands Terrace La. G12	H14	20
Julian Av.		
Redlawood Pl., G72	P25	68
Redlawood Rd.		
Redlawood Rd. G72	P25	68
Redmoss Rd., Clyde.	C 6	4
Redmoss St. G22	G16	21
Rednock St. G22	H17	22
Redpath Dr. G52	L10	32
Redwood Pl., Lenz.	C22	12
Redwood Rd., Cumb.	C 4	71
Reelick Av. G13	F 9	18
Reelick Quad. G13	F 9	18
Regent Moray St. G3	J14	34
Regent Park Sq. G41	N15	51
Regent Park Ter. G41	N15	51
Pollokshaws Rd.		
Regent Pl., Dalm.	D 6	4
Regent Sq., Lenz.	D23	13
Regent St., Dalm.	D 6	4
Regent St., Pais.	L 7	31
Regents Gate, Both.	Q27	69
Regwood St. G41	O14	50
Reid Av., Bear.	C13	8
Reid Av., Linw.	L 1	28
Reid Pl. G40	M18	52
Muslin St.		
Reid St. G40	M18	52
Reid St. G73	O19	53
Reidhouse St. G21	H18	22
Muir St.		
Reids Row, Bail.	M26	56
Reidvale St. G31	L18	36
Renfield St. G2	K16	35
Renfield St., Renf.	H 8	17
Renfrew Ct. G2	K16	35
Renfrew St.		
Renfrew La. G2	K16	35
Renfield St.		
Renfrew Rd. G51	J10	32
Renfrew Rd., Pais.	L 6	30
Renfrew Rd., Renf.	J10	32
Renfrew St. G3	J16	35
Rennies Rd., Renf.	F 5	16
Renshaw Dr. G52	L10	32
Renshaw Rd., John.	N 2	44
Renton St. G4	J17	36
Renwick St. G41	L15	35
Scotland St.		
Residdl Rd. G33	G24	25
Reston Dr. G52	L10	32
Revoch Dr. G13	F10	18
Rhannan Rd. G44	P16	63
Rhannan Ter. G44	P16	63
Rhindmuir Av., Bail.	L26	40
Rhindmuir Rd., Bail.	L26	40
Rhinds St., Coat.	M28	57
Rhinsdale Cres., Bail.	L26	40
Rhumhor Gdns., John.	N08	43
Rhymer St. G21	J18	36
Rhymie Rd. G32	M23	55
Rhynie Dr. G51	L13	34
Riccarton St. G42	N17	52
Riccartsbar Av., Pais.	M 5	46
Richard St., Renf.	H 8	17
Richmond Ct. G73	O20	53
Richmond Dr. G72	P21	66
Richmond Dr. G73	O20	53
Richmond Dr., Bish. G64	D19	11
Richmond Dr., Linw.	K 1	28
Richmond Gdns., Chr.	E25	14
Richmond Pl. G73	O20	53
Richmond St. G1	K17	36
Richmond St., Clyde.	E 8	5
Riddell St., Clyde.	D 8	5
Riddon Av. G13	F 9	18
Riddrie Cres. G33	K21	38
Riddrie Knowes G33	K21	38
Riddrie Ter. G33	H20	23
Provanmill Rd.		
Riddrievale Ct. G33	J21	38
Riddrievale St. G33	J21	38
Rigby St. G32	L20	37
Rigg Pl. G33	K24	39
Rigghead Av., Cumb.	A 3	71
Riggside Rd. G33	J23	39
Riggside St. G33	J23	39
Riglands Way, Renf.	H 8	17
Riglaw Pl. G13	F10	18
Rigmuir Rd. G51	L11	33
Rimsdale St. G40	L19	37
Ringford St. G21	H18	22
Ripon Dr. G12	G13	20
Risk St. G40	L18	36
Risk St., Dalm.	D 6	4
Ristol Rd. G13	G11	19
Anniesland Rd.		
Ritchie Cres., John.	M 2	44
Ritchie Pk., John.	M 1	44
Ritchie St. G5	M16	51
River Rd. G32	O22	54
River Rd. Mansion-house Rd. G41	O15	51
Riverbank St. G43	O14	50
Riverford Rd. G43	O14	50

Street	Ref	Page
Riverford Rd. G73	N20	53
Riversdale Cotts G14	G 9	18
Dumbarton Rd.		
Riversdale La. G14	G 9	18
Dumbarton Rd.		
Riverside Ct. G44	R16	63
Riverside Pk. G44	R16	63
Linnpark Av.		
Riverside Pl. G72	P24	67
Riverside Rd. G43	O15	51
Riverview Av. G5	L16	35
West St.		
Riverview Dr. G5	L16	35
Riverview Gdns. G5	L16	35
Riverview Pl. G5	L16	35
Roaden Av., Pais.	O 3	45
Roaden Rd., Pais.	O 3	45
Roadside, Cumb.	A 3	71
Robb St. G21	H18	22
Robert Burns Av., Clyde.	D 8	5
Robert St. G51	K13	34
Robert Templeton Dr. G72	P23	67
Roberton Av. G41	N14	50
Roberts St., Dalm.	D 6	4
Robertson La. G2	K16	35
Robertson St.		
Robertson St. G2	K16	35
Robertson St., Barr.	Q 7	59
Robertson Ter., Bail.	L26	40
Edinburgh Rd.		
Robin Way G32	O23	55
Robroyston Av. G33	H21	24
Robroyston Rd. G33	G21	24
Robslee Cres., Thorn.	Q13	62
Robslee Dr., Giff.	Q13	62
Robslee Rd., Thorn.	R13	62
Robson Gro. G42	N16	51
Rock Dr. G78	N 7	42
Rock St. G4	H16	21
Rockall Dr. G44	Q17	64
Rockbank Pl. G40	L19	37
Broad St.		
Rockbank Pl., Clyde.	C 7	5
Glasgow Rd.		
Rockbank St. G40	L19	37
Rockburn Dr., Clark.	S14	62
Rockcliffe St. G40	M18	52
Rockfield Pl. G21	G20	23
Rockfield Rd. G21	G20	23
Rockmount Av., Barr.	R 8	59
Rockmount Av., Thorn.	Q13	62
Rockwell Av., Pais.	O 5	46
Rodger Dr. G73	P19	65
Rodger Pl., Ruth.	P19	65
Rodil Av. G44	Q17	64
Rodney St. G4	J16	35
Roebank Dr., Barr.	R 8	59
Roebank St. G31	K19	37
Roffey Park Rd., Pais.	L 8	31
Rogart St. G40	L18	36
Rogerfield Rd., Bail.	K26	40
Rokeby Ter. G12	H14	20
Great Western Rd.		
Roman Av. G15	E10	6
Roman Av., Bear.	C12	7
Roman Ct., Bear.	C12	7
Roman Dr., Bear.	C12	7
Roman Gdns., Bear.	C12	7
Roman Rd., Bear.	C12	7
Roman Rd., Clyde.	C 7	5
Romney Av. G44	P17	64
Rona St. G21	J19	37
Rona Ter. G72	Q21	66
Ronaldsay Dr., Bish.	E20	11
Ronaldsay Pl., Cumb.	D 1	70
Ronaldsay St. G22	F17	22
Ronay St. G22	F17	22
Rooksdell Av., Pais.	N 5	46
Rose Cotts. G13	G12	19
Crow Rd.		
Rose Dale, Bish.	F19	23
Rose Knowe G73	N18	52
Rose St. G3	K16	35
Rosebank Av., Blan.	R27	69
Rosebank Dr. G72	Q23	67
Rosebank Ter., Bail.	M27	57
Roseberg Pl., Clyde.	E 7	5
Kilbowie Rd.		
Rosebery Pl., Clyde.	E 7	5
Miller St.		
Rosebery St. G5	N18	52
Rosedale Av. G78	O 2	44
Rosedale Dr., Bail.	M25	56
Rosedale Gdns. G20	F14	20
Rosefield Gdns., Udd.	O27	57
Roselea Gdns. G13	F12	19
Roselea Pl., Blan.	R26	68
Rosemount Meadows, Both.	R27	69
Rosemount Cres. G21	J19	37
Rosemount St. G21	J18	36
Rosemount Ter. G51	L15	35
Paisley Rd. W.		
Rosemount, Cumb.	A 2	70
Rosevale Rd., Bear.	D12	7
Rosevale St. G11	J13	34
Rosewood Av., Pais.	N 4	45
Rosewood St. G13	F12	19
Roslea Dr. G31	K19	37
Roslyn Dr., Bail.	L27	41
Rosneath St. G51	K13	34
Ross Av., Renf.	J 7	31
Ross Hall Pl., Renf.	H 8	17
Ross St. G40	L17	36
Ross St., Pais.	M 7	47
Rossendale Rd. G43	O14	50
Rosshall Av., Pais.	M 8	47
Rosshill Av. G52	L 9	32
Rosshill Rd. G52	L 9	32
Rossie Cres., Bish.	F20	23
Rosslea Dr., Giff.	R14	62
Rosslyn Av. G73	O19	53
Rosslyn Rd., Bear.	C10	6
Rosslyn Ter. G12	H14	20
Horslethill Rd.		
Rostan Rd. G43	P14	62
Rosyth Rd. G5	N18	52
Rosyth St. G5	N18	52
Rotherwick Dr., Pais.	M 9	48
Rotherwood Av. G13	E11	7
Rotherwood Av., Pais.	O 3	45
Rotherwood La. G13	E11	7
Rotherwood Av.		
Rotherwood Pl. G13	F11	19
Rothes Dr. G23	E14	8
Rothes Pl. G23	E14	8
Rothlinn Av., Lenz.	B24	13
Rottenrow East G4	K17	36
Rottenrow G4	K17	36
Roual Ter., Pais.	L 7	31
Greenlaw Av.		
Rouken Glen Rd., Thorn.& Giff.	R12	61
Roukenburn St. G46	Q12	61
Roundhill Dr., John.	M 3	45
Rowallan Gdns. G11	H13	20
Rowallan La. E. G11	H13	20
Churchill Dr.		
Rowallan La. G11	H13	20
Churchill Dr.		
Rowallan Rd., Thorn.	R12	61
Rowallan Ter. G33	H22	24
Rowan Av., Renf.	H 8	17
Rowan Cres., Lenz.	C23	13
Rowan Dr., Dalm.	D 6	4
Rowan Gate, Pais.	N 6	46
Rowan Gdns. G41	M13	50
Rowan Gdns. G71	Q28	69
Rowan Pl. G72	P22	66
Allison Dr.		
Rowan Pl. G72	P23	67
Caledonian Circuit		
Rowan Pl., Blan.	S26	68
Rowan Rd. G41	M13	50
Rowan Rd., Cumb.	B 4	71
Rowan Rd., Linw.	K 1	28
Rowan St., Pais.	N 6	46
Rowand Av. Giff.	R14	62
Rowandale Av., Bail.	M25	56
Rowanlea Av. G78	O 3	45
Rowanlea Dr., Giff.	Q14	62
Rowanpark Dr., Barr.	P 7	59
Rowans Gdns., Both.	Q28	69
Rowans, The, Bish.	E18	10
Rowantree Av. G73	P19	65
Rowantree Gdns. G73	P19	65
Rowantree Rd., John.	N09	43
Rowchester St. G40	L19	37
Rowena Av. G13	E11	7
Roxburgh Dr., Bear.	B12	7
Roxburgh La. G12	H14	20
Saltoun St.		
Roxburgh Rd., Pais.	O 2	44
Roxburgh St. G12	H14	20
Roy St. G21	H17	22
Royal Bank Pl. G1	K17	36
Buchanan St.		
Royal Cres. G3	J15	35
Royal Cres. G42	N16	51
Royal Exchange Bldgs. G1	K17	36
Royal Exchange Sq.		
Royal Exchange Ct. G1	K17	36
Queen St.		
Royal Exchange Sq. G1	K17	36
Royal Inch Cres., Renf.	G 8	17
Campbell St.		
Royal Inch Ter., Renf.	G 8	17
Royal Ter. G3	J15	35
Royal Ter. G42	N16	51
Queens Dr.		
Royal Terrace La. G3	J15	35
North Claremont St.		
Royston Rd. G21	J18	36
Royston Sq. G21	J18	36
Rozelle Av. G15	D10	6
Rubislaw Dr., Bear.	D12	7
Ruby St. G40	M19	53
Ruchazie Pl. G33	K21	38
Ruchazie Rd. G32	L21	38
Ruchill Pl. G20	G15	21
Ruchill St. G20	G15	21
Ruel St. G44	O16	51
Rufflees Av., Barr.	Q 8	59
Rugby Av. G13	F10	18
Rullion Pl. G33	K21	38
Rumford St. G40	M18	52
Rupert St. G4	J15	35
Rushyhill St. G21	H19	23
Cockmuir St.		
Ruskin La. G12	H15	21
Ruskin Pl. G12	H14	20
Great Western Rd.		
Ruskin Sq., Bish.	E19	11
Ruskin Ter. G12	H15	21
Ruskin Ter. G73	N19	53
Russel Pl., Linw.	L 1	28
Gilmerton Rd.		
Russell Cres. G81	B 6	4
Russell Cres., Bail.	M26	56
Russell Dr., Bear.	C12	7
Russell Rd., Clyde.	C 6	4
Russell St. G11	J13	34
Vine St.		
Russell St., John.	M 1	44
Russell St., Pais.	K 5	30
Rutaerford Av., Chr. & Waterside	C25	14
Chryston Rd.		
Rutherford La. G2	K16	35
Hope St.		
Rutherglen Rd. G5	L17	36
Ruthven Av., Giff.	R14	62
Ruthven La. G12	H14	20
Downside St.		
Ruthven Pl., Bish.	F20	23
Ruthven St. G12	H14	20
Rutland Cres. G51	L15	35
Rutland La. G51	L15	35
Govan Rd.		
Rutland Pl. G51	L15	35
Ryan Rd., Bish.	E19	11
Ryan Way G73	Q20	65
Rye Cres. G21	G20	23
Rye Rd. G21	G20	23
Rye Way, Pais.	N 3	45
Ryebank Rd. G21	G20	23
Ryecroft Dr., Bail.	L25	40
Ryedale Pl., G15	D10	6
Ryefield Av., John.	NO8	43
Ryefield Pl., John.	NO8	43
Ryefield Rd. G21	G19	23
Ryehill Gdns. G21	G20	23
Ryehill Pl. G21	G20	23
Ryehill Rd. G21	G20	23
Ryemount Rd. G21	G20	23
Ryeside Rd. G21	G19	23

Street	Grid	No.
Second Av., Clyde.	D 7	5
Second Av., Lenz.	E23	13
Second Av., Renf.	J 8	31
Second Av., Udd.	N27	57
Second Gdns. G41	M13	50
Second St., Udd.	O27	57
Seedhill Rd., Pais.	M 6	46
Seggielea La. G13	G11	19
Helensburgh Dr.		
Seggielea Rd. G13	G11	19
Seil Dr. G44	Q17	64
Selborne Pl. G13	G12	19
Selborne Rd.		
Selborne Place La. G13	G12	19
Selborne Rd.		
Selborne Rd. G13	G12	19
Selby Gdns. G32	L24	39
Selkirk Av. G52	M11	49
Selkirk Av., Pais.	N 4	45
Selkirk Dr. G73	O20	53
Sella Rd., Bish.	E20	11
Selvieland Rd. G52	L 9	32
Semple Pl., Linw.	K 1	28
Seres Rd., Clark.	S14	62
Sergeantlaw Rd., Pais.	P 4	45
Seton Ter. G31	K18	36
Settle Gdns., Bail.	M24	55
Seven Sisters, Lenz.	L24	13
Seventh Av., Udd.	O27	57
Seyton Av., Giff.	R14	62
Shaftesbury St., Dalm.	E 6	4
Shafton Pl. G13	F12	19
Shafton Rd. G13	F12	19
Shaftsbury St. G3	K15	35
Shakespeare Av., Clyde.	D 6	4
Shakespeare St. G20	G15	21
Shamrock Cotts. G13	G12	19
Crow Rd.		
Shamrock St. G4	J16	35
Shandon St. G51	K14	34
Govan Rd.		
Shandwick St. G34	K25	40
Shanks Av., Barr.	R 8	59
Shanks Cres., John.	N09	43
Shanks St. G20	G15	21
Shannon St. G20	G15	21
Shapinsay St. G22	F17	22
Sharp St. G51	K13	34
Sharrocks St. G51	L14	34
Clifford St.		
Shaw Pl., Linw.	L 1	28
Shaw St. G51	K13	34
Shawbridge St. G43	O14	50
Shawfield Dr. G5	N18	52
Shawfield Rd. G5	N18	52
Shawhill Rd. G43	O14	50
Shawholm Cres. G43	O13	50
Shawlands Arcade G41	O15	51
Shawlands Sq. G41	O15	51
Shawmoss Rd. G41	N14	50
Shawpark St. G20	G15	21
Shearer La. G5	L15	35
Shearer Pl. G5	L15	35
Sheepburn Rd., Udd.	O27	57
Sheila St. G33	H21	24
Sheldrake Pl., John.	O08	43
Shelley Ct. G12	G13	20
Shelley Rd.		
Shelley Dr., Clyde.	D 7	5
Shelley Rd. G12	G12	19
Shelly Dr., Udd.	Q28	69
Sheppard St. G21	H18	22
Cowlairs Rd.		
Sherbrooke Av. G41	M14	50
Sherbrooke Dr. G41	M14	50
Sherburn Gdns., Bail.	M24	55
Sheriff Park Av. G73	O19	53
Sherwood Av., Pais.	L 7	31
Sherwood Av., Udd.	P28	69
Sherwood Dr. G46	Q13	62
Sherwood Pl. G15	D10	6
Shetland Dr. G44	Q17	64
Shettleston Rd. G31	L20	37
Shettleston Sheddings G31	L21	38
Shiel Ct., Barr.	P 7	59
Shiel Rd., Bish.	E19	11
Shieldaig Dr. G73	Q19	65
Shieldaig Rd. G22	F16	21
Shieldburn Rd. G51	K11	33
Shieldhall Gdns. G51	K11	33
Shieldhall Rd. G51	K11	33
Shields Rd. G41	L15	35
Shilford Av. G13	F10	18
Shillay St. G22	F18	22
Shilton Dr. G53	P10	60
Shinwell Av., Clyde.	E 8	5
Shipbank La. G1	L17	36
Clyde St.		
Shiskine Dr. G20	F14	20
Shore St. G40	N18	52
Shortbridge St. G20	G15	21
Shanks St.		
Shortroods Av., Pais.	K 6	30
Shortroods Cres., Pais.	K 6	30
Shortroods Rd., Pais.	K 5	30
Shotts St. G33	K23	39
Shuna Pl. G20	G15	21
Shuna St. G20	G15	21
Shuttle La. G1	K17	36
George St.		
Shuttle St. G1	K17	36
Shuttle St., Kilb.	M07	42
Shuttle St., Pais.	M 6	46
Sidelaw Av., Barr.	R 8	59
Ochil Dr.		
Sidland Rd. G21	G20	23
Sidlaw Rd., Bear.	B10	6
Sielga Pl. G34	K25	40
Siemens Pl. G21	J19	37
Siemens St. G21	J19	37
Sievewright St. G73	N20	53
Hunter Rd.		
Silk St., Pais.	L 6	30
Silkin Av., Clyde.	E 8	5
Silverburn St. G33	K21	38
Silverdale St. G31	M20	53
Silverfir St. G5	M17	52
Silvergrove St. G40	L18	36
Silverwells Cres., Both.	R28	69
Silverwells, Both.	R28	69
Simons Cres., Renf.	G 8	17
Simpson Ct., Udd.	P27	69
Simpson St. G20	H15	21
Simshill Rd. G44	Q16	63
Sinclair Av., Bear.	C12	7
Sinclair Dr. G42	O15	51
Sinclair St., Clyde.	F 8	17
Singer Rd., Dalm. & Clyde.	D 6	4
Singer St., Clyde.	D 7	5
Sir Michael Pl., Pais.	M 5	46
Sixth Av., Renf.	J 8	31
Sixth St., Udd.	N27	57
Skaethorn Rd. G20	F13	20
Skaterig La. G13	G12	19
Skaterigg Rd. G13	G12	19
Crow Rd.		
Skelbo Path G34	J26	40
Auchengill Rd.		
Skelbo Pl. G34	J26	40
Skene Rd. G51	L13	34
Skerray Quad. G22	F17	22
Skerray St. G22	F17	22
Skerryvore Pl. G33	K22	38
Skerryvore Rd. G33	K22	38
Skibo Dr. G46	Q12	61
Skibo La. G46	Q12	61
Skipness Dr. G51	K12	33
Skirsa Ct. G23	F16	21
Skirsa Pl. G23	F15	21
Skirsa Sq. G23	F15	21
Skirsa St. G23	F15	21
Skirving St. G41	O15	51
Skye Av. G67	J 8	31
Skye Cres., Pais.	O 5	46
Skye Ct., Cumb.	D 1	70
Skye Dr., Cumb.	D 1	70
Skye Gdns., Bear.	C10	6
Skye Pl., Cumb.	D 1	70
Skye Rd. G73	Q20	65
Skye Rd., Cumb.	D 1	70
Skye St. G20	F14	20
Bantaskin St.		
Slakiewood Av., Gart.	F27	27
Slatefield St. G31	L19	37
Sleads St. G41	L15	35
Sloy St. G22	H17	22
Smeaton St. G20	G15	21
Smith Cres., Clyde.	C 7	5
Smith St. G14	J12	33
Smith Ter. G73	N19	53
Smithhills St., Pais.	L 6	30
Smiths La., Pais.	L 6	30
Smithy Ends, Cumb.	A 3	71
Smithycroft Rd. G33	J21	38
Snaefell Av. G73	Q20	65
Snaefell Cres. G73	P20	65
Society St. G31	L19	37
Soho St. G40	L19	37
Sollas Pl. G13	F 9	18
Solway Pl., Chr.	E26	14
Solway Rd., Bish.	E20	11
Solway St. G40	N18	52
Somerford Rd., Bear.	E12	7
Somerled Av., Renf.	J 7	31
Somerset Pl. G3	J15	35
Somerset Place Meuse G3	J15	35
Elderslie St.		
Somervell St. G72	P21	66
Somerville Dr. G42	O16	51
Somerville St., Clyde.	E 7	5
Sorby St. G31	L20	37
Sorn St. G40	M19	53
Souter La., Clyde.	D 8	5
South Annandale St. G42	N16	51
South Av., Clyde.	E 7	5
South Av., Pais.	O 6	46
South Av., Renf.	H 8	17
South Bank St., Clyde.	F 8	17
South Brook St., Clyde.	D 6	4
South Campbell St., Pais.	M 6	46
South Carbrain Rd., Cumb.	D 3	71
South Carmyle Av.	O22	54
South Chester St. G32	L22	38
South Cotts. G14	J12	33
Curle St.		
South Croft St., Pais.	L 6	30
Lawn St.		
South Crosshill Rd., Bish.	E19	11
South Deanpark Av., Udd.	R28	69
South Douglas St., Clyde.	F 8	17
South Dr., Linw.	L 1	28
South Elgin Pl., Clyde.	F 8	17
South Elgin St.		
South Elgin St., Clyde.	F 8	17
South Erskine Pk., Bear.	C11	7
South Exchange Ct. G1	K17	36
Queen St.		
South Frederick St. G1	K17	36
South Frederick St. G1	K17	36
Ingram St.		
South Hill Av. G73	P20	65
South Moraine La. G15	E11	7
Moraine Av.		
South Muirhead Rd., Cumb.	C 3	71
South Park Av., Pais.	N 6	46
South Portland St. G5	L16	35
South Scott St., Bail.	M25	56
South Spiers Wf. G4	J16	35
South St. G14	H10	18
South Vesalius St. G32	L22	38
South Vw., Blan.	R26	68
South Vw., Dalm.	D 6	4
South Vw., Lenz.	E23	13
Gadloch Av.		
South Wardpark Ct., Cumb.	A 4	71
Wardpark Rd.		
South Wardpark Pl., Cumb.	A 4	71
South William St., John.	N09	43
South Woodside Rd. G4	J15	35
Southampton Dr. G12	G13	20
Southbank St. G31	L20	37
Sorby St.		
Southbar Av. G13	F10	18
Southbrae Dr. G13	G11	19
Southbrae La. G13	G12	19
Milner Rd.		
Southcroft Rd. G73	N18	52
Southcroft St. G51	K13	34

Street	Grid	Page
Southdeen Av. G15	D10	6
Southdeen Rd. G15	D10	6
Southend Rd., Clyde.	C 7	5
Southern Av. G73	P19	65
Southesk Av., Bish.	E18	10
Southesk Gdns., Bish.	D18	19
Southfield Av., Pais.	O 6	46
Southfield Cres. G53	O11	49
Southfield Rd., Cumb.	C 1	70
Southinch Av. G14	G 9	18
Southinch La. G14	G 9	18
Tweedvale Av.		
Southlea Av. G46	Q13	62
Southlock St. G20	H18	22
Southmuir Pl. G20	G14	20
Southpark Av. G12	J14	34
Southpark La. G12	H15	21
Glasgow St.		
Southpark Ter. G12	J15	35
Southpark Av.		
Southview St. G64	F18	22
Southview Dr., Bear.	C11	7
Southview Pl., Gart.	G27	27
Southview Ter. G21	F18	22
Southwold Rd., Pais.	L 9	32
Southwood Dr. G44	P17	64
Spateston Rd., John.	OO8	43
Spean St. G44	O16	51
Speirs Pl., Linw.	K 1	28
Speirs Rd., John.	M 1	44
Spence St. G20	F14	20
Spencer Dr. G78	O 2	44
Spencer St. G13	F12	19
Spencer St., Clyde.	D 7	5
Spey Av., Pais.	N 3	45
Spey Dr., Renf.	J 9	32
Almond Av.		
Spey Pl., John.	OO8	43
Spey Rd., Bear.	E11	7
Spey St. G33	K21	38
Spiers Clo. G14	G 9	18
Spiers Rd., Bear.	D13	8
Spiers Ter. G14	G 9	18
Spiersbridge Av., Thorn.	Q12	61
Spiersbridge La. G46	Q12	61
Spiersbridge Rd., Thorn.	R12	61
Spiersbridge Ter. G46	Q12	61
Spindlehowe Rd., Udd.	P27	69
Spingburn Way G21	H18	22
Spinner Gdns., Pais.	M 4	45
Spinners La., Clyde.	B 7	5
Faifley Rd.		
Spinners Row, John.	NO8	43
Spittal Rd. G73	Q18	64
Spittal Ter. G72	R25	68
Spoutmouth G1	L17	36
Spring La. G5	M17	52
Lawmoor St.		
Springbank Rd., Pais.	K 5	30
Springbank St. G20	H15	21
Springbank Ter., Pais.	K 5	30
Springboig Av. G32	L23	39
Springboig Rd. G32	K23	39
Springburn Rd. G21	G18	22
Springburn Way G21	H18	22
Springfield Av., Bish.	F19	23
Springfield Av., Pais.	M 8	47
Springfield Av., Udd.	P27	69
Springfield Cres., Bish.	F19	23
Springfield Ct. G1	K17	36
Springfield Dr., Barr.	R 9	60
Springfield Park Rd. G73	P20	65
Springfield Pk., John.	N 1	44
Springfield Rd. G40	M19	53
Springfield Rd., Barr.	S 8	59
Springfield Rd., Bish.	E19	11
Springfield Rd., Cumb.	B 3	71
Springfield Sq., Bish.	F19	23
Springhill Gdns. G41	N15	51
Springhill Rd., Bail.	L24	39
Springhill Rd., Barr.	R 7	59
Springkell Av. G41	M14	50
Springkell Dr. G41	M13	50
Springkell Gate G41	N14	50
Springkell Gdns. G41	N14	50
Springside Pl. G15	D10	6
Springvale Ter. G21	H18	22
Hillkirk Pl.		
Spruce Av., Blan.	S26	68
Spruce Av., John.	N 1	44
Spruce Dr., Lenz.	C22	12
Spruce Rd., Cumb.	B 4	71
Spruce St. G22	G17	22
Spynie Pl., Bish.	E20	11
Squire St. G14	J12	33
Staffa Av., Renf.	J 8	31
Staffa Dr., Pais.	O 6	46
Staffa Rd. G72	Q21	66
Staffa St. G31	K19	37
Staffa Ter. G72	Q21	66
Staffin Dr. G23	E14	8
Staffin St. G23	E15	9
Stag St. G51	K14	34
Stair St. G20	H15	21
Stamford St. G40	L19	37
Stamperland Av., Clark.	S15	63
Stamperland Dr., Clark.	S15	63
Stamperland Gdns., Clark.	S15	63
Stamperland Hill, Clark.	S15	63
Stanalane St. G46	Q12	61
Standburn Rd. G21	F20	23
Stanely Av., Pais.	N 4	45
Stanely Cres., Pais.	O 4	45
Stanely Ct., Pais.	N 4	45
Stanely Dr., Pais.	N 5	46
Stanely Rd., Pais.	N 5	46
Stanford St., Clyde.	E 8	5
Stanhope Dr. G73	P20	65
Stanley Dr., Bish.	D19	11
Stanley Pl., Blan.	R26	68
Stanley St. G41	L15	35
Stanley Street La. G41	L15	35
Milnpark St.		
Stanmore Rd. G42	O16	51
Stark Av., Clyde.	C 6	4
Startpoint St. G33	K22	38
Station Rd. G20	F14	20
Station Rd. G33	G22	24
Station Rd. Step. G33	G23	25
Station Rd., Bail.	M26	56
Station Rd., Bear.	D11	7
Station Rd., Blan.	R27	69
Station Rd., Both.	R28	69
Station Rd., Chr.	G26	26
Station Rd., Giff.	Q14	62
Fenwick Rd.		
Station Rd., Kilb.	NO7	42
Station Rd., Pais.	M 4	45
Station Rd., Renf.	H 8	17
Station Rd., Udd.	P27	69
Station Way, Udd.	P28	69
Mansefield Dr.		
Station Wynd G78	N 7	42
Steel St. G1	L17	36
Steeple St., Kilb.	MO7	42
Stenton St. G32	K21	38
Stepford Path G33	K25	40
Stepford Rd.		
Stepford Pl. G33	K24	39
Stepford Rd. G33	K24	39
Stephen Cres., Bail.	L24	39
Stephenson St. G52	K 9	32
Stepps Rd. G33	J23	39
Stepps Rd., Lenz.	E24	13
Steppshill Ter. G33	G23	25
Stevbrae, Lenz.	C24	13
Stevenson St. G40	L18	36
Stevenson St., Dalm.	D 6	4
Stevenson St., Pais.	M 6	46
Stewart Av., Renf.	J 7	31
Stewart Ct., Barr.	Q 8	59
Stewart St.		
Stewart Dr., Bail.	L28	41
Coatbridge Rd.		
Stewart Dr., Clyde.	C 7	5
Stewart Rd., Pais.	O 6	46
Stewart St. G4	J16	35
Stewart St., Barr.	Q 8	59
Stewart St., Dalm.	D 6	4
Stewarton Dr. G72	P21	66
Stewarton Rd., Thorn.	R12	61
Stewartville St. G11	J13	34
Stirling Av., Bear.	E12	7
Stirling Dr. G73	P19	65
Stirling Dr., Bear.	C11	7
Stirling Dr., Bish.	D18	10
Stirling Dr., John.	NO8	43
Stirling Dr., Linw.	L 1	28
Stirling Fauld Pl. G5	L16	35
Stirling Gdns., Bish.	D18	10
Stirling Rd. G4	K17	36
Stirling St., Cumb.	B 3	71
Stirling Way, Renf.	J 8	31
York Way		
Stirrat St. G20	G14	20
Stirrat St., Pais.	K 4	29
Stobcross Rd. G3	K15	35
Stobhill Rd. G21	F18	22
Stobs Dr., Barr.	P 7	59
Stobs Pl. G34	J26	40
Stock Av., Pais.	N 6	46
Stock St., Pais.	N 6	46
Stockholm Cres., Pais.	M 6	46
Stockiemuir Av., Bear.	B11	7
Stockwell Pl. G1	L17	36
Stockwell St. G1	L17	36
Stoddard Sq., John.	M 2	44
Glenpatrick Rd.		
Stonefield Av. G12	G14	20
Stonefield Av., Pais.	N 6	46
Stonefield Cres., Pais.	N 6	46
Stonefield Dr., Pais.	N 6	46
Stonelaw Dr. G73	O19	53
Stonelaw Rd. G73	O19	53
Stoneside Dr. G43	P13	62
Stoneside Sq. G43	P13	62
Stoney Brae, Pais.	L 6	30
Stoneyetts Cotts., Chr.	D27	15
Stony Brae, Pais.	O 6	46
Stonyhurst St. G22	H16	21
Stonylee Rd., Cumb.	C 3	71
Storie St., Pais.	M 6	46
Stormyland Way., Barr.	R 8	59
Stornoway St. G22	F17	22
Stow Brae, Pais.	M 6	46
Stow St., Pais.	M 6	46
Strachur St. G22	F16	21
Straiton St. G32	K21	38
Stranka Av., Pais.	M 5	46
Stranraer Dr. G15	E11	7
Moraine Av.		
Stratford St. G20	G15	21
Strathallan La. G12	J14	34
Highburgh Rd.		
Strathallan Ter. G12	J14	34
Caledon St.		
Strathallon Pl. G73	Q20	65
Ranald Gdns.		
Strathbran St. G31	M20	53
Strathcarron Pl. G20	G14	20
Gelnfinnan Rd.		
Strathcarron Rd., Pais.	N 7	47
Strathclyde Dr.	O19	53
Strathclyde Path, Udd.	P27	69
Strathclyde St. G40	N19	53
Strathclyde Vw. G71	R28	69
Strathcona Dr. G13	F12	19
Strathcona Gdns. G13	F13	20
Strathcona Pl. G73	Q20	65
Strathcona St. G13	G12	19
Strathdee Av., Clyde.	C 7	5
Strathdee Rd. G44	R15	63
Strathdon Av. G44	R15	63
Strathdon Av., Pais.	N 5	46
Strathdon Dr. G44	R15	63
Strathendrick Dr. G44	Q15	63
Strathmore Av., Blan.	R26	68
Strathmore Av., Pais.	M 8	47
Strathmore Gdns. G12	J15	35
Gibson St.		
Strathmore Gdns. G73	Q20	65
Strathmore Rd. G22	F16	21
Strathord Pl., Chr.	D28	15
Strathord St. G32	M22	54
Strathtay Av. G44	R15	63
Strathview Gdns., Bear.	D11	7
Strathview Gro. G44	R15	63
Strathview Pk. G44	R15	63
Strathy Pl. G20	G14	20
Glenfinnan Rd.		
Strathyre Gdns., Bear.	C13	8
Strathyre Gdns., Chr.	E28	15
Heathfield Av.		
Strathyre St. G41	O15	51
Stratton Dr., Giff.	R13	62
Strauss Av., Clyde.	E 9	6
Stravanan Av. G45	R17	64
Stravanan Rd. G45	R17	64
Stravanan St. G45	R17	64

Street	Grid	Page
Strenabey Av. G73	Q20	65
Striven Gdns. G20	H15	21
Stroma St. G21	J19	37
Stromness St. G5	M16	51
Strone Rd. G33	K22	38
Stronend St. G22	G16	21
Stronsay Pl., Bish.	E20	11
Stronsay St. G21	J19	37
Stronvar Dr. G14	H10	18
Stronvar La. G14	H10	18
Larchfield Av.		
Strowan Cres. G32	M22	54
Strowan St. G32	M22	54
Struan Av., Giff.	Q13	62
Struan Gdns. G44	P16	63
Struan Rd. G44	P16	63
Struie St. G34	K25	40
Stuart Av. G73	P19	65
Stuart Dr., Bish.	F18	22
Succoth St. G13	F12	19
Suffolk St. G40	L18	36
Kent St.		
Sugworth Av., Bail.	L25	40
Sumburgh St. G33	K21	38
Summer St. G40	L18	36
Summerfield Cotts. G14	J12	33
Smith St.		
Summerfield Pl. G40	M19	53
Ardenlea St.		
Summerfield St. G40	N19	53
Summerhill Rd. G15	D10	6
Summerlee Rd., Thorn.	Q12	61
Summerlee St. G33	K23	39
Summertown Rd. G51	K13	34
Sunart Av., Renf.	H 7	17
Sunart Gdns., Bish.	E19	11
Sunart Rd. G52	L12	33
Sunart Rd., Bish.	E19	11
Sunningdale Rd. G23	F14	20
Sunningdale Wynd, Both.	Q27	69
Sunnybank St. G40	M19	53
Sunnylaw Dr. G78	N 4	45
Sunnylaw St. G22	H16	21
Sunnyside Av., Udd.	P27	69
Sunnyside Dr. G15	E10	6
Sunnyside Dr., Bail.	L27	41
Sunnyside Pl. G15	E10	6
Sunnyside Dr.		
Sunnyside Pl., Barr.	R 7	59
Sunnyside Rd., Pais.	N 5	46
Surrey La. G5	M16	51
Pollokshaws Rd.		
Sussex St. G41	L15	35
Sutcliffe Rd. G13	F12	19
Sutherland Av. G41	M14	50
Sutherland Av., Bear.	B12	7
Sutherland Dr., Giff.	R14	62
Sutherland Rd., Clyde	E 7	5
Sutherland St., Pais.	L 5	30
Swan La. G4	J17	36
Swan Pl., John.	O08	43
Swan St., Clyde.	D 6	4
Swanston St. G40	N19	53
Sween Dr. G44	Q16	63
Sweethope Pl., Booth.	Q28	69
Swift Pl., John.	O08	43
Swindon St., Dalm.	D 6	4
Swinton Cres., Bail.	L26	40
Swinton Cres., Coat.	M28	57
Swinton Dr. G52	L10	32
Swinton Pl. G52	L10	32
Swinton Rd., Bail.	L25	40
Switchback Rd., Bear.	E12	7
Sword St. G31	L18	36
Swordale Path G34	K25	40
Swordale Pl.		
Swordale Pl.	K25	40
Sycamore Av., John.	N 1	44
Sycamore Av., Lenz.	C23	13
Sycamore Dr., Dalm.	D 7	5
Sydenham La. G12	H13	20
Crown Rd. S.		
Sydenham Rd. G12	H14	20
Sydney Ct. G2	K16	35
Argyle St.		
Sydney St. G31	L18	36
Sydney St., Dalm.	D 5	4
Sylvania Way S., Clyde.	E 7	5
Sylvania Way, Clyde.	E 7	5
Symington Dr., Clyde.	E 7	5
Syriam Pl. G21	H18	22
Syriam St.		
Syriam St. G21	H18	22
Tabard Pl. G13	F11	19
Tabard Pl. N. G13	F11	19
Tabard Rd.		
Tabard Pl. S. G13	F11	19
Tabard Rd.		
Tabard Rd. G13	F11	19
Tabernacle La. G72	P22	66
Tabernacle St. G72	P22	66
Tain Pl. G34	K26	40
Tait Av., Barr.	Q 8	59
Talbot Dr. G13	G10	18
Talbot Pl. G13	G10	18
Talbot Ter., G13	G10	18
Talbot Ter., Udd.	O27	57
Talisman Rd. G13	G11	19
Talisman Rd., Pais.	O 3	45
Talla Rd. G52	L10	32
Tallant Rd. G15	D10	6
Tallant Ter. G15	D11	7
Tallisman, Clyde.	E 8	5
Onslow Rd.		
Tambowie St. G13	F12	19
Tamshill St. G20	G15	21
Tamworth St. G40	L19	37
Rimsdale St.		
Tanar Av., Renf.	J 9	32
Tanar Way, Renf.	J 9	32
Tandlehill Rd., Kilb.	N07	42
Tanera Av. G44	Q17	64
Tanfield Av. G32	K23	39
Tanfield Pl. G32	K23	39
Tanfield Av.		
Tankerland Rd. G44	P16	63
Tanna Dr. G52	M12	49
Tannadice Av. G52	M11	49
Tannahall Rd., Pais.	L 4	29
Tannahall Ter., Pais.	L 4	29
Tannahill Cres., John.	N09	43
Tannahill Rd. G43	P15	63
Tannoch Dr. G67	D 3	71
Tannoch Pl. G67	D 3	71
Tannock St. G22	H16	21
Tantallon Dr., Pais.	N 4	45
Tantallon Rd. G41	O15	51
Tantallon Rd., Bail.	M25	56
Tanzieknowe Av. G72	Q22	66
Tanzieknowe Dr. G72	Q22	66
Tanzieknowe Pl. G72	Q22	66
Tanzieknowe Rd. G72	Q22	66
Taransay St. G51	K13	34
Tarbert Av., Blan.	R26	68
Tarbolton Dr., Clyde.	D 8	5
Tarbolton Rd. G43	P14	62
Tarbolton Rd., Cumb.	C 3	71
Tarbolton Sq., Clyde.	D 8	5
Tarbolton Dr.		
Tarfside Av. G52	M11	49
Tarfside Gdns. G52	M11	49
Tarfside Oval G52	M11	49
Tarland St. G51	L12	33
Tarras Dr., Renf.	J 9	32
Tarras Pl. G72	P23	67
Tassie St. G41	O14	50
Tattershall Rd. G33	J23	39
Tavistock Dr. G43	P14	62
Tay Av., Pais.	N 3	45
Tay Av., Renf.	H 9	18
Tay Cres. G33	J21	38
Tay Cres., Bish.	E19	11
Tay Pl., John.	O08	43
Tay Rd., Bear.	E11	7
Tay Rd., Bish.	E19	11
Taylor Av. G78	M06	42
Taylor Pl. G4	K17	36
Taylor St. G4	K17	36
Taylor St., Clyde.	F 8	17
Taymouth St. G32	M22	54
Taynish Dr. G44	Q17	64
Tealing Av. G52	M11	49
Tealing Cres. G52	M11	49
Teasel Av. G53	Q10	60
Teith Av., Renf.	J 9	32
Teith Dr., Bear.	D11	7
Teith Pl. G72	P23	67
Teith St. G33	J21	38
Telford Pl. G67	D 3	71
Telford Rd., Cumb.	D 3	71
Templar Av. G13	E11	7
Temple Gdns. G13	F12	19
Temple Pl. G13	F12	19
Temple Rd. G13	F13	20
Templeland Av. G53	N11	49
Templeland Rd. G53	N11	49
Templeton St. G40	L18	36
Tennant Rd., Pais.	L 4	29
Tennant St., Renf.	G 8	17
Campbell St.		
Tennant St., Renf.	H 8	17
Tennyson Dr. G31	M21	54
Tern Pl., John.	O08	43
Terrace Pl. G72	P24	67
Terregles Av., G41	N14	50
Terregles Cres. G41	N14	50
Terregles Dr. G41	N14	50
Teviot Av., Bish.	D19	11
Teviot Av., Pais.	O 3	45
Teviot Cres., Bear.	E11	7
Teviot St. G3	K14	34
Teviot Ter. G20	H15	21
Sanda St.		
Teviot Ter., John.	O08	43
Thane Rd. G13	G11	19
Tharsis St. G21	J18	36
Third Av. G33	G22	24
Third Av. G44	O16	51
Third Av., Lenz.	E23	13
Third Av., Renf.	J 8	31
Third Gdns. G41	M13	50
Third St., Udd.	O27	57
Thirdpart Cres. G13	F 9	18
Thistle Bank, Lenz.	D23	13
Thistle Cotts. G13	G12	19
Crow Rd.		
Thistle St. G5	L17	36
Thistle St., Pais.	N 5	46
Thomas Muir Av., Bish.	F19	23
Thomas St., Pais.	M 4	45
Thompson Pl., Clyde.	C 8	5
Thomson Av., John.	M09	43
Thomson Dr., Bear.	C12	7
Thomson St. G31	L19	37
Thomson St., John.	N09	43
Thomson St., Renf.	J 8	31
Thorn Brae, John.	M 1	44
Thorn Dr. G73	Q20	65
Thorn Dr., Bear.	C11	7
Thorn Rd. G46	P13	62
Thorn Rd., Bear.	C11	7
Thorn St. G11	J13	34
Dumbarton Rd.		
Thornbank St. G3	J14	34
Yorkhill Parade		
Thornbridge Av. G12	G14	20
Balcarres Av.		
Thornbridge Av., Bail.	L25	40
Bannercross Dr.		
Thornbridge Gdns., Bail.	L25	40
Thornbridge Rd., Bail.	L25	40
Thorncliffe Gdns. G4	N15	51
Thorncliffe La. G41	M15	51
Thorncroft Dr. G44	Q17	64
Thornden Cotts. G14	G 9	18
Dumbarton Rd.		
Thornden La. G14	G 9	18
Dumbarton Rd.		
Thorndene, John.	M 1	44
Thornhill Av., Blan.	S26	68
Thornhill Av., John.	N 1	44
Thornhill Dr. G78	N 1	44
Thornhill Path G31	L20	37
Beattock St.		
Thornhill Path G31	L20	37
Grier Path		
Thornhill, John.	N 1	44
Thorniewood Gdns., Udd.	O28	57
Thorniewood Rd., Udd.	O27	57
Thornlea Dr., Giff.	Q14	62
Thornley Av. G13	Q10	18
Thornliebank Rd. G46	Q13	62
Thornliebank Rd., Thorn., Giff. & G43	R11	61
Thornly Park Av., Pais.	O 6	46
Thornly Park Dr., Pais.	O 6	46
Thornly Park Rd., Pais.	O 6	46

Street	Ref		Street	Ref		Street	Ref
Thornside Rd., John.	M 1 44		Torridon Av. G41	M13 50		Tweedsmuir Cres., Bear.	B12 7
Thornton La. G20	F15 21		Torrin Rd. G23	E14 8		Tweedsmuir Rd. G52	M10 48
Thornton St. G20	F15 21		Torrington Av., Giff.	S13 62		Tweedsmuir, Bish.	E20 11
Thorntree Way, Udd.	Q28 69		Torrington Cres. G32	M23 55		Tweedvale Av. G14	G 9 18
Thornwood Av. G11	J13 34		Torrisdale St. G42	N15 51		Tweedvale Pl. G14	G 9 18
Thornwood Av., Lenz.	C22 12		Torryburn Rd. G21	H20 23		Twinlaw St. G34	J26 40
Thornwood Cres. G11	H11 19		Torwood La., Chr.	E28 15		Tylnley Rd., Pais.	L 8 31
Thornwood Dr.			*Burnbrae Av.*			Tyndrum Rd., Bear.	C13 8
Thornwood Dr., G11	J12 33		Toryglen Rd. G73	O18 52		Tyndrum St. G4	J17 36
Thornwood Dr., Pais.	N 4 45		Toryglen St. G5	N17 52		Tyne St. G14	J11 33
Thornwood Gdns. G11	J13 34		Toward Rd. G33	K23 39		Tynecastle Cres. G32	K22 38
Thornwood Pl. G11	H13 20		Tower Av., Barr.	Q 8 59		Tynecastle Pl. G32	K22 38
Thornwood Quadrant G11	H11 19		Tower Cres., Renf.	J 7 31		Tynecastle St. G32	K22 38
Thornwood Dr.			Tower Dr., Renf.	J 7 31		Tynwald Av. G73	Q20 65
Thornwood Rd. G11	J12 33		Tower Pl. G20	G14 20			
Thornwood Ter. G11	J12 33		*Glenfinnan Dr.*			Uddingston Rd., Both.	Q28 69
Thornyburn Dr., Bail.	M26 56		Tower Pl., John.	N 1 44		Uig Pl. G33	L24 39
Thornyburn Pla., Bail.	M26 56		Tower Rd., John.	N09 43		Uist Cres. G33	H24 25
Three Ell Rd. G51	K14 34		Tower St. G41	L15 35		Uist St. G51	K12 33
Govan Rd.			Tower Ter., Pais.	M 5 46		Ulundi Rd., John.	N09 43
Threestonehill Av. G32	L22 38		Towerhill Rd. G13	E11 7		Ulva St. G52	L12 33
Thrums Av., Bish.	E20 11		Towerhill Ter. G21	H19 23		Unden Pl. G13	F12 19
Thrums Gdns., Bish.	E20 11		*Broomfield Rd.*			Underwood La., Pais.	L 5 30
Thrush Pl., John.	O08 43		Towerside Cres. G53	N10 48		Underwood Rd. G41	O15 51
Thrushcraig Cres., Pais.	N 6 46		Towerside Rd. G53	N10 48		*Tantallon Rd.*	
Thurso St. G11	J14 34		Towie Pl., Udd.	P27 69		Underwood Rd. G73	P20 65
Dumbarton Rd.			Townhead Rd., Gart.	J28 41		Underwood Rd., Pais.	L 5 30
Thurston Rd. G52	L10 32		Townhead Ter., Pais.	M 5 46		Union Pl. G1	K16 35
Tibbermore Rd. G11	H13 20		Townmill Rd. G31	K18 36		*Gordon St.*	
Tillet Oval, Pais.	K 5 30		Townsend St. G4	J17 36		Union St. G1	K16 35
Tillie St. G20	H15 21		Tradeston St. G5	L16 35		Union St., Clyde.	F 8 17
Tillycairn Dr. G33	J23 39		Trafalgar St. G40	M18 52		Union St., Pais.	N 6 46
Tilt St. G33	J21 38		Trafalgar St., Dalm.	D 6 4		Unity Pl. G4	J16 35
Tintagel Gdns., Chr.	D27 15		Trainard Av. G32	M21 54		*St. Peters St.*	
Tinto Dr., Barr.	S 8 59		Tranent Pl. G33	K21 38		University Av. G12	J14 34
Tinto Rd. G43	P14 62		Traquair Av. G78	O 3 45		University Gdns. G12	J14 34
Tinto Rd., Bear.	C10 6		Traquair Dr. G52	M10 48		University Pl. G12	J14 34
Tinto Rd., Bish.	E20 11		Treeburn Av., Giff.	Q13 62		Unsted Pl., Pais.	M 7 47
Fintry Cres.			Trees Park Av., Barr.	Q 7 59		Uphall Pl. G33	K21 38
Tinto Sq., Renf.	J 7 31		Trefoil Av. G41	O14 50		Upland Rd. G14	H11 19
Ochil Rd.			Tresta Rd. G23	F16 21		Upper Bourtree Ct. G73	Q20 65
Tinwald Av. G52	L 9 32		Trident Way, Renf.	J 8 31		*Upper Bourtree Dr.*	
Tinwald Path G52	L10 32		*Newmains Rd.*			Upper Bourtree Dr. G73	Q19 65
Tiree Av., Pais.	O 5 46		Trinity Av. G52	M11 49		Upper Glenburn Rd., Bear.	C11 7
Tiree Av., Renf.	J 8 31		Trinity Dr. G72	Q23 67		Ure Pl. G4	K17 36
Tiree Ct., Cumb.	D 1 70		Trinley Brae G13	E11 7		*Montrose St.*	
Tiree Dr., Cumb.	D 1 70		Trinley Rd. G13	E11 7		Urquhart Cres., Renf.	J 8 31
Tiree Gdns., Bear.	C10 6		Tronda Pl. G33	K24 39		Urrdale Rd. G41	L13 34
Tiree Rd., Cumb.	D 1 70		Tronda Rd. G33	K24 39		Usmore Pl. G33	L24 39
Tiree St. G21	J20 37		Trondra Path G33	K24 39			
Tirry Way, Renf.	J 9 32		Trongate G1	L17 36		Vaila Pl. G23	F15 21
Morriston Cres.			Troon St. G40	M19 53		*Vaila St.*	
Titwood Rd. G41	N14 50		Trossachs Rd. G73	R20 65		Vaila St. G23	F15 21
Tiverton Av. G32	M23 55		Trossachs St. G20	H16 21		Vale Wk., Bish.	F20 23
Tobago Pl. G40	L18 36		Troubridge Av., John.	O07 42		Valetta Pl., Dalm.	D 5 4
Tobago St. G40	L18 36		Troubridge Cres. G78	N07 42		Valeview Ter. G42	O16 51
Tobermory Rd. G73	R20 65		Troubridge Cres., John.	O07 42		Vallay St. G22	F17 22
Todburn Dr., Pais.	O 6 46		Truce Rd. G13	F10 18		Valley Vw. G72	P23 67
Todd St. G31	K20 37		Truro Rd., Chr.	D27 15		*Caledonian Circuit*	
Todholm Rd., Pais.	N 7 47		Tryst Rd. G67	C 2 70		Valleyfield St. G21	H18 22
Todholm Ter., Pais.	N 7 47		Tudor La. S. G14	H11 19		Van St. G31	L20 37
Toll La. G51	L14 34		*Orleans Av.*			Vancouver Pl., Dalm.	D 5 4
Paisley Rd. W.			Tudor Rd. G14	H12 19		Vancouver Rd. G14	H11 19
Tollcross Rd. G31	L20 37		Tudor St., Bail.	M24 55		Vanguard St., Clyde.	E 8 5
Tolsta St. G23	E15 9		Tufthill Av., Bish.	E18 10		Vanguard St., Renf.	J 8 31
Tontine La. G1	L17 36		Tufthill Gdns., Bish.	E18 10		Varna La. G14	H12 19
Bell St.			Tullis Ct. G40	M18 52		Varna Rd. G14	H12 19
Tontine Pl. G73	Q21 66		Tullis St. G40	M18 52		Veitchs Ct., Clyde.	C 6 4
Toppersfield, John.	O08 43		Tulloch St. G44	P16 63		*Dumbarton Rd.*	
Torbreck St. G52	L12 33		Tullochard Pl. G73	Q20 65		Vennacher Rd., Renf.	H 7 17
Torbrex Rd., Cumb.	C 3 71		Tummel St. G33	J21 38		Vennard Gdns. G41	N15 51
Torburn Av., Giff.	Q13 62		Tummel Way, Pais.	N 3 45		Vere St. G22	H17 22
Tordene Path, Cumb.	B 1 70		Tunnel St. G3	K15 35		Vermont Av. G73	O19 53
Torgyle St. G23	E14 8		Turnberry Av. G11	H13 20		Vermont St. G41	L15 35
Tormore St. G51	L11 33		Turnberry Dr. G72	P18 64		Vernon Dr., Linw.	L 1 28
Tormusk Dr. G45	Q19 65		Turnberry Gdns., Cumb.	A 2 70		Verona Av. G14	H11 19
Tormusk Rd. G45	Q19 65		Turnberry Pl. G73	P18 64		Vesalius St. G32	L22 38
Torness St. G11	J14 34		Turnberry Rd. G11	H13 20		Vicarfield Pl. G51	K13 34
Torogay Pl. G22	F18 22		Turnberry Wynd, Both.	Q27 69		*Vicarfield St.*	
Torogay St. G22	F17 22		Turnbull St. G1	L17 36		Vicarfield St. G51	K13 34
Torogay Ter. G22	F17 22		Turnlaw Rd. G72	R22 66		Vicarland Pl. G72	Q22 66
Toronto Wk. G32	O23 55		Turnlaw St. G5	M17 52		Vicarland Rd. G72	P22 66
Torphin Cres. G32	L22 38		Turret Cres. G13	F11 19		Vicars Wk. G72	P22 66
Torphin Wk. G32	L22 38		Turret Rd. G13	F11 19		Victoria Circus G12	H14 20
Torr Rd., Bish.	E20 11		Turriff St. G5	M16 51		Victoria Cres. G12	H14 20
Torr St. G22	H17 22		Tweed Av., Pais.	N 3 45		*Downside Rd.*	
Torran Rd. G33	K24 39		Tweed Cres. G33	J21 38		Victoria Cres. La. G12	H14 20
Torrance Rd., Bish.	C20 11		Tweed Cres., Renf.	H 9 18		*Victoria Crescent Rd.*	
Torrance St. G21	H18 22		Tweed Dr., Bear.	D11 7		Victoria Cres. Rd. G12	H14 20
			Tweed Pl., John.	O08 43			

Name	Grid	Page
Victoria Cross G42	N16	51
Victoria Rd.		
Victoria Dr. E., Renf.	J 8	31
Victoria Dr., Renf.	H 7	17
Victoria Park Corner G14	H11	19
Victoria Park Dr. N. G14	H12	19
Victoria Park Dr. S. G11	H11	19
Victoria Park Gdns. N. G11	H12	19
Victoria Park Gdns. S. G11	H12	19
Victoria Park La. N. G14	H11	19
Victoria Park La. S. G14	H11	19
Westland Dr.		
Victoria Park St. G14	H11	19
Victoria Rd. G33	G23	25
Victoria Rd. G42	N16	51
Victoria Rd. G73	P19	65
Victoria Rd., Barr.	Q 7	59
Victoria Rd., Lenz.	D23	13
Victoria Rd., Pais.	N 5	46
Victoria St. G73	O19	53
Victoria St., Clyde.	E 8	5
Victory Dr., Kilb.	M07	42
Glentyan Av.		
Viewbank, Thorn.	Q13	62
Viewfield Av., Bail.	L24	39
Viewfield Av., Bish.	F18	22
Viewfield Av., Blan.	R27	69
Viewfield Av., Lenz.	C23	13
Viewfield Dr., Bail.	L24	39
Viewfield Dr., Bish.	F18	22
Viewfield La., G12	J15	35
Gibson St.		
Viewfield Rd., Bish.	F18	22
Viewfield Rd., Coat.	M28	57
Viewfield Ter. G12	J15	35
Southpark Av.		
Viewmount Dr. G20	F14	20
Viewpark Av. G31	K19	37
Viewpark Dr. G73	P19	65
Viewpoint Pl. G21	G18	22
Viewpoint Rd. G21	G18	22
Viking Way, Renf.	J 8	31
Vanguard Way		
Villafield Av., Bish.	D19	11
Villafield Dr., Bish.	D19	11
Villafield Loan, Bish.	D19	11
Village Rd. G72	P24	67
Villiers Ct. G31	L18	36
Sword St.		
Vine St. G11	J13	34
Vinegarhill St. G31	L19	37
Vinicombe La. G12	H14	20
Vinicombe St.		
Vinicombe St. G12	H14	20
Vintner St. G4	J17	36
Violet St., Pais.	M 7	47
Virginia Bldgs. G1	K17	36
Virginia St.		
Virginia Ct. G1	K17	36
Virginia St.		
Virginia Pl. G1	K17	36
Virginia St. G1	K17	36
Viscount Av., Renf.	J 8	31
Voil Dr. G44	Q16	63
Vorlich Ct., Barr.	R 8	59
Vulcan St. G21	H18	22
Waddel Ct. G5	L17	36
Waddel St. G5	M17	52
Waldemar Rd. G13	F11	19
Waldo St. G13	F12	19
Walker Ct. G11	J13	34
Walker St.		
Walker Dr., John.	N 1	44
Walker Sq. G20	F14	20
Bantaskin St.		
Walker St. G11	J13	34
Walker St., Pais.	M 5	46
Walkerburn Rd. G52	M10	48
Walkinshaw Cres., Pais.	L 4	29
Ferguslie Park Av.		
Walkinshaw Rd., Renf.	H 5	16
Walkinshaw St. G40	M19	53
Walkinshaw St., John.	M09	43
Walkinshaw Way, Pais.	K 5	30
Broomdyke Way		
Wallace Av., John.	N 2	44
Wallace Pl., Blan.	R27	69
Wallace Rd., Renf.	J 7	31
Wallace St. G5	L16	35
Wallace St. G73	O19	53
Wallace St., Clyde.	F 7	17
Wallace St., Pais.	L 6	30
Wallacewell Cres. G21	G19	23
Wallacewell Pl. G21	G19	23
Wallacewell Quad. G21	G20	23
Wallacewell Rd. G21	G19	23
Wallbrae Rd., Cumb.	D 3	71
Wallneuk Rd., Pais.	L 6	30
Wallneuk, Pais.	L 6	30
Incle St.		
Walls St. G1	K17	36
Walmer Cres. G51	L14	34
Walmer Ter. G51	L14	34
Paisley Rd. W.		
Walnut Cres. G22	G17	22
Walnut Cres., John.	N 1	44
Walnut Dr., Lenz.	C22	12
Walnut Pl. G22	G17	22
Walnut Rd. G22	G17	22
Walter St. G31	K20	37
Walton St. G41	O15	51
Walton St., Barr.	Q 8	59
Wamba Av. G13	F12	19
Wamba Pl. G13	F12	19
Wandilla Av., Clyde.	E 8	5
Wanlock St. G51	K13	34
Warden Rd. G13	F11	19
Wardhill Rd. G21	G19	23
Wardhouse Rd., Pais.	O 5	46
Wardie Pl. G33	K25	40
Wardie Path G33	K24	39
Wardie Rd. G33	K25	40
Wardlaw Av. G73	O19	53
Wardlaw Dr. G73	O19	53
Wardlaw Rd., Bear.	E12	7
Wardpark Rd., Cumb.	A 4	71
Wardrop St. G51	K13	34
Wardrop St., Pais.	M 6	46
Ware Path G33	K25	40
Ware Rd. G33	K24	39
Warilda Av., Clyde.	E 8	5
Warp La. G3	K15	35
Argyle St.		
Warren St. G42	N16	51
Warrington St. G20	G15	21
Warriston Cres. G33	K20	37
Warriston Pl. G32	K22	38
Warriston St. G33	K20	37
Warroch St. G3	K15	35
Washington Rd., Renf.	K 6	30
Washington St. G3	K16	35
Water Brae, Pais.	L 6	30
Smithhills St.		
Water Brae, Pais.	M 6	46
Forbes Pl.		
Water Rd., Barr.	Q 8	59
Waterfoot Av. G53	O11	49
Waterford Rd., Giff.	Q13	62
Waterloo La. G2	K16	35
Waterloo St.		
Waterloo St. G2	K16	35
Watermill Av., Lenz.	D23	13
Waterside La., Kilb.	N08	43
Kilbarchan Rd.		
Waterside St. G5	M17	52
Waterside Ter., Kilb.	N08	43
Kilbarchan Rd.		
Watling St., Udd.	O27	57
Watson Av. G73	O18	52
Watson Av., Linw.	L 1	28
Watson St., G1	L17	36
Watson St., Udd.	P27	69
Watt Low Av. G73	P19	65
Watt Rd. G52	K 9	32
Watt St. G5	L15	35
Waukglen Dr. G53	Q10	60
Waukglen Path G53	Q10	60
Waulkmill Av., Barr.	Q 8	59
Waulkmill St., Thorn.	Q12	61
Waverley Cres., Cumb.	D 1	70
Waverley Ct., Udd.	R28	69
Waverley Dr. G73	O20	53
Waverley Gdns. G41	N15	51
Waverley Gdns., John.	N 2	44
Waverley Rd., Pais.	O 3	45
Waverley St. G41	N15	51
Waverley Ter. G31	L19	37
Whitevale St.		
Waverley Way, Pais.	O 3	45
Waverley Rd.		
Waverley, Clyde.	E 8	5
Onslow Rd.		
Weardale La. G33	K23	39
Weardale St. G33	K23	39
Weaver La., Kilb.	M07	42
Glentyan Av.		
Weaver St. G4	K17	36
Weaver Ter., Pais.	M 7	47
Weavers Av., Pais.	M 4	45
Weavers Rd., Pais.	M 4	45
Webster St. G40	M19	53
Webster St., Clyde.	F 9	18
Wedderlea Dr. G52	L10	32
Weensmoor Pl. G53	Q10	60
Weensmoor Rd. G53	P10	60
Weeple Dr., Linw.	L 1	28
Weighhouse Clo., Pais.	M 5	46
Weir Av., Barr.	R 8	59
Weir Rd., Linw.	K 1	28
Weir St. G5	L16	35
Weir St., Pais.	L 6	30
Weirwood Av., Bail.	M24	55
Weirwood Gdns., Bail.	M24	55
Welbeck Rd. G53	P10	60
Welfare Av. G72	Q23	67
Well Grn. G43	O14	50
Well Rd., Kilb.	M07	42
Well St. G40	L18	36
Well St., Pais.	L 5	30
Wellbank Pl., Udd.	P27	69
Church St.		
Wellbrae Ter., Chr.	E27	15
Wellcroft Pl. G5	M16	51
Wellfield Av., Giff.	Q13	62
Wellfield St. G21	H18	22
Wellhouse Cres. G33	K24	39
Wellhouse Path G33	K24	39
Wellhouse Rd. G33	K24	39
Wellington La. G2	K16	35
West Campbell St.		
Wellington Pl., Dalm.	D 5	4
Wellington Rd., Bish.	D20	11
Wellington St. E. G31	L20	37
Wellington St. G2	K16	35
Wellington St., Pais.	L 5	30
Calendonia St.		
Wellington Way, Renf.	J 8	31
Tiree Av.		
Wellmeadow Rd. G43	P13	62
Wellmeadow St., Pais.	M 5	46
Wellpark G31	K18	36
Wellpark St. G31	K18	36
Wellshot Dr. G72	P21	66
Wellshot Rd. G32	M21	54
Wellside Dr. G72	Q23	67
Wemyss Gdns., Bail.	M25	56
Wendur Way, Pais.	K 5	30
Abbotsburn Way		
Wenloch Rd., Pais.	N 6	46
Wentworth Dr. G23	E15	9
West Av. G33	G23	25
West Av., Renf.	H 8	17
West Av., Udd.	P28	69
West Brae, Pais.	M 5	46
West Campbell St. G2	K16	35
West Campbell St., Pais.	M 4	45
West Chapelton Av., Bear.	D12	7
West Chapelton Cres., Bear.	D12	7
West Chapelton Dr., Bear.	D12	7
West Chapelton La., Bear.	D12	7
West Chapelton Av.		
West Coats Rd. G72	Q21	66
West Cotts., Gart.	H25	26
West Ct., Dalm.	D 6	4
Little Holm		
West Duntiblae Rd., Lenz.	B25	14
West George La. G2	K16	35
West Campbell St.		
West George St. G32	K16	35
West Graham St. G4	J16	35

Street	Grid	Page
West Greenhill Pl. G3	K15	35
West La., Pais.	M 4	45
West Lodge Rd., Renf.	H 7	17
West Nile St. G2	K16	35
West Princes St. G4	J15	35
West Regent La. G2	K16	35
Renfield St.		
West Regent St. G2	K16	35
West St. G5	L16	35
West St. G5	M16	51
West St., Clyde.	F 9	18
West St., Kilb.	M07	42
West St., Pais.	M 5	46
West Thomson St., Clyde.	D 7	5
West Whitby St. G31	M20	53
Westbank La. G12	J15	35
Gibson St.		
Westbank Quad. G12	J15	35
Gibson St.		
Westbank Ter. G12	J15	35
Gibson St.		
Westbourne Cres., Bear.	C11	7
Westbourne Dr., Bear.	C11	7
Westbourne Gdns. La. G12	H14	20
Lorraine Rd.		
Westbourne Gdns. N. G12	H14	20
Westbourne Gdns. S. G12	H14	20
Westbourne Gdns. W. G12	H14	20
Westbourne Rd. G12	H13	20
Westbourne Ter. La. G12	H13	20
Westbourne Rd.		
Westbrae Dr. G14	H12	19
Westburn	P24	67
Westburn Av. G72	P23	67
Westburn Av., Pais.	L 4	29
Westburn Cres. G73	O18	52
Westburn Dr. G72	P22	66
Westburn Farm Rd. G72	P22	66
Westburn Rd. G72	P25	68
Westclyffe St. G41	N15	51
Westend Park St. G3	J15	35
Westend, Bear.	E13	8
Maryhill Rd.		
Wester Cleddens Rd., Bish.	E19	11
Wester Common Dr. G22	H16	21
Wester Common Rd. G22	H16	21
Wester Common Ter. G22	H16	21
Wester Rd. G32	M23	55
Westerburn St. G32	K21	38
Carntynehall Rd.		
Westercraigs G31	K18	36
Westergreens Av., Lenz.	C23	13
Parkburn Av.		
Westerhill Rd., Bish.	D19	11
Westerhill St. G22	H17	22
Westerhouse Rd. G34	J25	40
Westerkirk Dr. G23	E15	9
Western Av. G73	O18	52
Western Rd. G72	Q21	66
Westerton Av., Bear.	F12	19
Westfield Av. G73	O18	52
Westfield Cres., Bear.	E12	7
Westfield Dr. G52	L10	32
Westfield Dr., Bear.	E12	7
Westfield Rd., Thorn.	R12	61
Westfield Villas G73	O18	52
Westfields, Bish.	D18	10
Westhouse Av. G73	O18	52
Westhouse Gdns. G73	O18	52
Westknowe Gdns. G73	P19	65
Westland Dr. G14	H11	19
Westland Drive La. G14	H11	19
Westland Dr.		
Westlands Gdns., Pais.	N 5	46
Westlands, Bish.	D18	10
Westminster Gdns. G12	H14	20
Kersland St.		
Westminster Ter. G3	K15	35
Claremont St.		
Westmoreland St. G42	N16	51
Westmuir Pl. G73	O18	52
Westmuir St. G31	L20	37
Westpark Dr., Pais.	L 4	29
Westray Circus G22	G17	22
Westray Ct., Cumb.	D 2	70
Westray Pl. G22	F17	22
Westray Pl., Bish.	E20	11
Ronaldsay Dr.		
Westray Rd., Cumb.	D 2	70
Westray Sq. G22	F17	22
Westray St. G22	F17	22
Westwood Av., Giff.	Q13	62
Westwood Quad., Clyde.	E 8	5
Westwood Rd. G43	P13	62
Weymouth Dr. G12	G13	20
Whamflet Av., Bail.	K26	40
Wheatfield Rd., Bear.	E11	7
Wheatlands Dr., Kilb.	M07	42
Wheatlands Farm Rd., Kilb.	M07	42
Whin Dr., Barr.	Q 7	59
Whin St., Clyde.	D 7	5
Whinfield Path G53	Q10	60
Whinfield Rd. G53	Q10	60
Whinfold Av. G72	O21	54
Whinhill Rd. G53	M10	48
Whinhill Rd., Pais.	N 7	47
Whins Rd. G41	N14	50
Whirlow Gdns., Bail.	L25	40
Whirlow Rd., Bail.	L25	40
Whistlefield, Bear.	D12	7
Whitacres Path G53	Q10	60
Whitacres Pl. G53	Q10	60
Whitacres Rd. G53	Q10	60
Whitburn St. G32	K21	38
White St. G11	J13	34
White St., Clyde.	F 8	17
Whitecraigs Pl. G23	F15	21
Whitefield Av. G72	Q22	66
Whitefield Rd. G51	L14	34
Whiteford Rd., Pais.	N 7	47
Whitehall Ct. G3	K15	35
Whitehall St. G3	K15	35
Whitehaugh Av., Pais.	L 7	31
Whitehaugh Cres. G53	Q10	60
Whitehaugh Dr., Pais.	L 7	31
Whitehaugh Path G53	Q10	60
Whitehaugh Rd. G53	Q10	60
Whitehill Av., Cumb.	C 1	70
Whitehill Av., G33	G23	25
Whitehill Farm Rd. G33	G23	25
Whitehill Gdns. G31	K19	37
Garthland Dr.		
Whitehill La., Bear.	D11	7
Whitehill Rd.		
Whitehill Rd. G33	F23	25
Whitehill Rd., Bear.	C11	7
Whitehill St. G31	K19	37
Whitehurst, Bear.	C11	7
Whitekirk Pl. G15	E10	6
Whitelaw St. G20	F14	20
Whitelawburn Av. G72	Q21	66
Whitelawburn Rd. G72	Q21	66
Whitelawburn Ter. G72	Q21	66
Whitelaws Loan, Both.	Q28	69
Whiteloans, Udd.	Q28	69
Wordsworth Way		
Whitemoss Av. G44	Q15	63
Whitestone Av., Cumb.	B 1	70
Dungoil Av.		
Whitevale St. G31	L19	37
Whithope Rd. G53	Q 9	60
Whithope Ter. G53	Q 9	60
Whitriggs Rd. G53	P 9	60
Whitslade St. G34	J25	40
Whittingehame Dr. G12	G12	19
Whittingehame Gdns. G12	G13	20
Whittliemuir Av. G44	Q15	63
Whitton Dr., Giff.	Q14	62
Whitton St. G20	F14	20
Whitworth Dr., Clyde.	E 7	5
Whitworth St. G20	G16	21
Whyte Av. G72	P21	66
Wick St. G51	K13	34
Wickets, The, Pais.	M 7	47
Wigton St. G4	H16	21
Wigtoun Pl., Cumb.	B 3	71
Wilderness Brae, Cumb.	B 3	71
Wilfred Av. G13	F11	19
Wilkie Rd., Udd.	P28	69
Wilkie St. G31	L19	37
William St. G2	K16	35
William St., Clyde.	C 7	5
William St., John.	M09	43
William St., Pais.	M 5	46
Williamson Park W. G44	R15	63
Williamson Pl., John.	N 1	44
Williamson St. G31	M20	53
Williamson St., Clyde.	D 7	5
Williamwood Dr. G44	R15	63
Williamwood Pk. G44	R15	63
Willoughby Dr. G13	G12	19
Willow Av., Bish.	F19	23
Willow Av., John.	N 2	44
Hillview Rd.		
Willow Av., Lenz.	C23	13
Willow Dr., Blan.	S26	68
Willow Dr., John.	N09	43
Willow St. G13	F12	19
Willowbank Cres. G3	J15	35
Willowbank St. G3	J15	35
Willowdale Cres., Bail.	M25	56
Willowdale Gdns., Bail.	M25	56
Willowford Rd. G53	Q 9	60
Wilmot Rd. G13	G11	19
Wilson Av., Linw.	L 1	28
Wilson St. G1	K17	36
Wilson St., Pais.	M 5	46
William St.		
Wilson St., Renf.	H 8	17
Wilsons Pl., Pais.	M 6	46
Seedhill		
Wilton Cres. G20	H15	21
Wilton Crescent La. G20	H15	21
Wilton Cres.		
Wilton Ct. G20	H15	21
Wilton Dr. G20	H15	21
Wilton Gdns. G20	H15	21
Wilton Mansions G20	H15	21
Wilton Dr.		
Wilton St. G20	H15	21
Wiltonburn Path G53	Q10	60
Wiltonburn Rd. G53	Q10	60
Wilverton Rd. G13	F12	19
Winchester Dr. G12	G13	20
Windhill Pl. G43	P14	62
Windhill Rd.		
Windhill Rd. G43	P13	62
Windlaw Ct. G45	R17	64
Windlaw Gdns. G44	Q15	63
Windlaw Park Gdns. G44	Q15	63
Windmill Cres. G43	P13	62
Windmill Rd.		
Windmill Pl. G43	P14	62
Windmill Rd.		
Windmillcroft Quay G5	L16	35
Windsor Cres., Clyde.	D 7	5
Windsor Cres., John.	N 1	44
Windsor Cres., Pais.	L 7	31
Windsor Rd., Renf.	J 8	31
Windsor St. G20	J16	35
Windsor St. G32	L23	39
Windsor Ter. G20	J16	35
Windsor Wk., Udd.	O28	57
Windyedge Cres. G13	G11	19
Windyedge Pl. G13	G11	19
Wingfield Gdns., Both.	R28	69
Blairston Av.		
Winifred St. G33	H20	23
Winning Ct., Blan.	R27	69
Ness Dr.		
Winning Row G31	L21	38
Winton Av., Giff.	R14	62
Winton Dr. G12	G14	20
Winton Gdns., Udd.	O27	57
Winton La. G12	G14	20
Wirran Pl. G13	F 9	18
Wishart St. G4	K18	36
Wisner Ct., Thorn.	Q12	61
Wiston St. G72	P24	67
Woddrop St. G40	N19	53
Wolseley St. G5	M17	52
Wood Farm Rd., Giff.	R13	62
Wood La., Bish.	F19	23
Wood Quad., Clyde.	F 9	18
Wood St. G31	K19	37
Wood St., Pais.	M 7	47
Woodbank Cres., John.	N09	43

Street	Grid	Col	Row
Woodbank Ter. Gart.	G27		27
Woodburn Av., Blan.	S27		69
Woodburn Rd. G43	P14		62
Woodburn Rd., Cumb.	C 1		70
Woodcroft Av. G11	H12		19
Woodcroft Ter. G11	H12		19
Crow Rd.			
Woodend Ct. G32	N24		55
Woodend Dr. G13	G12		19
Woodend Dr., Pais.	M 8		47
Woodend Gdns. G32	N24		55
Woodend Pl., John.	N 1		44
Malloch Cres.			
Woodend Rd. G32	N23		55
Woodend Rd. G73	Q19		65
Woodend, Giff.	R13		62
Milverton Rd.			
Woodfield Av., Bish.	E19		11
Woodfoot Path G53	Q10		60
Woodfoot Pl. G53	Q10		60
Woodfoot Quad. G53	Q10		60
Woodfoot Rd. G53	Q10		60
Woodford Pl., Linw.	L 1		28
Woodford St. G41	O15		51
Woodgreen Av. G44	P17		64
Woodhall St. G40	N19		53
Woodhead Av. G71	R28		69
Old Bothwell Rd.			
Woodhead Cres., Both.	S28		69
Woodhead Cres., Udd.	O27		57
Woodhead Path G53	P10		60
Woodhead Rd. G53	P 9		60
Woodhead Rd., Chr.	G25		26
Woodhead Ter., Chr.	F25		26
Woodhill Rd. G21	G19		23
Woodhill Rd., Bish.	E19		11
Woodholm Av. G44	P17		64
Woodhouse St. G13	F12		19
Woodilee Cotts., Lenz.	C24		13
Woodilee Rd., Lenz.	C24		13
Woodland Av., Gart.	F27		27
Woodland Av., Pais.	O 6		46
Woodland Cres. G72	Q22		66
Woodland Vw., Cumb.	B 3		71
Braehead Rd.			
Woodland Way, Cumb.	B 3		71
Woodlands Av., Both.	Q28		69
Woodlands Cres., Both.	Q28		69
Woodlands Cres., Thorn.	Q12		61
Woodlands Dr. G4	J15		35
Woodlands Gate G3	J15		35
Woodlands Gate, Thorn.	Q12		61
Woodlands Gdns., Udd.	Q27		69
Woodlands Pk., Thorn.	R12		61
Woodlands Rd. G3	J15		35
Woodlands Rd., Thorn.	R12		61
Woodlands Ter. G3	J15		35
Woodlands Ter., Both.	Q28		69
Woodlea Dr., Giff.	Q14		62
Woodlinn Av. G44	P16		63
Woodneuk Av., Gart.	G28		27
Woodneuk Rd. G53	P10		60
Woodneuk Rd., Gart.	G27		27
Woodrow Circus G41	M14		50
Woodrow Pl. G41	M14		50
Maxwell Dr.			
Woodrow Rd. G41	M14		50
Woods La., Renf.	H 8		17
Woodside Av. G73	O20		53
Woodside Av., Lenz.	C23		13
Woodside Av., Thorn.	Q13		62
Woodside Cres. G3	J15		35
Woodside Cres., Barr.	R 8		59
Woodside Cres., Pais.	M 5		46
William St.			
Woodside Pl. G3	J15		35
Woodside Place La. G3	J15		35
Elderslie St.			
Woodside Rd. G20	H15		21
Woodside Ter. G3	J15		35
Woodside Ter., Bish.	D17		10
Woodside Terrace La. G3	J15		35
Woodlands Rd.			
Woodstock Av. G41	N14		50
Woodstock Av., Pais.	O 3		45
Woodvale Av., Bear.	E13		8
Woodvale Av., Giff.	S13		62
Woodvale Dr., Pais.	L 4		29
Woodville St. G5	L13		34
Wordsworth Way, Udd.	Q28		69
Works Av. G72	P24		67
Wraes Av., Barr.	Q 8		59
Wren Pl., John.	O08		43
Wright Av., Barr.	R 7		59
Wright St. G4	K18		36
Wright St., Renf.	J 7		31
Wrightlands Cres., Renf.	F 6		16
Wykeham Pl. G13	G11		19
Wykeham Rd. G13	G11		19
Wynd, The, Cumb.	A 3		71
Wyndford Dr. G20	G14		20
Wyndford Pl. G20	G14		20
Wyndford Rd.			
Wyndford Rd. G20	G14		20
Wyndham St. G12	H14		20
Wynford Ter., Udd.	O28		57
Wyper Pl. G40	L19		37
Gallowgate			
Wyvil Av. G13	E12		7
Wyvis Av. G13	F 9		18
Wyvis Pl. G13	F 9		18
Wyvis Quad. G13	F 9		18
Yair Dr. G52	L10		32
Yarrow Ct., Cumb.	P23		67
Yarrow Gdns. G20	H15		21
Yarrow Rd., Bish.	D19		11
Yate St. G31	L19		37
Yetholm St. G14	G 9		18
Yew Pl., John.	N 1		44
Yoker Ferry Rd. G14	G 9		18
Yoker Mill Gdns. G13	F 9		18
Yoker Mill Rd. G13	F 9		18
Yokerburn Ter., Clyde.	F 8		17
York Dr. G73	P20		65
York La. G2	K16		35
York St.			
York St. G2	K16		35
York St., Clyde.	E 8		5
York Way, Renf.	J 8		31
Yorkhill La. G3	K14		34
Yorkhill St.			
Yorkhill Par. G3	J14		34
Yorkhill St. G3	K14		34
Young St., Clyde.	D 7		5
Young Ter. G21	H19		23
Zambesi Dr., Blan.	R26		68
Zena Cres. G33	H20		23
Zena Pl. G33	H20		23
Zena St. G33	H20		23
Zetland Rd. G52	K 9		32

ADDENDUM The street names listed below should be added to the main index to street names:

Street	Grid	Col	Row
Aird's La., G1	L17		36
Bridgegate			
Auchengreoch Av., John.	O08		43
Auchengreoch Rd., John.	O08		43
Bellshaugh Gdns. G12	G14		20
Bonawe St. G20	H15		21
Broom Path., Bail.	M24		55
Tudor St.			
Bute Rd., Pais.	J 5		30
Church Vw. G72	O22		54
Campsie Dr., Pais.	J 6		30
Cunningham Rd., G73	O18		53
Dalhouse Rd., Udd.	N25		56
Dover St. G3	K14		35
Drumclog Gdns. G33	G21		24
Drysdale St. G14	G 9		18
Duich Gdns. G23	E15		9
Dunalistair Dr. G33	G22		24
Edinburgh Rd. G33	K20		37
Edzell Ct. G14	J11		33
Edzell Pl. G14	J11		33
Foundary St. G21	H18		22
Gallowflat St. G73	O19		53
Reid St.			
Gartartan Rd., Pais.	L 9		32
Katrine Pl. G72	P22		66
Kelso Pl. G14	G 9		18
Kilkerran Dr. G33	G21		24
Kincaid Gdns. G72	P22		66
Lauder Dr. G73	P20		65
Laurieston Rd. G5	L17		36
Letterfearn Dr. G23	E15		9
Lloyd St. G73	N19		53
Lockerbie Av. G43	P15		63
Manse Av., Both.	R28		69
Marine Cres. G51	L15		35
Mansionhouse Rd. G41	O15		51
Mavisbank Gdns. G51	L15		35
McDonald St. G73	O19		53
Greenhill Rd.			
Melrose Ct. G73	O19		53
Dunard Rd.			
Morrison Park Dr. G72	O22		54
Moss Path., Bail.	M24		55
Castle St.			
Mossvale Rd. G33	J23		39
Newpark Ct. G72	O22		54
Olifard Av., Both.	Q28		69
Orbiston Gdns. G32	L22		38
Balintore St.			
Orion Way G72	P22		66
Parsonage Row G1	K17		36
Parsonage Sq.G1	K17		36
Pinewood Sq. G15	D 9		6
Plantation Pk. Gdns. G51	L14		34
Reuther Av. G73	O19		53
Richmond Gro. G73	O20		53
St. Andrews Dr. W., Pais.	J 5		30
St. Bride's Way, Udd.	Q28		69
Sandyford Pl., G3	K15		35
Shieldbridge Gdns. G23	E15		9
Shiskine Pl. G20	F14		20
Shiskine Dr.			
Speirshall Clo. G14	G 9		18
Speirshall Ter. G14	G 9		18
Springfield Quay G51	L15		35
Thomson Gro. G72	O22		54
Trossachs Ct. G20	H16		21
Trossachs St.			
Victoria Pl. G73	O19		53
Greenbank St.			
Watt Low Av. G73	P18		64
William St. G3	K15		35
Yarrow Gdns. La. G20	H15		21
Yarrow Gdns			

ADDENDUM The street names listed below should be deleted from the main index to street names:

Street	Grid	Col	Row
Auckengreoch Av.,John.	008		43
Auckengreoch Rd.,John.	008		43
Bonawe St. G20	H15		21
Kirkland St.			
Cartartan Rd., Pais.	L 9		32
Cunningham Rd. G73	020		53
Cambuslang Rd			
Drumclog Gdns. G33	G21		24
Auchinleck Av.			
Dunalistair Av. G33	G22		24
Edzell Ct. G14	J11		3
Edzell St.			
Ennerdale St. G32	L21		38
Gallowflat St. G73	019		53
General Terminus Quay G51	L15		35
India St. G73	019		53
Langholm St. G14	G 9		18
Lauder Dr. G73	020		53
Locherbie Av. G43	P15		63
Mause Av., Both.	R28		69
Mossvale Rd. G33	H22		24
Olifard Av., Udd.	Q28		69
Peebles Dr. G73	P20		65
St. Bride's Way, Both.	Q28		69
Sandiefield Rd., G5	M17		52
Sandyford Pl. G3	K15		35
Sauchiehall St.			
Spiers Clo. G14	G 9		18
Spiers Ter. G14	G 9		18
Watt Low Av. G73	P19		65

Personal Information

Name	Address	Tel. No.	Notes
	Post Code		
	Post Code		
	Post Code		
	Post Code		
	Post Code		
	Post Code		
	Post Code		
	Post Code		
	Post Code		
	Post Code		

Personal Information

Name	Address	Tel. No.	Notes
	Post Code		
	Post Code		
	Post Code		
	Post Code		
	Post Code		
	Post Code		
	Post Code		
	Post Code		
	Post Code		
	Post Code		

Personal Information

Name	Address	Tel. No.	Notes
	Post Code		
	Post Code		
	Post Code		
	Post Code		
	Post Code		
	Post Code		
	Post Code		
	Post Code		
	Post Code		
	Post Code		

Personal Information

Name	Address	Tel. No.	Notes
	Post Code		
	Post Code		
	Post Code		
	Post Code		
	Post Code		
	Post Code		
	Post Code		
	Post Code		
	Post Code		
	Post Code		

Personal Information

Name	Address	Tel. No.	Notes
	Post Code		
	Post Code		
	Post Code		
	Post Code		
	Post Code		
	Post Code		
	Post Code		
	Post Code		
	Post Code		
	Post Code		